Jewelry Making

Jewelry Making

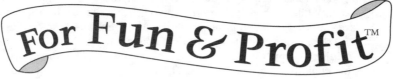
For Fun & Profit™

Lynda S. Musante

Maria Given Nerius

PRIMA HOME
An Imprint of Prima Publishing
3000 Lava Ridge Court • Roseville, California 95661
(800) 632-8676 • www.primalifestyles.com

FOR FUN & PROFIT and PRIMA HOME are trademarks of Prima Communications, Inc. PRIMA PUBLISHING and colophon are registered trademarks of Prima Communications, Inc.

Interior illustrations by Laurie Baker McNeile

Special thanks to Joyce Roark for her valuable contribution to this book.

Prima Publishing and the author hope that you enjoy the projects discussed in this book. While we believe the projects to be safe and fun if proper safety precautions are followed, all such projects are done at the reader's sole risk. Prima Publishing and the author cannot accept any responsibility or liability for any damages, loss, or injury arising from use, misuse, or misconception of the information provided in this book. In addition, business and legal information provided in this book is for reference purposes only, and is not intended to be legal or business advice. You should always consult a legal professional regarding the laws that may apply to your business.

Library of Congress Cataloging-in-Publication Data

Musante, Lynda S.
        Jewelry making for fun & profit / Lynda S. Musante and
  Maria Given Nerius.
        p.   cm. – (For fun & profit series)
  Includes index.
  ISBN 0-7615-2044-9
    1. Jewelry making. 2. Home-based businesses. I. Title: Jewelry making for fun and profit. II. Title.
TT212.M87   2000
745.594'2—dc21   00-058000

00 01 02 03 04 ii 10 9 8 7 6 5 4 3 2 1
Printed in the United States of America

How to Order

Single copies may be ordered from Prima Publishing,
3000 Lava Ridge Court, Roseville, CA 95661; telephone (800) 632-8676,
ext. 4444. Quantity discounts are also available. On your letterhead,
include information concerning the intended use of the books and
the number of books you wish to purchase.

Visit us online at www.primalifestyles.com

Contents

Introduction

MAKING YOUR OWN JEWELRY is a wonderful way to express yourself creatively. You can make gifts for friends and family, or begin a home-based business. Jewelry making can be very satisfying in that it is portable for the designer on the go, and profitable for those who want to sell their art.

I specialize in wire jewelry, but thoroughly enjoy all aspects of jewelry making: beading, modeling materials, fabric embellishment, and assemblage of found items (multimedia jewelry). For me, the exploration of techniques, self-expression, and development of skills are as satisfying as wearing the finished piece. I try many different mediums and combine a wide variety of materials in some of my pieces. I sometimes rescue a piece that I originally thought to be a failure by applying another technique or using different materials, and sometimes I need to put a piece down and work on something else. It is always a challenge to take an idea and make it into a three-dimensional item.

You may have heard jewelry defined into the categories of *fine* jewelry and *craft* jewelry. Finc jewelry generally refers to pieces created with gold or silver and precious gemstones, like diamonds, rubies, and sapphires. The processes used to create fine jewelry require a great deal of education, tools, time, and practice. This book covers information about craft jewelry, or multimedia jewelry, which can be just as elegant, valuable, and beautiful as fine jewelry, particularly today, when so many materials are available to the designer. Many of the pieces I have made or purchased from other designers are as valuable to me as some of the fine jewelry pieces I own.

The wonderful thing about making your own jewelry is putting your own imprint onto the pieces you make. Sometimes, I make a piece of jewelry to accessorize an outfit I purchased. Other times, I purchase an outfit to go along with a piece of jewelry I've just finished! You'll discover an inner satisfaction when your jewelry is admired and appreciated by others.

This book, your hands, and a few items from your home and the local arts and crafts store are all you need to get started. In fact, you can get started with just a needle, thread, and some fabric. Many of the basic techniques in this book can be used in making many different types and styles of jewelry. You'll learn how to use different tools, combine materials, and the basic principles of design.

A Brief History of Jewelry

Since ancient times, people have adorned themselves with jewelry. The first jewelry probably consisted of sinew or cording strung with stones or pebbles with holes, or claws, teeth, or bones from animals. As man evolved, so did his adornment. Jewelry has changed throughout the ages to reflect the values and trends of the times. Guilds developed to educate apprentices and to protect and preserve the techniques of fine jewelry making. (Even today, jewelers become apprentices in order to reach the highest skill levels.) Folks who couldn't afford the education or costly materials to make fine jewelry continued to make their own adornments.

Many cultures have influenced today's jewelry designs. Some regions of the world have become famous for their native materials, used in making jewelry. Some examples are Tibetan jade, African glass trading beads, Egyptian scarabs, Asian pearls, and Australian opals. Your own preferences for certain styles or materials may be influenced by where you live or the places you have visited.

In the late twentieth century, new materials such as Bakelite and other plastics, polymer clay, and Precious Metal Clay (PMC) were developed and became available to crafters. The line between fine jewelry and craft jewelry thus became blurred as new materials and techniques allowed designers to create sophisticated looking jewelry without years of study. Even so, much of today's fine and craft jewelry is created using techniques that were employed centuries ago.

How to Use This Book

This book is designed with the beginner in mind, but the accomplished jewelry maker can also use it to expand his or her skills or to try a new technique. Use this book as a guide to setting up your work area, and choosing and using tools and materials. Follow the project instructions to learn about using four distinctly different categories of materials. You'll find many sources for materials and additional education in this book, as well as explanations of techniques and styles. You'll also explore methods and concerns for mass production for retail sales, retail display ideas, and most importantly, how to create your jewelry in a safe manner.

There are so many ways to create jewelry—you'll want to try many of them in order to discover which ones you prefer and what challenges you. And most of all, you'll have fun in the process. Enjoy!

Basic Tools for Jewelry Making

1 Clay rolling pin
2 Round nose pliers
3 Wire cutters
4 Jewelry jig
5 Tiger tail wire

6 Ruler
7 Scissors
8 Fabric marker
9 Tapestry needle
10 Cutting knife

11 Chain nose pliers
12 Base metal wire
13 Coated wire
14 Cord for
    stringing beads

Part One

For Fun

The Joy of Jewelry Making

▼▼

DO YOU REMEMBER YOUR FIRST piece of jewelry? Was it a food-coloring dyed macaroni necklace you proudly wore home from Sunday school? Or was it a delicate filigreed brooch handed down to you from your grandmother? Jewelry can represent many things. Rings can be promises of friendship, symbols of engagement, or expressions of the bliss of marriage. Necklaces might be trophies of success or statements of personal style. A bracelet of charms might stand for personal milestones and interests. Any one of these items might become an heirloom that passes from one generation to another.

A Passion

For many of us, jewelry is a passion—tokens to admire and cherish. I've loved beads since I was a small child and my grandmother allowed me to select a few pieces from her jewelry box to wear when I played dress-up. I began my jewelry creations by stringing beads, then I went on to more complex beaded projects. After graduating from college, I was living on my own and working for a craft

NANCEE'S STORY

Nancee McAteer of Palm Bay, Florida loves pins and brooches. "They became my trademark of sorts," she explains. "I never leave home without some type of brooch or pin to make my outfit complete. I've quite a collection. Since it is so well known that I wear this type of jewelry, my family and friends usually give me a new piece to add to my collection for birthdays and Christmas. I've got pieces from all over the world. My husband is retired army and we did a bit of traveling during his career. My jewelry was easy to pack and move.

"I've always loved art and craft projects. I like trying new products and techniques. I enjoy working with color, too. I like whimsical, bright, and bold pieces. Jewelry making is great for this need I have to create. I not only get to play with my crafts, but I end up with pretty pins and brooches for myself and as gifts I can give friends. Recently I've been hooked on rubberstamping. I've learned about using my rubberstamps with shrink plastic, polymer clay, and even paper to create some really cool earrings and pins. It's amazing how many mediums can help you create fun jewelry.

"I did sell my work a few years ago, but the family scheduling has gotten so hectic that now I don't have the time to do shows. Yet, I think I'm happier just making jewelry for fun. I still sell an occasional piece to an old customer or to someone who sees a pin I'm wearing and just has to have it. Jewelry is something that catches the attention of people. We all have fond memories associated with jewelry, or we can find a design or motif that makes us smile. It's a great ice-breaker when I go to my son's school or attend a church event. Jewelry is challenging, but the best part of this art and craft is that I can make great pieces to share with my friends.

"I thoroughly enjoyed coming up with different finished pieces to wear to work and just for fun. I was especially pleased that many of my own creations cost considerably less than those I saw at department store jewelry counters, art galleries, and art and craft shows. Soon I was making and selling jewelry to friends and family, as well as through a local gallery. I was thrilled that my "hobby" was making money. In fact it even paid for a couple of trips to craft shows to look at others' work and buy materials. Once I began to sell more of my own creations, I began making a profit, and found myself in business. As a business,

my jewelry making required dutiful record keeping and filing certain paperwork with my local and state governments. As I produced more pieces, I also had to organize my work area more efficiently. (You'll learn about the business side of jewelry making in Part Two of this book.)

"Eventually, I began to search for a way to make my jewelry different than anyone else's and I discovered the joy of working with polymer clay. Polymer clay refers to a new clay, manufactured in a brilliant rainbow of colors. This type of clay was specifically designed for the artist and craftsperson. One advantage to using polymer clay is that there is no need to buy an expensive kiln or to pay a ceramics shop to fire (make the clay hard) your clay jewelry pieces. An added bonus is that the colors of the clay can have a soothing effect on you as you knead and shape it for a project. Yet another advantage of using polymer clay is that there is a wide variety of techniques you can use in this medium. I enjoy using all of them. I also enjoy making jewelry using fabric, needles, and thread—plus beads, of course. While I was growing up, my mother sewed many of my clothes and we always had lots of material around. I learned to sew and I experimented with making coordinating jewelry for some of my outfits. (You'll find projects using polymer clay, fabric, and beads in chapter 4.)

industry manufacturer. While attending industry trade shows, I saw delightful displays of jewelry, created by the leading artists and craftsmen in the art, craft, and creative industries. These pieces included the latest trendy items and mainstay classics. I also saw the materials and tools that created these masterpieces. As a designer, I was given samples of products to work with, and as a professional crafter, I was able to order supplies at the shows. Seeing and handling all those materials fired my imagination and I went home and experimented, first by following the instructions of other designers, and then by branching out to create my own designs. You can use the how-to's and projects in this book to create your first pieces, then go on to experiment with your own ideas and creativity. Before long, you will find yourself mixing and matching different styles and techniques. You may even combine different materials, such as wire and fabric, or you might coordinate colors, such as gold and red or silver and blue.

General Helpful Terms

It's important to familiarize yourself with out-of-the-ordinary terms you'll hear while you try to experience yourself with making jewelry. I've provided a list of these commonly used terms so you can communicate with others and understand anything you run into along the way.

Alloy: Metal made up of a mixture of two or more different metals. Common examples of alloys include bronze (a mixture of copper and tin), brass (copper and zinc), and pewter (tin with antimony, copper, and sometimes lead).

Annealed: Softened by heat.

Aspic cutters: Tools used to cut decorative shapes in aspic, a tomato-based gelatin food. These tools are similar to cookie cutters, only significantly smaller.

Bail: Metal triangle used to attach a bead or a pendant to a necklace.

Baroque: Irregular, rounded stone, glass, or bead.

Base metal: Non-precious metal used as a core in plated and gold-filled items. Brass and nickel are common base metals used in jewelry making.

Bead loom: Wood or plastic frame used to stretch warp threads for bead weaving.

Bead tip: Jewelry finding used to attach thread to a clasp. A knot sits inside a small concave shape attached to a bent metal loop.

Beeswax: Waxy substance used to strengthen and smooth beading thread.

Bell cap: Jewelry finding used to convert a bead or stone with no hole into a pendant, using glue.

Bicone: Bead shape that tapers to a cone at each end.

Bib: Necklace that fits close to the base of the neck and extends over the chest in the shape of child's bib.

Bugle: Small, glass, tubular bead.

Burr: Roughness left by a tool when cutting wire or metal.

Cabochon: Round or oval stone, cut and polished with one flat side (the back) and one smooth, domed side (the front or face). A faceted cabochon is cut with faceted surfaces around the edges of the stone.

Chatoyancy: Having a changeable luster, like a cat's eye.

Choker: Short necklace, usually 15 inches long, that fits snugly at the base of the neck. Popular in the 1950s and revived in the 1970s with the addition of ornaments cascading to cover the chest.

Coil: Flat spiral of wire or metal.

Crimp bead: Small, soft metal bead that is squeezed shut to secure a loop of threaded material onto a clasp.

Dog collar: Wide choker, worn tightly around the neck. Popular in the 1930s and 1960s.

Eyepin: Wire finding with a loop at one end. Used for linking beads or beaded links.

Facet: Flat, polished surface cut into a stone or bead.

Finding: Catch-all term used to describe metal jewelry components. Clasps; connecting rings; and the pins that hold the beads, ear wires, and posts are all findings.

Gauge: Measure of dimension.

Gold: Yellow-colored, soft, shiny metal commonly used in jewelry. The purity of gold is measured in "karats." 24 karat (24K) denotes pure or fine gold; 12K is 50% gold; 14K is about 58% gold. Gold that is less than 24K is actually an alloy.

Gold-filled: Thin layer of gold bonded to a base metal core. In gold-filled products, the gold layer must be at least 5% of the overall product, by weight.

Gold-plated: Very thin layer of gold bonded to a base metal core. The layer of gold in gold-plating is only required to be seven-millionths of an inch thick. (The layer of gold in gold-filled products is about one hundred times thicker than in gold-plating.)

Lampwork: Technique for making glass beads by hand. A glass rod or cane is held to a flame or "lamp" and wound around a mandrel. The bead is shaped or smoothed by rotating the mandrel through the flame.

Lapidary: Cutting, shaping, polishing, and creating jewelry from precious and semiprecious stones.

Lavaliere: Necklace with a drop of a single stone suspended from a chain, also called a neglige.

Lazy stitch: Bead embroidery stitch that attaches several small beads on each short stitch.

Loaf: Block of clay with a pattern throughout; usually a square shape.

Log: Roll of clay that is thicker than a cane.

Matinee: Necklace 24 to 26 inches long; in Europe, 30 to 35 inches.

Opera: Necklace 28 to 30 inches long; in Europe, 48 to 90 inches, can extend to 120 inches.

Opacity: Quality of not allowing light to pass through (the quality of being opaque).

Opaque: Not allowing light to pass through; solid.

Papier roule: Beads made of rolled up paper triangles.

Parure: Set of several matching types of jewelry such as a necklace, earrings, and bracelet.

Paste: Jewelry made of glass, imitating faceted gemstones.

Perfumed beads: Beads that release a scent when warmed by the body.

Peyote stitch: Honeycomb beadwork stitch, worked in a spiral fashion to produce a beadwork tunnel.

Princess: Necklace 20 to 21 inches long.

Sautoir: Long necklace popular in the 1920s; usually made of chains, beads, or pearls and ending in a tassel or fringe.

Silver: White-colored, soft, shiny metal, commonly used in jewelry. Like gold, silver is available in different levels of purity: the purest form, fine silver, is 99.9% silver. Sterling silver is 92.5% silver, with other metals (usually copper) making up the remaining 7.5%. Coin silver is 90% silver with 10% copper. Nickel silver is an alloy of copper (65%), nickel, and zinc—no silver at all.

Silver-plated: A very thin layer of silver bonded to a base metal core.

Split ring: Small base metal finding resembling a key-ring.

Torsade: Combination of several strands of pearls, chains, or beads twisted together into a single necklace.

Translucent: Allowing some light to pass through; objects seen through translucent material are diffused or indistinct.

Transparent: Easily seen through; allowing light to pass through without obscuring the ability to see objects on the other side.

Create According to Your Own Desires

Do you know what you want to make? Do you know how far you want to go? Think about what kind of jewelry you like to wear. Look in your jewelry box. What do you see? Do you prefer long, dangling earrings or studs? Delicate, small necklaces or bold statement pieces? Thin bangles or wide cuffs? Each jewelry style has it own design elements and requires certain skills to make quality pieces. What do you like to do? What materials attract you in the craft or fabric stores? What techniques appeal to you? What equipment are you able to use? Does drilling intimidate you? Are you comfortable with a sewing machine? Whatever your answers are to these questions, there are materials and techniques that will fit your own likes and abilities.

A Sense of Satisfaction

Part of the fun of creating your own quality jewelry is the sense of satisfaction you feel when a piece turns out as you imagined it would. The compliments of friends, family, and even strangers will build your self-confidence and encourage you to try new techniques and designs.

Birthstones

Month	Stone	Color
January	Garnet	Dark Red
February	Amethyst	Dark Purple
March	Bloodstone, Aquamarine	Light Blue
April	Diamond, Cubic Zirconia	Clear
May	Emerald	Deep Green
June	Alexandrite, Pearl, Moonstone	Light Purple
July	Ruby	Red
August	Sardonyx, Peridot	Light Green
September	Sapphire	Deep Blue/Violet
October	Tourmaline, Opal	Rose
November	Topaz, Citrine	Yellow/Amber
December	Turquoise, Blue Zircon	Light Blue

Gathering Your Resources

You can get design ideas by looking at consumer magazines and catalogues, from those focused on arts and crafts to those with a broader focus on fashion and home décor. In addition to looking for jewelry designs, look closely at the ads to see what the advertising world is using to show off style. I often tear out pages that show colors and motifs that appeal to me. I save these pages in folders, so when I'm looking for ideas, I can page through the folders to see what jumps out at me.

There are also many organizations or guilds for jewelry makers. Perhaps there are some in your area. Since polymer clay is a fairly recent addition to the art and craft world, many polymer clay groups and guilds have been formed to help the enthusiast network and share ideas with other enthusiasts. These organizations often have newsletters for their memberships to learn about upcoming meetings, techniques, shows, competitions, and seminars. (See Resources for more about these organizations, including contact information.)

▼▼▼▼▼▼▼▼▼▼▼▼▼▼▼▼▼▼▼▼▼▼▼

Did you know???

Jewelry making has become one of the most widely practiced crafts.

▲▲▲▲▲▲▲▲▲▲▲▲▲▲▲▲▲▲▲▲▲▲▲▲▲▲

Your local library or bookstore is yet another resource for books on jewelry making. The number of books published on jewelry design and techniques is rapidly growing. Read everything you can. Learn about a wide variety of styles and techniques. This will help you decide where to begin.

The Internet is another wonderful source of inspiration, resources, and information about techniques and technology you can use in making your own jewelry. Many Internet businesses offer catalogs as well. You can view and purchase most of the materials you need to begin and have them delivered to your doorstep.

Get a notebook to take notes on what you read and see. You'll find it much easier to return to a source of inspiration or knowledge. Keep a list of the books you read or own in your notebook. You may want to record the addresses of Internet Web sites that you may wish to order from or revisit. It's so frustrating to see or read something and then not be able to find it again. I even keep a notebook in my purse so that I am always ready to write down an idea, sketch a design motif, or record a resource that I discover while I'm away from my studio.

The number of people making jewelry or items to be used in jewelry making is growing. This growth is increasing the need for individual originality in design and workmanship. You will find you have favorite artists who have created work that particularly appeals to you. Although it is tempting to make pieces that are similar or evocative, it is important to develop your own style. By keeping notes on where your ideas originate, you'll be building a portfolio and have a wonderful resource for developing new jewelry designs. Many artists copyright their pieces as they develop a particular look in order to prevent others from profiting from their ideas. The jewelry community is very close and artists will alert one another if they believe that someone is encroaching on another artist's style. If you plan to develop your hobby into a business you will want to be certain that your reputation is sparkling.

Financial Benefits

You'll enjoy a great feeling of accomplishment when you wear jewelry that you've created for much less than the cost of comparable pieces in style today. If you pursue jewelry making as a business, you will be more competitive if you can keep your production costs low. One way to do this is to develop the skills to do as much of your own work as efficiently as possible. One of the wonderful things about jewelry making is that you can constantly learn and develop your skills, yet you don't have to purchase large or expensive pieces of equipment to create professional, quality pieces. As you learn and grow, your interests may change and you'll find the confidence to explore working with new materials. Advancing technology is constantly introducing new materials that allow the jewelry designer to create professional looking pieces.

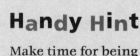

Handy Hint

Make time for being creative.

Anniversary Gifts Chart

First Year: paper, clocks

Second Year: cotton, china

Third Year: leather, crystal, glass

Fourth Year: linen silk, appliances

Fifth Year: wood, silverware

Sixth Year: iron, wood objects

Seventh Year: wool, copper, desk sets

Eighth Year: bronze, linens, lace

Ninth Year: pottery, china, leather goods

Tenth Year: tin, aluminum, diamonds

Eleventh Year: steel, fashion jewelry

Twelfth Year: silk, pearls, colored gems

Thirteenth Year: lace, textiles, furs

Fourteenth Year: ivory, gold jewelry

Fifteenth Year: crystal, watches

Twentieth Year: china, platinum

Twenty-Fifth Year: silver, sterling silver

Thirtieth Year: pearl, diamond

Thirty-Fifth Year: coral, jade

Fortieth Year: ruby

Fiftieth Year: gold

Sixtieth Year: diamond

Grow Your Creativity

In today's world, much of our time is focused on work and family. Developing a leisure time hobby that is fun and profitable is a great opportunity for self-expression, relaxation, and enjoyment. I find that when I'm working on a project I'm excited about, I'm so focused that the hours can fly by without my noticing. In sports, that's called being in *the zone.* That feeling of timelessness when you're in touch with your creativity is a wonderful experience. Many books have been written on the subject of developing, exploring, acknowledging, and growing one's creativity. Reading one or more of these books can help you determine your goals as you begin jewelry making.

Self-Discovery

Why are you considering jewelry making as a new hobby? Are you looking for an outlet for your creativity? Are you looking for an opportunity for self-expression? Do you want a second income? Will making gifts for friends and family be the primary goal for your new hobby? How do you feel about dedicating time and space in your home to your new hobby? How will your family and friends regard this new venture? Will they value the time you will spend working and developing your skills? How seriously are you willing to pursue your successes and how determined are you to overcome any failures? These questions may seem overwhelming when all you want are some instructions for making earrings or a necklace. But, by spending some time on self-examination, you'll be able to determine how much time, energy, and money you're willing to spend on this new venture.

> **Handy Hint**
>
> Take the time to explain your goals to your family and friends. Sometimes people feel threatened or confused when a loved one takes off in a new creative direction.

As in any new hobby—creative or not—there are up-front costs, including tools, materials, and your time. In fact, one of the most important things to consider when you begin any creative venture is that your time must have value. If your hobby evolves into a business, you will need to track, guard, and charge for your time. Answering the above questions can help you become comfortable with your creativity and enhance your enjoyment of jewelry making.

Holidays and Celebrations for Jewelry Gift Giving

Birthdays

Anniversaries

Retirement

Promotions/work advancement

Graduation

Milestones

Engagements/weddings

New family member/births

Thank-you/appreciation

I love you/love

Networking

Consider seeking out successful jewelry makers in your community. Most established artists and craftspeople are very generous and will help each other and newcomers by sharing information and techniques. Be sure to appreciate their time and energy spent on your behalf! Make sure the relationship is not one-sided, or it will end quickly. I have developed many relationships in my community with other artists. Sometimes we share problem-solving methods with a particular technique, or discuss sources of inspiration. This exchange of information with other artists has often helped me in the development of a design. Some of my friends don't work in the same medium I do, but we still share many of the same creative challenges. I know one artist who uses fish skeletons

Valentine's Day: February 14

St. Patrick's Day: March 17

Mother's Day: second Sunday in May

Father's Day: third Sunday in June

Halloween: October 31

New Year's Day: January 1

Memorial Day: last Monday in May

United States of America's Independence Day: July 4

Thanksgiving Day: fourth Thursday in November

Christmas Day: December 25

and chicken feet in her designs. While those materials don't appeal to me, I admire her work and we have had great conversations while sharing ideas about composition, design, and style. Another friend is an incredible quilter and she began working in polymer clay to make buttons and embellishments for her quilted garments. Now she mostly works with polymer clay because she enjoys it so much. So start conversations with people who are wearing or doing interesting things. You never know where it will take you, but it will be worth the trip! I've always found that making the time for relationships with other jewelry makers and creative thinkers helps me grow my own business and skills in many ways. Sometimes even a simple suggestion for improving a design can be very helpful, or just watching someone else demonstrate a new technique that I've been struggling to master, can make a big difference.

If you design without any interaction with other jewelry makers or feedback from your community, you may find yourself developing pieces that only appeal to you! Feedback is essential if you want your jewelry to appeal to a wide customer base. Feedback, if constructive, may be painful at first, but it will help you define your style and develop jewelry that will be desired by others. It is difficult at first to separate yourself from your art when hearing criticism, and having a thick skin about a new creative venture can feel almost impossible. But stick with it!

Handy Hint

Network with other artists to share tips and explore new techniques.

What Can You Expect After Learning to Make Jewelry?

You'll look around with new eyes and consider how you can include common, everyday materials in your designs. You'll look at motifs, trends, and styles and plan how you can distill what you see into an element of your own design. You'll develop the ability to focus on what works for you. You'll learn to prioritize what you're going to work on first, and develop the skills to accomplish your goals. Your reward will be the joy of becoming an artist.

Getting Started

JEWELRY MAKING ENCOMPASSES a wide range of materials and tools. This chapter focuses on the materials and tools needed for making jewelry in five different mediums: clay, wire, beads, fabric, and found objects. You can use each of these mediums to create stunning jewelry.

Many accomplished jewelry artists focus their talents in one area, such as clay. Some jewelry artists specialize to the point of using one brand of material or creating one type of jewelry. These artists have worked with a wide variety of materials before selecting a specialty. You, too, should try out all of the materials before settling on a favorite. Only by experimenting will you learn about the properties and limitations of the various materials, and you may even discover a new application that will become a unique element of your designs.

Clay

Clay is a wonderful material to work with because it provides many possibilities in jewelry design. There are many types of clay available, and each one has its own unique properties.

Polymer Clay

Polymer clay is an innovative and relatively new product in jewelry design that has dramatically grown in popularity over the past 20 years. Polymer clay is a plastic-based substance composed of polyvinyl chloride, suspended in a plasticizer that fuses into a hard, durable plastic when heated to the proper temperature. For the first time, a hobbyist doesn't need professional equipment to fire and cure the material, but can, instead, use a conventional oven or even a toaster oven.

An outstanding characteristic of artists working in polymer clay is the way they share their knowledge and discoveries. Many of the top designers in polymer clay experiment and teach new techniques to others in order to foster the growth and acceptance of this product as a legitimate material.

There are several brands of polymer clay available to the jewelry designer. Each brand has different properties such as firmness, color variety, strength, translucency, or opacity. After much experimentation, I have come to prefer FIMO Soft that is manufactured by Eberhard Faber. It is a strong clay that is easy to condition.

Other types of polymer clay that are readily available are Cernit, FIMO, Sculpey III, Premo, and Liquid Sculpey (even though this product is a liquid, it is a polymer clay and can be used for wonderful special effects). If you have stiff hands or lack strength in your fingers, you might choose a softer clay that will be easier to condition. Some soft types of clay have a tendency to become sticky or to smear if cut when warm. You should plan to let soft clay rest, or cool, before cutting it.

Work Surface

A smooth work surface is very important when working with polymer clay. A smooth surface is easy to clean and won't mark your clay as you work. A sheet of glass with the edges taped or sanded, a smooth cutting board, a ceramic tile, or a Teflon cookie sheet are all good work surfaces that have the added advantage of being portable. A glass surface provides you with the option to slide a drawn pattern or sheet of graph paper (for measuring) beneath it. Smooth, small ceramic tiles are useful for curing small projects, and they can then be placed in the oven. If your project is flat, sandwiching the clay between the smooth sides of two tiles will keep it flat through the baking and cooling steps. (If you use this technique, add at least 10 minutes to the curing time to accommodate the tile's absorption of heat.)

Conditioning

Polymer clay must be conditioned before use, to ensure that the ingredients are completely mixed so the clay will cure properly. You can condition the clay by removing it from the packaging and kneading, folding, twisting, and rolling it. Repeat and continue the conditioning until the clay is soft and malleable. Never skip conditioning the clay, even when it appears to be soft, right out of the packaging. You can roll older clay and chop it into smaller pieces, then roll it until it's soft and malleable. You can also put clay through a pasta machine to condition it. In this case, you should no longer use the pasta machine for making pasta or other food uses. Polymer clay will harden with age and should be stored in a cool location. For some brands and older clay, it may be necessary to add a softening product to assist in the conditioning. Clay that isn't conditioned will be weak and brittle after baking, which may result in a piece of jewelry that disappoints a customer.

Polymer clay is nontoxic at temperatures under 265 degrees Fahrenheit, but as with any art product, you should exercise care to be sure that the clay does not come in contact with food.

Inclusions

You can achieve many interesting effects by kneading other materials (especially translucent clay) into polymer clay. Embossing powders, mica powders, glitter, shaved crayons, and cooking spices can add a nice touch. You can mix powders into translucent clay, or brush powders onto the surface of clay for embellishment. These inclusions make it possible to use polymer clay to create realistic facsimiles of semiprecious stones, such as turquoise, lapis lazuli, ivory, jade, rose quartz, and granite.

You can also add an elegant luster to a piece by combining polymer clay with imitation gold leaf. Since gold leaf can be costly, you can use plastic-backed foils to get a similar look. The foils will adhere to polymer clay when the wrong side of the foil is placed onto the clay and firmly scraped on the other side. These foils are available in many colors and patterns at art, craft, and rubberstamp supply stores. You can also order them from Web sites that sell art and craft supplies.

Handy Hint

If you are conditioning several colors of clay, begin with the lightest clay and end with the darkest. It may be necessary to clean your hands and work surface between colors as they may stain your hands, tools, and work surface and thus be transferred to your next color of clay.

Curing

Once conditioned, polymer clay remains soft and flexible until cured with heat. FIMO Soft cures at 265 degrees Fahrenheit. Most types of polymer clay cure between 235 degrees Fahrenheit and 285 degrees Fahrenheit. Once the clay is cured and cooled, it has chemically changed and cannot be returned to a soft state. The properties of the different clay brands can affect the hardness or flexibility of the cured clay. Never put your project into the oven until the oven has reached the proper temperatures. Darkening or burning of the clay can occur if the oven temperature varies from 265 degrees Fahrenheit. (Some colors become darker with curing.) Even though polymer clay is nontoxic when cured at the specified temperatures, it can emit toxic fumes or smoke if the oven temperature rises above 265 degrees Fahrenheit. Many ovens heat up by spiking the temperature much higher than called for, and then cool down to the proper temperature. Any clay inside the oven during this process can burn or smoke, releasing potentially toxic fumes. To prevent this problem, preheat your oven to 250 degrees Fahrenheit, then place a meat thermometer in the oven on a cookie sheet. Wait 15 minutes, remove the thermometer, and read the gauge. This will give you a base line for knowing how hot your oven is. Please note that a lower temperature means you will need to "cook" the clay longer, but there will be no danger of overheating. Overheating will burn the item.

When using your kitchen oven, you need to take special precautions to ensure that the clay is properly covered while curing to prevent any residue adhering to your oven's walls, then possibly contaminating food when you next use your oven at a higher temperature. If you are using your kitchen oven to cure your polymer clay and want to protect your oven from any fumes, place the items you're baking inside of a metal pie pan. Cover and seal the pan with aluminum foil while baking. If there should be a problem, all of the fumes and smoke will be contained within the pan. You must also thoroughly clean your oven after any polymer clay use! As a safer alternative, consider purchasing a toaster oven to use for the sole purpose of baking your clay projects.

> ## Handy Hint
>
> An old food processor works well to chop up stiff clay into small uniform pieces for conditioning.

Glue

You will need either a cyanoacrylate glue or two-part epoxy to join two pieces of cured polymer clay or to attach the clay to a jewelry finding. Cyanoacrylate glues are commonly marketed under the brand names Zap-A-Gap or Super Glue. If you are coating another object with polymer clay, first coat the object with PVA glue (white glue) and allow it to dry. The clay will adhere more securely during the baking process. A small amount of PVA glue will help two raw pieces of clay adhere better, as well.

Air Drying Clay

This category of clay cures when it is shaped and left out to dry. Some types of air drying clay can be reconstituted with water if they dry out prematurely. Be sure to read the specifications on the packaging of each brand you try.

Paper Clay

Paper clay is a great option for beginners. This type of clay can be shaped in a similar manner to polymer clay and can yield a porcelain-like appearance if sanded after drying. Paper clay can also be painted with water-based paints and is lightweight when dry. One disadvantage of paper clay is that it doesn't have the strength and durability of polymer clay, which is an important factor to consider when designing jewelry for sale.

Mexican Clay

You may remember Mexican clay from your elementary school days. This clay is a rich, orange-red color and may remind you of the terra cotta clay used in making flower pots. Mexican clay is coarser in texture than air drying clay and polymer clay, but can be used to great effect. Like paper clay, Mexican clay is not as strong as polymer clay, so may not be suitable for some jewelry designs.

Clay Tools

The right tools for the job can save you time, frustration, and add the perfect finishing touches to your jewelry. Some tools can be found in most home toolboxes, but some are specifically designed to aid the jewelry artist. You can add tools as your interests and designs go from simple to complex.

Cutting Tools

Caution and safety are imperative when using sharp tools to cut polymer clay. Many beginning designers start out by using wallpaper scraper blades to cut through the clay. Mark the dull side of the blade with nail polish or paint, so you don't accidentally pick up the blade by the cutting edge.

There are cutting blades manufactured expressly for polymer clay. One line is the Nu-Blade line, designed by master polymer clay artist, Donna Kato. The Nu-Blade is 6 inches long, extremely sharp, and available in a flexible or stiff blade. These blades are similar to the blades used in medicine for cutting human tissue.

A craft knife is useful for cutting flattened clay, or cutting around templates. If you are repeatedly cutting out small shapes, there are steel cutting punches marketed just for this purpose. These punches are often sold in sets of varying sizes. You can use cookie cutters for this purpose as well.

Needle Tools

You can use needle tools to pierce or texture your polymer clay creations. Needle tools are particularly useful when creating beads. You can purchase commercial needle tools, or use tapestry needles and sewing needles of varying lengths and diameters.

Texturing Tools

Many designers create visual interest in their pieces by adding texture. You can easily add texture to polymer clay by pressing just about any object onto the surface. Some items to consider are rubberstamps, lace, plastic canvas, screen, sandpaper, or fabric. You

Making Handles for Blades and Needles

You can use clay to make handles for a variety of blades and needles. To make a handle for a wallpaper scraper, roll a small amount of clay into a snake, embed the dull side of the blade in the clay, and bake it to cure the clay. You can also use clay to make a customized handle for a replacement craft blade by embedding one end of the blade in clay, molding the clay to fit your hand, and baking it. Make needles easier to use by embedding them in waste clay and curing the clay. When you shape handles to your fingers, you increase your comfort and control when using the tools. You can use waste clay to make handles for your tools. Some artists take the time to design beautiful handles for their tools.

can buy texturing sheets or you can make your own texturing tools. For example, you can imprint a square of clay with a piece of plastic canvas, and then cure the clay. To use your new tool, press the square of cured clay onto the surface of the raw clay. If you coat your texturing tools (and molds) with a light dusting of corn starch or baby powder, they will release better from the raw clay.

You can also use many basic household tools to texture and shape polymer clay. A few examples are toothpicks, paperclips, cookie cutters, aspic cutters, toothbrushes, paint brushes, vegetable brushes, a garlic press, and hair combs and brushes. Some dental tools are useful when working with clay. These can be purchased at drugstores or flea markets, or you can ask your dentist or dental hygienist to order them for you.

Warning: Once a tool, utensil, or household item is used on polymer clay, it should never be used for food preparation or come in contact with food.

Rolling Tools

Many polymer clay techniques require that you start with a uniformly flat sheet of clay. You can achieve a thin, flat sheet by using a rolling pin, a section of PVC or acrylic pipe, a brayer, or a cylindrical drinking glass. An advantage to the drinking glass and acrylic pipe is that you can see through them to the clay. Many polymer clay artists use a pasta machine for rolling out clay into sheets, or blending clay. The pasta machine helps condition the clay at the same time. Pasta machines have several settings to vary the thickness of the clay. Most are operated with a hand crank on one side, but some brands are equipped with a motor that operates the rollers. If you plan to work extensively with polymer clay, consider purchasing a pasta machine. It will greatly decrease the amount of time you spend conditioning and rolling out clay. As previously cautioned, don't use the pasta maker for food after you have used it for clay.

Handy Hint

To accurately measure clay, after conditioning it, roll it into a snake, then measure it and cut off lengths. Remember to record the amounts for future reference.

Measuring Tools

Polymer clay colors, like acrylic paints, can be easily mixed together to greatly expand or customize the colors used in a project. In order to repeat a custom color you will have to measure each proportion of the clay. You can buy plastic templates manufactured for this purpose, or you can develop your own measurement system. For example, you can roll out your clay to a specified thickness, use a punch or cookie cutter to cut out a shape, and record exactly which tools you used and the steps you followed. Rulers are helpful for measuring length, and a draftsman's template is helpful for measuring ball sizes.

Finishing Tools

Polymer clay has a matte finish once it is cured and cooled. The finish on your project depends on the texturing or smoothness you leave on the surface before baking the clay. If you accidentally leave a fingerprint on the surface of the clay before you bake it, you'll need to sand the surface to remove the imprint.

To achieve a luster or shiny finish on your project, you need to sand the clay with several different grits of sandpaper and then buff it. Avoid inhaling the dust created by sanding by using a wet/dry sandpaper and by sanding under running water. Another option is to sand over a container of water and frequently dunk the piece into the water to remove the dust. Begin sanding with 320-grit sandpaper, then sand with 400 grit, then 600 grit. Once you achieve the amount of smoothness and shine you desire, you can stop, or you can continue with 1200-grit paper. Thoroughly rinse any dust from your piece and rub it lightly with a soft cloth. Using a buffing wheel can bring a mirror-like shine to the clay.

You can finish your piece with any number of lacquers manufactured expressly for polymer clay. Many artists recommend using a clear, water-based varnish or non-yellowing liquid floor wax as alternatives to lacquer.

Wire

Wire jewelry is growing in popularity and shows no signs of slowing. Silver and gold wires continue to be used in creating fine jewelry, but the increasing availability of new wire products offers more options to today's designers. Now you can create jewelry with the appearance of gold and silver, but for much less money by using coated wires.

When you begin working with wire, start out with an inexpensive, flexible wire to practice the basic techniques. Once you consis-

Summarized List of Polymer Clay Tools

Cutting Blades

wallpaper blades

Nu-Blades by Kato

craft knives

cutting punches

Texturing Tools

rubberstamps

lace

plastic canvas

screen

sandpaper

toothbrushes

paint brushes

garlic press

dental tools

Needle Tools

tapestry needles

knitting needles

sewing needles

Rolling Tools

rolling pin

pasta machine

acrylic tubing

cylindrical drinking glass

brayer

Measuring Tools

rulers

clay measuring templates

draftsman's templates

Baking Tools

oven

toaster oven

timer

baking thermometer

tin pie plate

aluminum foil

tently achieve satisfactory results, then you can try higher quality wires. Even now, when I experiment with a new design or technique, I practice first and save my good wire for making the finished product.

Wire is sold by gauges, a term referring to the wire's diameter or thickness. The higher the wire's gauge number, the smaller the wire's diameter. For example, 26-gauge wire is much thinner than 10-gauge wire. In wire project directions, the word *gauge* is usually abbreviated to *g.* Consider the need for strength, thickness, and flexibility of the wires in your design. If the wire in your design will be supporting weight, like several glass beads, use a 16-gauge or 18-gauge wire. If the wire is going to be a decorative element and wrapped around strung beads, you may only need a 26-gauge or 24-gauge wire. Decorative wires on the market range from 10 gauge up to 32 gauge. It's possible to crochet and make tatted jewelry with the thinnest wires.

The hardness of the wire affects your choice and the application for your project. Dead soft wire is very flexible and best for wire wrapping, but dead soft wire does not have the strength to hold its shape if used for making links or shaped segments. Half-hard wire is recommended for creating wire segments that are shaped on a jig or with pliers. Hammering the wire will strengthen it as well. If you plan on making a variety of projects with wire, you should have both dead soft and half-hard wire on hand.

Copper Wire

Copper wire is commonly available and is less costly than other wires. It can be purchased at your local hardware store. Uncoated copper wire will tarnish, and can add an interesting patina to your jewelry. If you prefer the copper to remain shiny, you will need to polish it frequently or seal it by spraying or brushing on an acrylic sealant.

Base Metal Wire

Often manufactured from tin or brass, base metal wires are widely available in craft stores and are frequently used as embellishments

> **Handy Hint**
>
> You can use almost anything you can sew or glue onto your project as an embellishment. Some suggestions are: feathers, buttons, snaps, washers, and rubber o-rings.

to painted projects or projects with wire that is not worn. Base metal wires will eventually tarnish and may be brittle. Therefore, I don't recommend using them in jewelry creation, especially when making jewelry to sell. These wires do not add value to your jewelry and may also cause allergic skin reactions.

Coated Wire

Several manufacturers in the industry are producing types of coated wire; some have a shiny metallic coating and others have a matte finish. This wire usually has a copper or tin core, and the color is applied, then sealed. Although it is possible to scratch the color when working with sharp tools, the colors are permanent. Due to the great variety of colors and gauges, coated wire can be combined for great effects with all types of beads.

Plastic Coated Wire

This wire has a plastic coating similar to telephone wire and is manufactured in a variety of gauges. Plastic coated wire is manufactured with bright, shiny, and matte finishes. This is wonderful for children's jewelry and bright, fun designs.

Specialty Wire

Niobium and titanium wires have eye-popping colors and can add great interest and value to your pieces. You must protect the coating on the wire by taping or coating your tools. If the wire coating is damaged, the finish will fracture and eventually the color will peel away, leaving a dull, gray surface.

Basic Tools for Wire Bending

When working with wire, use tools that fit well in your hand, or have ergonomically shaped handles. When possible, choose hand tools with springs because the springs assist in opening the tools after they are engaged. These features can help keep your hands from tiring quickly.

Round nose pliers are used for bending curves and coiling wire. They are essential if you want to make jump rings, loops, and spirals.

Chain nose pliers can have smooth or serrated jaws. Use chain-nose pliers for sharp angles and geometric shaping.

There are different kinds of wire cutters. Use heavier wire cutters for thicker wires, as thicker wires may damage the cutting blades on lightweight cutters.

You will need a file for filing away any burs or sharp edges left by the cutters. Always file after cutting! Wire ends that are not filed may snag clothing or scratch skin.

Not-So-Basic Tools for Wire Bending

Jewelry jigs are versatile tools for bending wire, repetitively and precisely, as in the case of earring hooks. A transparent version, Olympus, can be used to replicate drawn patterns/designs. The jig base has holes in a grid pattern. The jewelry designer inserts pegs of varying diameters and follows a pattern to shape the wire.

Did you know???

Beads are measured in millimeters by their diameter.

Twist 'n' Curl is a very clever tool consisting of a crossbar and rod. It is used to create coils by spinning the crossbar and winding the wire around the rod. The deluxe version features rods in three diameters that can be used to create a variety of beads. Rods in other shapes such as oval, square, triangle, and flattened can be purchased separately.

Nylon jaw pliers won't mar the finish on coated wires, and the pliers can be used to straighten wire for shaping another time.

You can use crimping pliers to crush and form crimp beads in order to attach jewelry findings, or to anchor beads in position on a cord.

You might want to purchase a jeweler's hammer to add texture or flatten wire. Hammering wire can strengthen it somewhat. The hammer can be metal or nylon-faced. A nylon face will not mar the finish on coated wires.

Place wire on an anvil before hammering. A plastic anvil is especially useful when you're hammering coated wires. If you are hammering a segment where wires cross, place a piece of scrap leather or chamois under the wires. If you don't cushion the crossed wires while hammering, the intersections will be brittle, and may break if flexed.

Beads

There are many, many different kinds of beads available today. Following are some examples to give you an idea of some of the more common bead types and shapes.

Seed beads are very small round or tubular beads that are available in a wide variety of colors and finishes. Indian, Czech, and Japanese seed beads are popular, and each can be used in a variety of applications.

Bugle beads are tubular beads that are measured by their lengths. They are available in smooth cut and twisted finishes, and come in varied lengths.

Some other bead shapes are: bi-cone, button, cabochon, chip, cylinder, disk, filigree, heishi, oval, pony, side drilled, and tear drop.

> ## Handy Hint
>
> When buying materials for a project, string some of the beads you are using on a cord and take them to the store with you. You'll be sure that your additional purchases will coordinate with the items you already have.

Glass Beads

Glass beads come in many varieties. Lampworked beads are created, one at a time, by a glass bead artist using glass rods and a torch. These beads can be very plain, or incredibly complex. Often a glass-bead artist creates a focal bead and sets of plainer, coordinating beads to use in a project.

Miracle Beads

Miracle beads have a special luster, and add an elegant touch to any project. Manufactured in Japan, miracle beads have a metallic core that is encased in a clear acrylic coating, which magnifies the core. These beads are available in several diameters. There are inexpensive plastic versions of miracle beads on the market, as well.

Metal Beads

Metal beads can add dimension, texture, and interest to a jewelry piece. You can find beads made from brass, tin, copper, silver, and other metals. Some metal beads are plated with a thin layer of gold, silver, or vermeil (an alloy containing gold and silver). Other metal beads are stamped, or machine formed, while still others are manufactured individually. Many metal beads are imported from Bali, Taiwan, and Indonesia. When purchasing metal beads, be sure to question the vendor about the quality and origin of the beads.

Other Bead Materials

Other materials commonly used to make beads are: molded or pressed glass, wood, bone, metal, ceramic, seeds, shells, pearls, coral, and plastic. Beads are also manufactured from a wide variety of semiprecious stones that can add elegance to your finished jewelry. When purchasing semiprecious stones, be sure to inquire about the origin of the stones, as many imitations are manufactured.

Wires for Stringing Beads

This category of wire refers to extremely thin and flexible strands of stainless steel wire in a clear coating. These wires are used to string beads, especially heavy or rough-edged ones, like glass or ceramic beads. Some brands of stringing wires, such as Soft Flex, can be knotted, but I recommend finishing the ends of these wires with crimp beads in order to be secure. The strength and flexibility of these products are excellent for creating multistrand necklaces or bracelets. Some brands of wire are not as flexible as cords, and that can affect the drape of the piece on the body.

Cords for Stringing Beads

The type of thread or cord you choose for stringing your beads will depend on the size of the hole in the beads, and the number of times the cord will pass through the hole. Most cords are manufactured in a variety of diameters. When you choose one, keep in mind that you want to fill the bead's hole in order to prevent it from sliding and causing wear to the cord from friction.

Fishing line and monofilament cords are generally not used in creating jewelry, as they tend to stretch out and become brittle with time. Silk cords have been traditionally used in knotting pearl strands, but as a natural product, silk can also become brittle. Other products developed for stringing or stitching beads include Nymo, C-thru-B cord, elastic cords, and waxed linen. Elastic cords can be round or flat and come in varying diameters. These cords are often used in creating illusion or floating style necklaces, which are made with transparent string giving the "illusion" that a charm or bead is floating around a person's neck.

Tools for Working with Beads

There are some wonderful tools designed specifically to help you work with beads. These tools can help you bead the finest of seed beads or create wonderfully huge, one-of-a-kind beads.

Needles

You'll need special needles to stitch through beads. Beading needles are different from sewing needles, in that the eye of the needle is much smaller in order to fit through the beads. Beading needles are sold by sizes. As with wire, the higher the number, the smaller the needle size. The sharpness and length of the needle is important to your project. For example, you would need a larger needle to stitch through leather than through fabric. Some needles have large eyes for threading heavier cord.

Handy Hint

Tightly crumple aluminum foil into the basic shape you want, and coat it with thin pieces of clay. This will save clay and considerably lighten the weight of a necklace, making it easier to wear for long periods.

Chain

Adding chain to your bead designs can bring a quality element to your pieces. Chain can be used to space beads apart, or can be the base to which beads and other items are attached. Choose chain that has open links, as they are easier to thread or connect.

Findings

Jewelry findings are finishing pieces used in creating jewelry, for example pinbacks, clasps, and other items. Like wires, findings are manufactured in a variety of metals and finishes. Be sure to purchase the best quality findings you can. Findings take most of the wear and tear put on a piece of jewelry.

Pierced Earring

> Flat front post
> Ball and ring post
> Kidney ear wires

Lever-back ear wires
Comfort clutch

Clip Earring

Perforated disk

Necklace or Bracelet

Spring ring
Lobster catch
Chain tab
Clamshell knot cover (also called beaded clamshell, knot
     cup, or bead tips)
Crimp bead

Miscellaneous

Assorted pinbacks
Stick pins
End cones
Split rings
Jump rings
Head pins
Eye pins

Fabric Jewelry

Fabric jewelry can be fun and funky or elegant and refined. There's
no limit to the shapes and techniques that can be used to create
fabric-based jewelry. If you can sew on a button, you can create fabric jewelry, and if you can operate a sewing machine, then you have

even more options! Fabric can be the focus of your design, or it can be a canvas for beads and fibers.

Fabrics

Silk, cotton, velvet, ultra suede, lace, polar fleece, and satin are all fabrics you can use when making fabric jewelry. Select fabrics with a tight weave, like ultra suede, cottons, or silk for the base of your fabric jewelry. These fabrics will support the weight of beads and other embellishments. Also, these fabrics can be supported with interfacings that can be sewn or fused to the wrong side of the fabric. Use looser fabrics, such as lace, for embellishing the surface of your projects.

▼▼▼▼▼▼▼▼▼▼▼▼▼▼▼▼▼▼▼▼▼▼▼▼

Did you know???

Culling beads means to sort through them in order to set aside the damaged ones that may affect the quality of your finished item. Don't throw these beads away as they can be used in fringe.

▲▲▲▲▲▲▲▲▲▲▲▲▲▲▲▲▲▲▲▲▲▲▲▲

Embellishments

The true fun of jewelry making is the eye-pleasing and style-refreshing effects you can achieve by using a variety of embellishments. Some embellishments can be purchased at your local art and craft store, but many are already right there in your home!

Fibers

Metallic threads, blending filaments, and textured yarns make good embellishments because they can be stitched through and onto the surface of the project.

Beads

You can use beads, stitched on, one at a time, or in a bunch, to accent the pattern of your fabric. Or, you can make the beads the focus of the design. Choose beads with smooth edges that will not cut the threads used to stitch them in place. Bugle beads are wonderful and attract light, but beware: They are also notorious for irregular and sharp edges.

Paints

You can change or embellish any fabric with paints, dyes, or bleaches. Silk painting is an ancient craft and the results can be stunning. Silk painting is done in two steps. The first step is to apply a resist (keeps dyes from blending into each other) that is painted on to outline and define the areas for color to be applied. After the resist has dried, the second step is the application of dyes that are applied with a brush to the surface of the fabric. Be sure the paint you choose is formulated for fabrics. You can use acrylic paints on fabrics, but only after you mix a fabric medium into the paint. (The fabric medium bonds the paint to the fabric's fibers.)

Dimensional paints are usually squeezed out of a bottle and sit on top of the surface of the fabric. Use these paints to adhere flat-backed beads or rhinestones.

There are also rubberstamping inks, crayons, and markers formulated for fabric that become permanent once they are heat set.

> ### Handy Hint
>
> Be sure to have a dedicated pair of scissors for cutting fabric and ribbons. Don't use your fabric scissors on paper, as cutting paper will dull the blades. To sharpen blades, cut two or three times through a piece of fine grit sandpaper.

Tools for Fabric

When you're working with fabric, a whole new set of tools is required. It's good to have these things on hand.

Scissors

Sharp scissors are your number one tool when working with fabrics. You may also want to use pinking shears to cut fabrics that tend to ravel. Rotary cutters are great for cutting through several layers of fabric at once. They require a cutting mat to protect your work surface. Small manicure scissors can be useful for cutting out small areas of fabric.

Sewing Machines

Although it is not always necessary, most fabric jewelry can be created with a basic sewing machine. If you have a complex, computerized machine, then you also have the ability to add texture and specialty stitches to create unusual effects.

Needles

Use sharp needles when sewing your fabrics together, and be sure to use the appropriate needle for the task. For example, use a beading needle to attach beads, a strong needle for stitching through leather or suede, and a tapestry or embroidery needle for loosely woven fabrics. Needles are sized in a similar manner to wires; the larger the number, the smaller the needle.

Pins and Weights

Use stainless steel pins to prevent rust marks from appearing on your fabrics, especially if your design requires pressing or steaming. If you are cutting out large pieces of fabric, weights can be helpful to hold the fabric in place.

Hoops

Embroidery hoops are helpful for holding fabric and creating a taut surface for stitching. Be sure to remove your project from the hoop between work sessions so it doesn't stretch.

Fabric Markers

These markers are formulated to disappear with time or with the application of water. Fabric markers are helpful for drawing stitch-

Some Found Items You Might Use in Your Designs

Puzzle pieces	Beads	Fabric remnants
Kid's toys	Braids	Lace
Buttons	Bottle caps	Leaves
Earrings	Match boxes	Gum wrappers
Keys	Dice	Plastic whistles
Hardware	Spoons	Leather pieces
Gum ball machine toys	Wood turnings	Upholstery cording
Paper clips	Spools	

ing lines or marking details of patterns onto the fabric surface. If your are using a marker that is removed with water, be sure not to use it on fabric that is dry clean only.

Found Objects

Assembling found objects into jewelry can be a fun and challenging craft. Many designers use found objects to create jewelry that makes a strong statement, political or otherwise. Found object jewelry is whimsical, and it is a great way to use a scrap of fabric, a small toy, or that single earring. Combining found objects is also a good way to update jewelry—though I recommend that you don't start disassembling valuable pieces of jewelry in order to get materials. Garage sales, flea markets, and white elephant sales are great places to find items to include in your jewelry. Found object jewelry can be the most fun to make, but you still need to apply the principles of good design. The unpredictability of the materials requires that you be a master of basic jewelry assembling techniques.

Glues

You'll need a variety of glues to attach the different kinds of materials you combine when making found object jewelry. If items are not heat sensitive, then a high- or low-temperature glue gun can quickly adhere them to each other. If your piece will be subject to temperature changes, or if the materials you are using are heat sensitive, you may want to use white glue or other glues formulated for bonding materials. GOOP is a strong, all-purpose, white jewelry glue that will bond wood, metal, and fabric—yet it dries clear. Cyanoacrylate glues are appropriate for gluing small plastic and metal pieces.

Now that you know which tools and materials you need to begin creating jewelry, you're ready to set up shop. The following chapter will help you make your work area efficient and pleasurable.

Handy Hint

Tape or glue elements of a project you're working on to an index card. This makes a project card that you can carry with you when you shop for supplies. You'll be able to match colors and textures precisely.

Setting Up Your Personal Workspace

▼▼

YOUR WORKSPACE WILL REFLECT your own style of creativity. Some designers prefer a workspace that is clean, neat, and orderly. Others thrive on having all their materials in view and readily accessible. The location of your workspace may also dictate how your materials are organized. For example, a dining room table lets you spread everything out or stack it in piles.

Find a place in your home where you can leave work-in-progress undisturbed. Make your workspace a welcoming area where you want to spend time. If you don't like being in your workspace, you won't want to work there. If possible, hang pictures or photos that inspire you. Keep your resource books handy and your tools within easy reach.

Your Chair

You will be spending a lot of time in your chair, so it should be stable and comfortable, and support your back. Slumping while working can stress your back, arms, shoulders, and neck, which will make creating jewelry a misery instead of a pleasure. An adjustable

Safety Tip

It's important to stop working frequently to stretch your arms, neck, and back in order to avoid stiffness. Be sure to flex your wrists and fingers as well, to prevent developing a repetitive motion injury. Remember that your hands are your most important tools in creating jewelry. It is easy to ignore your body while you are intent on completing a project. I suggest setting a timer for 20- or 30-minute intervals as a reminder to take stretch breaks. You'll feel better, and be less likely to stress any joints.

chair is a good choice if your workspace surfaces have different heights. A chair that swivels or one that has wheels is useful if you need to move from one work area to another. Office supply stores are a good source for adjustable, ergonomic chairs. You may also want to purchase a plastic mat for the floor under your chair. The mat will keep the floor clean and make it easier to move your chair.

Your Work Surface

Your work surface can be a card table, your dining room table, or a lap desk, depending on the type of jewelry you are creating. A workbench or countertop is also a good work surface. If you work at your kitchen counter, cover it, as some shades of polymer clay can stain. Your work surface should be smooth, clean, and the proper height. To determine the right height for you, sit in your chair at your work surface. The top of the work surface should be slightly higher than your bent elbows. Often, you will need to steady an elbow on the table while working. If the table is too high or too low, this action will stress your back and shoulders. If you prefer to stand while you craft, make sure your work surface is at least waist high.

Stand on a cushioned mat and take frequent breaks to stretch your lower back.

Many designers use a white work surface as a neutral background for selecting colored items to use in your projects. This way, the color of your work table doesn't affect your perception of the jewelry elements you are combining. In my studio, I have two workspaces: one for beads and wire jewelry assembly and design; and the other for modeling materials, rubberstamping, and other messy techniques.

On my work surface, I have a self-healing cutting mat that has a grid and ruler printed on it. It protects my surface and is helpful when measuring materials. It is a bright green though, so I usually remove it while I select the elements I want to use in a project. A removable surface is great, too, when it's time to clean up. It's much easier to replace a self-healing cutting mat than a table top in case of an accident with paint or glue.

Lighting

Lighting is very important when you are creating jewelry and working with small items. Good lighting can prevent eyestrain and helps you select colors and materials. Fluorescent lighting can affect your perception of color, so it is best to avoid that type of lighting while making color selections. You can purchase specialty spectrum lights, or you can devise your own by purchasing full spectrum light bulbs that mimic natural sunlight. These are available in home improvement stores.

If you set up your workspace near a window, you'll benefit from the natural sunlight, especially when selecting colors.

If possible, set up your workspace so you have more than one source of light shining on your work. With two or more lights, you will not block your light while working on your project, and additional light can cut down on eyestrain when you are working on projects with small components.

Flooring

Many of us cannot control the flooring in our workspaces. If you are designing with messy materials, you may need to consider covering the floor in your workspace to prevent permanent damage from an accident. If you can choose the floor covering, look for a smooth, vinyl product that will wipe up easily if a spill occurs. Also, vinyl flooring makes it easy to recover small beads that fall. Avoid working on carpeting or plush rugs as it is hard to locate dropped beads. Keep your floor clean by immediately sweeping up any beads or supplies that might cause you to slip and fall.

Handy Hint

If you don't have natural light in your workspace, carry your project components outside or over to a window to check how well the colors match. You will be surprised how different things can look in different lighting.

Air Circulation

Several materials used in jewelry making, such as sealants or glues, can give off toxic fumes. Be sure to read the labels and heed the warnings. Small tabletop fans can be invaluable for removing fumes from your workspace. If you will be spraying paint, gluing, or working with other materials that give off an odor, do so outside, or in a garage with the large door open so you have adequate ventilation. Allow the sprayed or glued materials to dry before you take them back to your workspace. If you feel light-headed or have a headache when working with sprays or glues, leave the area immediately and stay away until you feel better. Go back later, look for the cause, and remove it. Safety is the top priority when working on any craft project.

Storage

It's frustrating when you can't find a certain tool or component, so it's helpful to store your materials so they're easy to find, use, and replace. If you work in several different craft mediums, you may have different storage requirements for each one. I organize my supplies first by technique, such as rubberstamping, polymer clay, or beading. Then I categorize materials by size and color.

Label all of your supplies and keep a notebook of what you have, so you can replace items as you run out. Keeping a record of your product inventory is valuable when you sell what you make, because you are able to see what materials you are replacing most frequently.

Organizing a Polymer Clay Workspace

1. Store unopened clay in a cool spot away from sunlight. Heat will damage the clay, and it will not perform properly.

2. Wrap opened or conditioned clay in wax paper, plastic wrap, or plastic bags. Wrapping opened clay in paper will cause the plasticizer to leach out of the clay into the paper. As a result, the clay will be less flexible and may require an additive to become malleable.

3. Store cutting knives and blades inside a separate plastic container. Be sure to store the container away from children.

4. Sort tools into plastic shoe boxes or baskets. Label the containers so your tools are easy to find, use, and return.

5. Store glues and lacquers with the lids tightly secured and away from heat and sunlight.

6. Keep your work surface clean and free of dust and particles.

Other Safety Tips for Your Workspace

1. Keep your workspace clean and free of dust.

2. Always use a wet cloth to wipe up after a project. A dry cloth will scatter dust and powders, which may find their way into another project, or into your eyes or lungs. Raw polymer clay will pick up any dust that comes in contact with it.

3. Do not eat or drink in your workspace. Aside from the hazard of spilling a drink on a project, you must also avoid ingesting any particles or stray pieces that may fall into a cup or onto your food.

4. Do not allow unsupervised children in your workspace, as there may be small particles, sharp tools, and toxic glues. Store all dangerous items out of reach and out of sight of children.

5. Wash your hands frequently while crafting. This will avoid contamination of supplies.

6. Avoid rubbing your face and eyes while crafting.

7. Store your supplies properly. Some materials must be stored in a cool place away from direct sunlight. Polymer clay will be affected if subjected to high temperatures.

8. Don't use powders if you have raw skin or cuts on your hands. Protect your hands when necessary with gloves or bandages.

9. When discarding any waste or leftover supplies, put the items into a plastic container and seal or knot the top. This will prevent the materials from dispersing into the air.

10. Never flush craft waste or pour it into your home's water system.

11. Take frequent breaks and stop when fatigued. Accidents occur most often when we're tired.

7. Keep a terry cloth towel or moistened wipes nearby to clean your hands, tools, and work surface.

8. Keep paintbrushes used for applying powders separate from brushes used for painting.

9. Keep toaster ovens unplugged when not in use, and keep an oven thermometer nearby to frequently check the accuracy of the thermostat.

10. Use a timer to monitor the curing time your clay is in the oven.

Organizing a Wire and Bead Workspace

The following suggestions for organizing a space to work with wire and beads can also be applied to organizing a space for making found object jewelry. There are many different kinds of containers available today. Any container used to store beads and findings must have lids that securely fasten to prevent spillage. The lids on multi-compartment containers should touch the top edge of each compartment to prevent the beads from spilling from one compartment to another if the container is tipped. Your local hardware store is a good source for organizers with multiple, small, clear plastic drawers. If you are making found object jewelry, you may need larger containers to organize your supplies.

Jewelry making supply catalogs offer many options for storing your tools and supplies. You can even order a jeweler's workbench. I have a work table covered with kitchen counter material. Around the edge of the work table I have several, multi-drawer, wooden boxes that hold tools, such as pliers, hammers, anvils, scissors, tweezers, and so on. I also have an organizer with see-through, tip-out compartments that hold a variety of findings.

For beads, I use clear, round, plastic containers that screw together. I organize my beads by color, then by size. Each stack of four or five containers contains a color family. You can find a wide variety of plastic organizer boxes at hardware and craft stores. Be sure to get the kind that you can see through. It is time-consuming to have to stack and unstack containers to look inside to find a particular bead. I use the organizer boxes for my collection of focal beads—

special beads that will be put in a place of prominence in a necklace or earrings. Ceramic watercolor dishes that have several wells for holding paint are great for holding beads as well.

If you want a project to be portable, you can use a fishing tackle box, or small toolbox (available at hardware and home improvement stores). Small, hard-shell cases with foam inserts are also handy.

When traveling, I put the ceramic watercolor dishes into one of these cases between the foam inserts. I place needles and thread conditioner under the foam inserts. When closed, the foam presses onto the beads in the dishes and keeps them from shifting. The case fits easily into a tote bag along with any other tools or materials I may need.

Handy Hint

If you spill beads on the floor, cover the end of your vacuum cleaner's hose with some pantyhose and then vacuum up the beads. The pantyhose will prevent the beads from going into the vacuum's bag. Stop frequently to slide the beads off the pantyhose into a container.

Organizing a Sewing Workspace

Be sure your sewing machine is placed on a table that is the right height for you. Many sewing machine vendors also sell tables manufactured for sewing machines. Some may have electrical features to raise and lower the sewing machine for storage or other tasks.

There are plastic organizers made for storing thread and bobbins. You should have a basic selection of thread colors for your projects including white, black, red, blue, green, and brown. Monofilament threads, elastic threads, and specialty threads, like metallic threads, are often sold on irregular-sized spools and may require an organizer box of a different size.

Sewing boxes range from the traditional style your grandmother may have used to store her buttons, needles, and other small items, to large cabinets.

Storing Sewing Supplies

It's important to store your fabric away from direct sunlight that may fade the surface or make the fabric brittle. Fabric also needs to be kept dry to prevent mold or mildew from growing. Excessive heat can damage the fibers. If you have a fabric in storage for a long time, take it out periodically, and refold it. Sometimes, it's a good idea to roll fabrics to prevent creases or cracking of the fibers. Velvet and suede fabrics should be hung so the textured fibers that make these fabrics so beautiful won't be crushed.

Purchase a pincushion so your pins will always be nearby. Magnetic pincushions are handy, but if you use them, be sure you purchase pins that are not aluminum.

Polyester stuffing and batting should be stored in the original plastic containers. Batting can also be rolled or folded and placed without packaging on a shelf. In jewelry making you will probably only need the thinnest batting.

Now that you know what kind of workspace you need, we can move on to the fun stuff. The next chapter contains all the how-to's of jewelry making. If you take the time to read this before you jump into the projects, you'll find that jewelry making is fun and simple!

Creative How-To's

▼▼▼

THERE ARE A LOT of standard techniques in jewelry making. Once you learn these techniques, each project will become easier, but please take the time to read this chapter thoroughly to familiarize yourself with all the how-to's before you dive into the projects.

Before You Start

Before you begin any technique, completely read the instructions and cover your work surface appropriately. Once your work surface is ready, assemble the needed materials and tools. Be certain you have the time for any step that must be monitored, such as baking polymer clay or allowing glue to dry. In general, jewelry making is a very convenient and portable craft, allowing you to stop and start working whenever you like.

Finding Inspiration

Where do you find the inspiration to create your own unique pieces? Glance through books to expand your knowledge of techniques. Look at the jewelry creations made by artists who work in mediums different than your own. Page through magazines you've never seen before, and check out the jewelry in the advertisements. Watch for jewelry that the actresses and actors wear on your favorite shows. Flip through home decorating magazines to find common design themes, colors, and shapes. Window shop at the mall, at galleries, and in artist co-ops. Surf the Internet for Web sites of successful jewelry businesses.

Once you see what's out there, try to figure out what's missing. If you can find a niche to fill, you will have more success than if you make your designs similar to another artist's work.

Will your jewelry be marketable, in light of the latest jewelry trends? For example, if delicate patterns and lightweight, sheer materials are in and you are creating large, long, and chunky pieces, how might your work be received?

Still looking for inspiration? Look out the window! Take a walk and carry a camera with you. Look at flowers, leaves, branches, rocks, and bark. Then look at them more closely. Can you see any unusual shapes, lines, or colors you want to include in your piece? Take lots of photos—close-ups and panoramic shots. Try looking at your pictures upside down and see if anything jumps out at you.

Sometimes you can find inspiration and the motivation to create by just taking a break from the outside world. If you can put your responsibilities on hold, such as making dental appointments, taking children to their after-school activities, paying bills, and so on, you will find it easier to enter the world of creativity. Jewelry design follows some basic guidelines, but there are also artists who have enjoyed success by breaking the "rules." Master the techniques that interest you. Learn the properties of the materials and their limitations. Then, go ahead and experiment. If you experiment with knowledge, you will not waste your materials—some of which can be very costly.

Planning Your Design

In college, I studied to become a reporter. A reporter's responsibility is to get the answers to who, what, when, where, and why questions, commonly referred to as the five W's. After creating jewelry for pleasure and profit for many years, I've found that I approach my jewelry designing using the same principles that I used to approach my writing—by answering the five W's and one additional question: how? Let's apply this technique toward the design of a necklace.

Who?

Who will be wearing the piece of jewelry? An adult? A child? Children require jewelry that looks delicate but is sturdy and will not come apart easily when worn. When you are designing adult jewelry, you must keep in mind that a piece that looks wonderful on you might be much too large for someone with a petite build or become lost on someone who is large-boned.

What?

What do you want to make? Earrings? A necklace? Or both? How about a bracelet to complete the set? If so, you'll need enough coordinating materials for three items. Deciding what you need before you get started will help you be well prepared to embark on your project. For example, if you are going to use a particularly large bead as the focal point in a necklace, what construction elements are going to be necessary to finish the project? What beads will coordinate with the focal bead? What tools do you need?

When?

When will you work on your design? If you are making a custom order, when will you need to deliver it? If you have a short time frame, you may choose to use a quick method of assembly, such as loading your needle with more than one bead at a time, rather than stitching them on one at a time.

Where?

Where will the piece be worn? Are you creating something for a formal occasion? Or is the piece going to be something that can be worn almost anywhere?

 If you're making jewelry to sell, where are you going to sell this particular item? Will the price of the materials put its final price in line with the market? For example, if you are going to sell your jewelry at the local weekend flea market, a necklace that includes 14K gold wires and several collectible glass beads may be too costly for the audience. That necklace would be better displayed at a gallery or boutique.

Why?

Why are you making this particular piece of jewelry? If your goal is to make a one-of-a-kind necklace that will be an exploration of techniques, appropriate for a gallery or showing, then you will want to use the best materials and take extra care with the construction of the piece. Sometimes you will want to use a certain bead or master a particular technique, which then becomes the reason for making the piece.

If you want to make several items to deliver to a gallery or retail store and want to meet a certain price point, then you will use less costly materials and create the pieces with simpler techniques that are less time-consuming.

How?

How will you make the piece? If, for example, you are making a brooch, you need to consider how the brooch will look to determine which design elements you are going to use.

Design Considerations

Some designers sketch out their projects before beginning. If you plan to work with beads, I recommend purchasing a bead board or using a dish towel to lay out the elements of your project before beginning.

> **Handy Hint**
>
> A bead board is usually rectangular and has a U-shaped trough to hold the beads. Use it to arrange your beads to see how you like the look. Rearrange your beads until you are satisfied with the appearance.

When you assemble the beads, you'll find that the actual necklace may vary slightly in length due to the technique used in assembly, which may affect where you place your beads. With practice, you will be able to anticipate these changes. For example, wire necklaces may turn out slightly longer, because of the loops and jump rings between the beads that connect everything together. Strung necklaces may be shorter because the beads are held tightly together on the cording.

Basic Polymer Clay Techniques

Once conditioned, polymer clay can be rolled, squeezed, and pressed into any bead shape you desire, such as ball, cone, bullet, bi-cone, disk, and oblong. Beads can be left smooth, textured, or embellished with canes. Once cured, and with the addition of inclusions, these beads can appear like semiprecious stones.

Piercing a Bead

Polymer beads weigh less than the real stones they are made to resemble, a helpful quality when making jewelry with numerous or large stones. Beads can be made from one color of clay or a number of colors blended together.

Materials

Conditioned clay
Needle tool, skewer, ice pick, nail, or other long, sharp object
Baking pan
Baking parchment or other plain white paper
Bamboo skewer or 16-gauge wire
Baking oven
Timer
Acrylic sealer, sand paper, wax, or other finishing substance

Instructions

1. Cut off a small amount of clay and roll it into a ball. This is the size of your bead. Add or remove clay, depending on the size you want your bead.

2. Hold the ball in one hand and your needle tool in the other.

3. Put your index finger on the ball where you want the tool to exit.

4. Using the needle tool or other sharp object, push the sharp point through the center of the ball, twisting the tool back and forth as you push.

5. When you feel the needle about to break through the opposite surface, stop pushing and remove it. Twist the tool as you pull the needle out.

6. Rotate the ball 180 degrees and insert the needle into the opposite side where the point of the tool started to exit.

7. Push the needle through the center of the bead, twisting the needle back and forth until the hole goes all the way through the bead. The diameter of the hole should be the same size as the material you will be using to string your beads.

8. To enlarge the hole, place the bead on the palm of your hand with the needle in the hole.

9. Gently press down on the tool while rolling the bead back and forth on your palm. Stop rolling when the hole size reaches the diameter you desire.

10. Reshape the bead as necessary.

11. Cover the baking pan with parchment or other white paper.

12. Suspend the beads from the sides of the baking pan with a bamboo skewer or 16-gauge wire to prevent the beads from developing flat or shiny spots from the baking surface.

13. Bake the beads in an oven according to manufacturer's instructions. Be sure to use a timer.

14. Once the baking is completed, remove the beads from the oven and let them cool before handling.

15. Finish the beads using one of the finishing techniques described in chapter 2.

Handy Hint

Use a small piece of clay to hold each end of the skewer or wire to the baking pan to prevent the beads from rolling off the pan when placing the pan into or removing it from the oven.

Making Canes

One unique characteristic of polymer clay is its use for creating and using canes. Canes are cylinders of clay, made by joining sheets of polymer clay into a roll. The ends of a cane are removed to show a pattern. When the cane is sliced, each piece will be the same pattern. A thick cane is called a *log;* a thin cane is called a *snake.*

Millefiori means thousands of flowers. Millefiori canes originated with ancient glass-making techniques in which pieces of glass were assembled to create a larger picture. Polymer clay can be assembled into canes to replicate patterns, much like the original glass techniques. Like glass, polymer clay canes can be reduced in diameter, and the image remains the same—with all the details proportionally smaller. The colors you choose can change the appearance of your jewelry dramatically. Experiment with color blending by mixing colors together. Be sure to record the amounts and what colors you use so you can repeat the results. For detailed information and instructions for making canes, see the reference section of this book.

Making canes is an advanced polymer clay technique, but the manufacturers have come to your rescue. Canes of many different patterns, colors, and sizes are available in packages at your craft store. They can be sliced and baked the same as the canes you would make yourself.

Making Beads from Polymer Clay Canes

Multicolor beads can be made easily from canes.

Materials

Polymer clay cane
Sharp knife
Skewer

Baking pan
Baking oven
Finishing materials

Instructions

1. Cut a slice of clay about ¼ inch thick off the cane (see step CB-1). The slice should look like the end of the cane only thinner (see figure 1).

2. The cane slice can be modified at this time for the bead. On a square cane, remove both colored outside edges, by cutting the colored edges off the slice on opposite sides (see step CB-2). This will leave two sides with a colored edge and two sides with only the design showing (see figure 2).

3. Wrap the slice around the skewer. The two sides that have only the design on them should meet (see step CB-3).

4. Press the edges of the cane slice together to form a smooth seam on the cane (see step CB-4).

5. Bake the beads according to manufacturer's instructions on the skewer suspended over the baking pan. Let cool before handling.

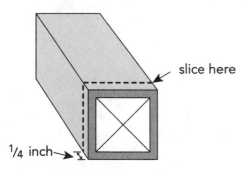

Step CB-1. Cut a slice of clay about ¼ inch thick off the cane.

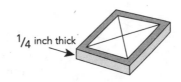

Figure 1. Slice from end of cane.

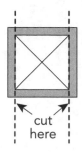

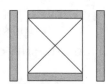

Step CB-2. On a square cane, remove both colored outside edges, by cutting the colored edges off the slice on opposite sides.

Figure 2. Cane slice with appropriate edges showing.

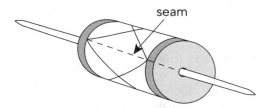

Step CB-3. Wrap the slice around the skewer. The two sides that have only the design on them should meet.

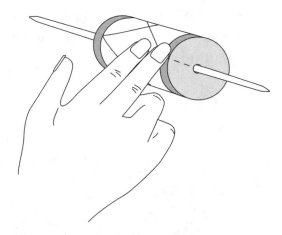

Step CB-4. Press the edges of the cane slice together to form a smooth seam on the cane.

Basic Wire-Bending Techniques

Wire has added a wonderfully wild dimension to jewelry making. It can be used in a frenzied fun manner, or it can be tamed to add sophisticated swirls and curls to your creations. With a little know-how, you'll love what wire can add to your jewelry adventures. For most designs you should use dead soft wire; however, when strength is needed, such as in findings, be sure to use half-hard wire.

Loops

Loops are the starting point for other wire-bending techniques. They are also used to connect two jewelry components together. The most common use is the end of a head pin or eye pin.

Materials

Head pin, eye pin, or a couple inches of 21- or 22-gauge wire
Round nose pliers
Flat nose pliers

Instructions

1. Grip the wire about ½ inch from the end with flat nose pliers and bend the wire slightly to the side (see step L-1). If this step isn't done, the loop will not be centered over the wire and most likely will be oval rather than round in shape.

2. Grasp the short (bent) end of the wire with the round nose pliers and twist the round nose pliers in the opposite direction of the bend to make a loop (see step L-2). You should see a horseshoe or U-shape in the wire (see figure 3).

3. Remove the pliers and grasp the tip end of the wire and close the loop by closing the wire against the original bend (see step L-3).

Step L-1. Grip the wire about 1/2 inch from the end with flat nose pliers and bend the wire slightly to the side

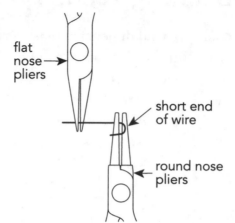

flat nose pliers

short end of wire

round nose pliers

Step L-2. Grasp the short (bent) end of the wire with the round nose pliers and twist the round nose pliers in the opposite direction of the bend to make a loop.

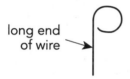

long end of wire

Figure 3. Wire bent into a horseshoe or u-shape.

original bend

end sticks up

tip end

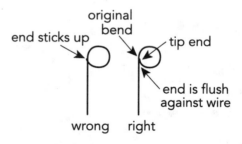

end is flush against wire

wrong   right

Step L-3. Remove the pliers and grasp the tip end of the wire and close the loop by closing the wire against the original bend.

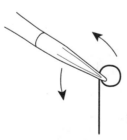

Step L-4. Grip the original bend with the chain nose pliers and adjust the entire loop.

Figure 4. Loop, centered over the length of wire.

4. Grip the original bend with the chain nose pliers and adjust the entire loop (see step L-4) until you have a loop centered over the long length of the wire (see figure 4).

Spirals and Rosettes

A spiral is used as an element in necklaces, bracelets, anklets, and other pieces of jewelry. The rosette is primarily for earrings. The short shaft is the earring post, and the rosette is the base used to glue cabochons to creating an earring.

Materials

2 pieces of 22-gauge wire, square or round, 6 inches long
   (The rosette will require half-hard wire.)
Round nose pliers
Wire cutters
Chain nose pliers
File

Instructions for the Spiral

1. Make a loop at the end of the wire with the round nose pliers (see step SR-1).

2. Grasp the loop between the jaws of the flat nose pliers and begin to tightly wrap the wire around the loop (see step SR-2). Shift the position of the pliers as needed.

3. Continue to wrap the wire until you have a spiral of the desired width. Cut off any excess wire.

4. With the chain nose pliers, press the cut end of the wire next to the spiral so the spiral is tight (see step SR-3). Smooth out the spiral so it looks even (see figure 5).

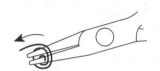

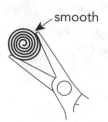

smooth

Step SR-1. Make a loop at the end of the wire with the round nose pliers.

Step SR-2. Grasp the loop between the jaws of the flat-nose pliers and begin to tightly wrap the wire around the loop.

Step SR-3. With the chain nose pliers, press the cut end of the wire next to the spiral so the spiral is tight

Figure 5. Finished, smoothed out spiral.

Instructions for the Rosette

The rosette is identical to the spiral, except it has a post.

1. Grasp the wire ½ inch from the end with the flat nose pliers and bend the wire to make a 90-degree bend (see step RS-1).

2. Use the chain nose pliers to grasp the short end of the wire, keeping the wire perfectly straight in the pliers (the short end of the wire will be the post) (see step RS-2). The tip of the pliers should be at the bend.

3. Begin wrapping the wire over the jaws of the pliers with your thumb (see step RS-3).

4. Bring the wire completely around the jaws of the pliers, forming a spiral (see step RS-4).

5. Remove the chain nose pliers and grasp the spiral with the flat nose pliers (see step RS-5).

6. Turn the wire around the spiral until the rosette is of the desired width, and clip off the excess wire (see step RS-6).

7. Use the chain nose pliers to press the cut end of the wire against the outer edge of the rosette (see step RS-7).

8. File the end of the ½-inch wire flat, and file off any burs.

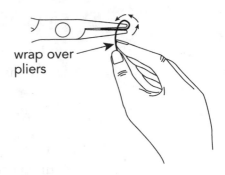

wrap over pliers

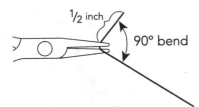

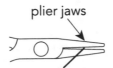

plier jaws

Step RS-1. Grasp the wire 1/2 inch from the end with the flat nose pliers and bend the wire to make a 90-degree bend.

Step RS-2. Use the chain nose pliers to grasp the short end of the wire, keeping the wire perfectly straight in the pliers (the short end of the wire will be the post).

Step RS-3. Begin wrapping the wire over the jaws of the pliers with your thumb.

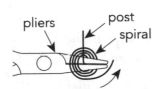

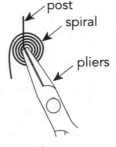

Step RS-4. Bring the wire completely around the jaws of the pliers, forming a spiral

Step RS-5. Remove the chain nose pliers and grasp the spiral with the flat nose pliers

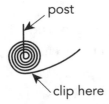

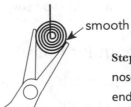

Step RS-6. Turn the wire around the spiral until the rosette is of the desired width, and clip off the excess wire.

Step RS-7. Use the chain nose pliers to press the cut end of the wire against the outer edge of the rosette.

Squared Coils

Squared coils are a variation of spirals. The spiral is made to look square instead of round.

Materials

1 piece of 22-gauge wire, 6 inches long, round or square
Round nose pliers
Flat nose pliers
Wire cutters
Chain nose pliers
File

Instructions

1. Make a loop in the wire using the round nose pliers (see step SC-1).

2. Grasp the wire next to the loop with the flat nose pliers and bend the wire to form a 90-degree angle (see step SC-2).

3. Grasp the wire with the flat nose pliers just past the bend, and bend the wire to form another 90-degree angle (see step SC-3). Continue to bend the wire around the loop forming 90-degree angles.

4. Repeat step 3 until the square coil is the size you desire, and clip off the excess wire.

5. With the chain nose pliers, press the cut end of the wire next to the coil (see step SC-4). File off any sharp areas.

Triangular Coils

Triangular coils are another variation of spirals. The coil is made the same as the squared coil except the angles are 60 degrees instead of 90 degrees.

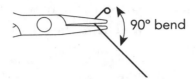

90° bend

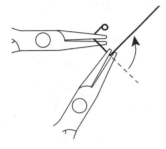

Step SC-1. Make a loop in the wire using the round nose pliers.

Step SC-2. Grasp the wire next to the loop with the flat nose pliers and bend the wire to form a 90-degree angle.

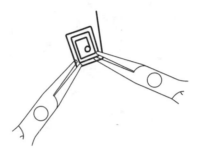

Step SC-3. Grasp the wire with the flat nose pliers just past the bend, and bend the wire to form another 90-degree angle.

Step SC-4. With the chain nose pliers, press the cut end of the wire next to the coil.

Materials

1 piece of 22-gauge wire, 6 inches long, round or square
Round nose pliers
Flat nose pliers
Wire cutters
Chain nose pliers
File

Instructions

1. Make a loop in the wire using the round nose pliers (see step TC-1).

2. Grasp the wire next to the loop with the flat nose pliers, and bend the wire at a 60-degree angle into a V-shape (see step TC-2).

3. Grasp the wire with the flat nose pliers just past the bend, and bend the wire to form another V-shaped, 60-degree angle (see step TC-3).

4. Repeat step 3 until the triangle is the size you need.

5. Cut off the excess wire near the end of the side of the coil.

6. With the chain nose pliers, press the end of the wire next to the coil (see step TC-4). File off any sharp areas.

Step TC-1. Make a loop in the wire using the round nose pliers.

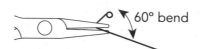

Step TC-2. Grasp the wire next to the loop with the flat nose pliers, and bend the wire at a 60-degree angle into a V-shape.

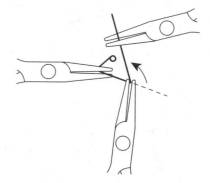

Step TC-3. Grasp the wire with the flat nose pliers just past the bend, and bend the wire to form another V-shaped, 60-degree angle.

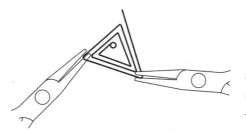

Step TC-4. With the chain nose pliers, press the end of the wire next to the coil.

3-D Coils

These are long coils that can be purchased already made, or you can make them yourself. They add whimsy to jewelry.

Materials

1 piece of 22-gauge wire, 6 inches long
Round nose pliers
1 pencil or other thin round object

Instructions

1. Make a loop at each end of the wire with the round nose pliers (see step 3D-1).

2. Starting at the top, wrap the piece of wire around the pencil (see step 3D-2).

3. Continue wrapping the wire until all the wire is wrapped around the pencil.

4. Remove the pencil. You have a coil in three dimensions (see figure 6).

5. Push the turns of the coil close together to create a tight coil (see step 3D-3).

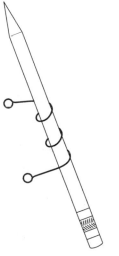

Step 3D-1. Make a loop at each end of the wire with the round nose pliers.

Step 3D-2. Starting at the top, wrap the piece of wire around the pencil.

Figure 6. A 3-D coil, after removing it from the pencil

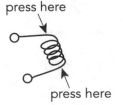

press here

press here

Step 3D-3. Push the turns of the coil close together to create a tight coil

Twisted Wire

A high-gauge wire may be too weak to hold a shape or object. Twisting the wire will increase its strength. If you use square wire instead of round wire, the twisting can add an interesting element to your design. This is usually done with dead soft wire.

Materials

Wire not more than 12 inches long
Pin vise
Chain nose pliers

Instructions

1. Place one end of the wire in the pin vise.

2. Tighten the vise around the wire so that the wire is secure.

3. Grasp the other end of the wire with the chain nose pliers, and hold the wire tight.

4. Hold the pliers stationary while you turn the pin vise with the wire held tightly (see step TW-1). The more the wire is twisted, the closer the twists will be together.

Note: A more advanced technique is a variation of this method that is used to twist longer wires.

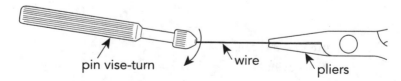

pin vise-turn   wire   pliers

Step TW-1. Hold the pliers stationary while you turn the pin vise with the wire held tightly.

French Earring Hook

The French hook is a variation of closed earring hooks. It is the most common ear wire worn.

Materials

2 pieces 22-gauge wire, half hard round or square, 2 inches long
Round nose pliers
Wire cutters
File

Instructions

1. Grasping the tip of the wire with the round nose pliers, make a loop in one end of the wire (see step FH-1).

2. Grasp the wire above the loop with the round nose pliers and bend the wire in the opposite direction to form a U or horseshoe shape (see step FH-2). The side without the loop will go through the ear.

3. When you have completed both French hooks, check to see whether they are the same length. Trim them with wire cutters to the same size if necessary.

4. Curve the straight end up slightly (see step FH-3).

5. Check the ends for rough areas, and file them smooth.

Step FH-1. Grasping the tip of the wire with the round nose pliers, make a loop in one end of the wire.

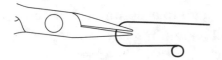

Step FH-2. Grasp the wire above the loop with the round nose pliers and bend the wire in the opposite direction to form a U or horseshoe shape.

curve slightly

Step FH-3. Curve the straight end up slightly.

Basic Bead Techniques

There are standard techniques associated with beads. You'll find, when working with beads, that you'll run into most or all of these techniques. If you master them, bead jewelry will be a breeze.

Bead Stringing

One of the easiest jewelry making techniques, bead stringing is the term used to describe beads strung on a cord or wire and beads strung on eye pins and connected together.

Bead Segments

Bead segments can add interest and dimension to your overall jewelry design. They're usually made using eye pins and beads. The eye pins are attached to other eye pins, jump rings, cords, etc.

Materials

Eye pins
Beads
Round nose pliers
Chain nose pliers

Instructions

1. Select an eye pin that is long enough to accommodate a few beads and still have about ½ inch extending beyond the beads.

2. Slide one or more beads onto the eye pin.

3. Grasp the tip of the eye pin with the round nose pliers and form a loop (refer to wire loop instructions).

4. Use the chain nose pliers to close the loop tightly (refer back to wire loop instructions).

Note: You can also wrap wire around itself to create one-of-a-kind beads, which can be used to enhance the appearance of inexpensive designs. Use 3-D uniform coils to enhance or enlarge the bead segments. The loops on the coils attach to the loops at the ends of the bead segments.

Attaching Necklace Findings with Crimp Beads

There are two popular ways to string beads. One is to put the clasp on one end of the cord, string the beads, and then attach the other end of the clasp. The second method is to loosely tie one end of the cord to an object that is too large to go through the beads, such as a pencil. String the beads, loosely tie the second end to another pencil, and then attach the clasp.

The last part of any jewelry project is attaching the findings. Crimp beads are an easy, inexpensive way to attach the clasp parts to the necklace, bracelet, or anklet. Crimp beads should not be used with wire because the metal in the crimp bead and the act of crimping the bead can damage the wire. Also, some metals react when they touch each other.

Materials

Cord (right size to fit through bead)
Clasp
2 crimp beads (Crimp beads come in different sizes. Be sure to have the one that is large enough for the cord you are using to pass through it twice.)
Crimping tool
Scissors
Adhesive

Instructions for Method One

1. Slide one end of the cord through a crimp bead and one end of the clasp (see step CMO-1).

2. Thread the cord back through the crimp bead, leaving a tail (see step CMO-2). Pull the cord so that the clasp is against the crimp bead; hold the cord tight.

3. Grip the crimp bead with the crimping pliers' second opening and squeeze firmly (step CMO-3). This will dent the crimp bead.

4. Move the crimp bead into the first opening on the crimping pliers and squeeze to reshape the crimp bead, crushing it so it holds the stringing materials tightly (step CMO-4).

5. String the first two beads over both sides of the cord, making sure that the tail of the stringing material is hidden inside the first two beads (see step CMO-5).

6. After stringing the first two beads, pull one side of the cord out of the way and cut it off next to the last bead, as close to the bead as possible (see step CMO-6). A drop of adhesive will help to prevent the cord from raveling or pulling out.

7. String the rest of the beads onto the remaining cord.

8. To finish the necklace, slide the crimp bead onto the stringing material up to the last bead (see step CMO-7).

9. Thread on the jump ring or whatever you're using to close the necklace (see step CMO-8).

10. Insert the tail back through the crimp bead, and push it through the last two beads (see step CMO-9).

11. Pull the stringing material tight, but not too tight, or the item you're making will be stiff.

12. Making sure that the stringing material stays tight, repeat steps 3 and 4.

13. Cut off any excess cord as close to the bead as possible and secure with a drop of adhesive.

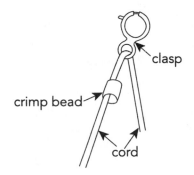

Step CMO-1. Slide one end of the cord through a crimp bead and one end of the clasp

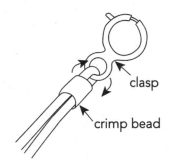

Step CMO-2. Thread the cord back through the crimp bead, leaving a tail

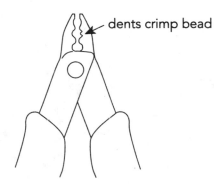

Step CMO-3. Grip the crimp bead with the crimping pliers' second opening and squeeze firmly.

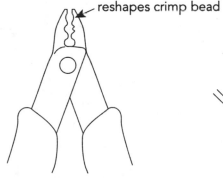

Step CMO-4. Move the crimp bead into the first opening on the crimping pliers and squeeze to reshape the crimp bead, crushing it so it holds the stringing materials tightly

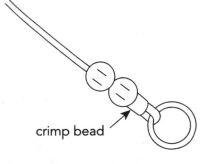

Step CMO-5. String the first two beads over both sides of the cord, making sure that the tail of the stringing material is hidden inside the first two beads

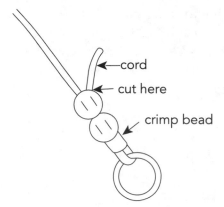

Step CMO-6. After stringing the first two beads, pull one side of the cord out of the way and cut it off next to the last bead, as close to the bead as possible

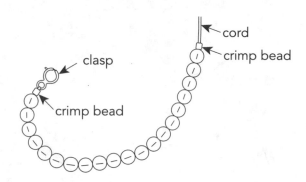

Step CMO-7. To finish the necklace, slide the crimp bead onto the stringing material up to the last bead

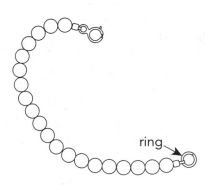

Step CMO-8. Thread on the jump ring or whatever you're using to close the necklace.

Step CMO-9. Insert the tail back through the crimp bead, and push it through the last two beads

Instructions for Method Two

1. Loosely tie one end of the cord to a pencil.

2. String the beads onto the cord.

3. Loosely tie the other end to a pencil.

4. Once you're sure your jewelry item is arranged the way you want it, untie one end of the cord. Thread the end of the cord through a crimp bead and one part of the clasp and back through the crimp bead and the last two beads (see step CMT-1). Hold the cord tight.

5. Follow the directions for crimping the bead in steps 3 and 4 of the instructions for method one.

6. Cut off extra cord and secure with a drop of adhesive.

7. Repeat for the other end of the clasp.

Step CMT-1. Insert the tail back through the crimp bead, and push it through the last two beads.

Earrings

Men and women are wearing earrings. Some like ear wires, others like posts, and still others like clips. Regardless of which you use, most procedures for making earrings are generally the same.

Materials

Ear wires, posts, or clips
Chain nose pliers
Jewelry segment

Instructions

1. Open the loop on the ear wires or clips with the chain nose pliers (see step ER-1). The loop on posts do not open. The loop on the jewelry segment will have to be opened if you are using posts.

2. Slide on the jewelry segment (or post), and close the loop with the pliers (see step ER-2).

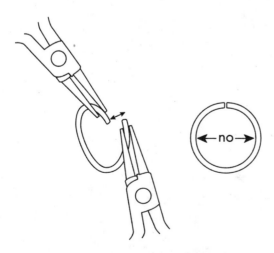

Step ER-1. Open the loop on the ear wires or clips with the chain nose pliers

Step ER-2. Slide on the jewelry segment (or post), and close the loop with the pliers.

Beaded Fabric Jewelry

You have seen wedding gowns and evening dresses that are covered with beads. The technique for making these beaded masterpieces is the same as beading on fabric jewelry. The difference is the number of beads needed and the size of the piece of fabric.

Applying a Single Bead

This technique is used when the beads are to be spaced apart. Whether the beads are evenly spaced or unevenly spaced on the fabric, the technique is the same.

Materials

Beading needle
Thread
Fabric piece
Beads
Scissors

Instructions

1. Thread a needle, and tie a small knot in the end of the thread.

2. Push the needle through the fabric from the wrong side to the right side where you want the bead to go.

3. Slip a bead over the needle and push the needle back through the fabric as close as possible to where the needle first came through the fabric (see step SB-1).

4. Pull the thread tight. The bead should be secure.

5. If this is the only bead to be attached, tie off and clip the thread with the scissors.

6. If more beads are to be sewn, push the needle up through the fabric where you want to attach the next bead. Repeat steps 3 and 4.

7. When all the beads are attached, tie and clip the thread.

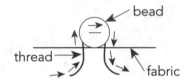

Step SB-1. Slip a bead over the needle and push the needle back through the fabric as close as possible to where the needle first came through the fabric.

Adding a String of Beads

This technique can be used to attach charms, large beads, or anything that has a hole in it to the fabric. It is also used to cover an area with beads that are close together.

Materials

Beading needle
Thread
Beads
Fabric
Scissors

Instructions

This technique is the same as for a single bead (see the Applying a Single Bead section on page 81), except that more than one bead is slipped over the needle before the needle is pushed back through the fabric. This technique can create two different looks—the difference is where the needle is pushed back through the fabric.

1. If the needle is pushed back through at about the same place it first came up, a loop of beads will be formed (see figure 7).

2. Push the needle through the fabric next to the first loop of beads and add another loop. A row of loops will create a fringe. The length of the loops is determined by the number of beads slipped onto the needle before it is pushed back through the fabric.

3. To add a charm, slip a few beads onto the needle, then slip on the charm and a few more beads before you push the needle back through the fabric.

4. After you have sewn on all the loops, tie the thread and clip.

5. If you want to add a row of beads to the fabric, push the needle through the fabric, slip on a few beads, and push the needle back through the fabric at the end of the line of beads (see figure 8). This technique can represent a flower stem, the edge of a square, or any place you want a line of beads.

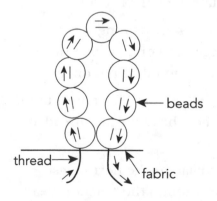

Figure 7. A loop of beads.

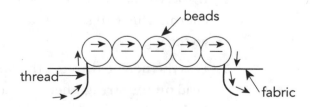

Figure 8. A row of beads

6. When all the beads are sewn on, tie and clip the thread.

Adding a Straight Fringe

This fringe varies from the loop fringe in that it is straight and can be just about any length. Also, the loop fringe is usually applied to the surface of the fabric, whereas the straight fringe is attached to the edge of the fabric.

Materials

Thread
Beading needle
Beads
Fabric
Scissors

Instructions

1. Using a piece of thread that is long enough to complete the project, usually about 24 inches, thread the needle and tie a knot.

2. Push the needle up through the fabric near the edge.

3. Slip on enough beads to make the fringe the length you want. You may want to have a large bead or charm at the end of the fringe. If so, this special item should be put on last.

4. If you've added a charm, add one more small bead next to the charm. This will serve as an "anchor" bead for the thread to go through.

5. Pass the needle through the large bead or the next to last bead on the string, then thread it through the "anchor" bead and continue to pass the needle back through all the beads on the string (see figure 9). The anchor bead is necessary to

prevent the beads from falling off when you string the thread back through. The needle should come out at the bead next to the fabric.

6. Push the needle through the right side of the first row of fringe, at about the same place the needle came through the fabric before the beads were added.

7. To make a fringe, repeat these strings of beads along the side of the fabric until you have added all that you want.

8. Tie and clip the thread.

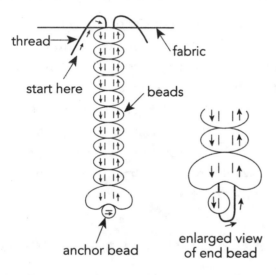

Figure 9. Threading the beads to make a row of fringe.

Variations in Jewelry

Pendants, single-strand necklaces, multistrand necklaces, pins, brooches, bracelets, anklets, and rings are all jewelry pieces, but each is different. Rings are an advanced jewelry making technique and so will not be covered here. However, the other jewelry items can be easy or complex. Your skill will determine how complex your designs are.

Pendant

A pendant is usually a single cord or chain that has one large focal object or bead. The cord can be covered with small filler beads or a combination of beads, cord, and chain.

Single-Strand versus Multistrand Necklaces

Single-strand jewelry pieces consist of beads that are all one size or graduated in size with the largest at center front. Multi-strand jewelry pieces are usually in graduated lengths. They may or may not contain the same beads, cord, or chains. They are usually hooked together at the clasp. However, some multistrand bead and pearl necklaces require spacer bars to keep the strands in place and to prevent damage to the beads or pearls. Multistrand jewelry pieces are not something you will want to start with.

Handy Hint

Consider using an acid-free glue for projects that include photos or papers. The acid-free glue will not harm the photo as the piece ages.

Lengths of Necklaces and Bracelets

Chokers are usually 15 to 17 inches long. However, the length will vary depending on the size of the individual's neck. It is best to measure the choker on the individual before completely attaching the clasp. However, this is not always possible. When designing chokers to sell, it's a good idea to include a clasp that can be adjusted for length.

Most necklaces are 18 to 24 inches in length. Individuals usually have a particular length necklace they like to wear. I have found that the best way to sell necklaces is to have a variety of lengths or to measure the necklace on an individual and finish it at that time with the length he or she desires. If you are at a craft fair, this is not difficult. However, if you are selling to a store, you may end up being asked to redo the necklace for a customer.

Lariat necklaces are very long, allowing them to be worn tied in a knot, looped over the head to appear as a multistrand necklace, or pinned off to the side in an asymmetrical look. Bracelets are usually 6½ to 8 inches in length, including the clasp. If you are designing a bracelet for an individual, measure the wrist where he or she likes to wear bracelets and add ½ inch.

Anklets are usually 2 inches longer than bracelets, but measure the individual's ankle and add 1 inch.

Pins and Brooches

A brooch is a large decorative pin. Just about anything can be worn as a pin or brooch. Pinbacks come in numerous finishes, lengths, and designs. Some pinbacks are glued to the back of the jewelry piece, while others are designed to be seen. If you are using a decorative pinback, the jewelry piece is attached with a jump ring or wire loop. The size of the glued pinback should be the largest possible without showing on the front of the piece. The larger the pinback, the better the stability of the brooch.

> ### Handy Hint
>
> To spread a smooth, thin layer of white glue, squeeze the glue onto the surface, then use an old credit card or a stiff piece of cardboard as a spatula to move the glue around.

Some pinbacks have bails attached that allow the piece to also be worn as a pendant. This feature was common in the nineteenth and early twentieth centuries. Historically the bail would turn down behind the piece while it was worn as a brooch. Today the bails are fixed, and care must be taken when gluing the pinback to the piece to ensure the bail will not show on the front.

An alternative to the pinback with an attached bail, which can be difficult to find, is the brooch converter. This is a tube with a loop (bail) attached that slides over the pin on the pinback.

Basic Found Object Jewelry Assembly

Many of the techniques outlined here can be used in making found object jewelry, especially pins and brooches. Once you know what you're making, the next step is figuring out how to assemble the piece so you can wear it comfortably.

Backing Materials

The backing materials you use for a pin will greatly affect the construction of the piece. They should be appropriate to the materials you are using in construction. For example, if you are assembling beads and polymer clay, I suggest using ultrasuede or leather for a backing. If your piece is primarily composed of paper, then a quality paper, or even felt, would be appropriate.

Glues

The weight and porosity of the items you are gluing together will determine the type of glue you use. There are specialty glues for fabrics, foam, craft foam, paper, and more.

White glue, also known as PVA glue, is usually water based. Use it on paper, wood, and small items like sequins, fabrics, and fibers. You can also use white glue to bond small pieces of china, ceramics, and metal.

Use cyanoacrylate glue for bonding nonporous items like metals or plastics. Work quickly, because this glue will instantly bond anything it touches, including your skin!

Goop or Surebonder brand glues are used on glass, ceramics, magnets, metal, plastics, vinyl, or florals. (A floral is any kind of a flower—dried, silk, fresh, or otherwise.) These glues give off fumes, so use them in a well-ventilated area. They often take up to 24 hours to dry.

Glue guns can hold hot- or low-temperature glue. The glue sets as soon as it cools off. Use low-temperature glue with heat-sensitive materials like foams and some fabrics.

Handy Hint

Use masking tape or props to hold pieces together temporarily so they don't shift while the glue dries.

Creating Your Jewelry Making Projects

▼▼

NOW THAT YOU'VE FAMILIARIZED yourself with the how-to's of creating jewelry and the tools you need, it's time to put it all into practice. By creating the projects in this chapter, you'll get a feel for the type (or types) of jewelry you prefer making. Remember, even when you're creating jewelry from instructions, you can add your own personal touch by making changes to suit your own likes. If you find some instructions that aren't clear, refer to chapter 4. Take some time and read over the directions completely and assemble all of your tools and supplies, then you'll be ready to go. See the color insert in the center of the book to see what your finished projects will look like.

Wire and Bead Jewelry

There are endless possibilities with wire and beads—necklaces, bracelets, earrings, anklets, and basically whatever else you like. The projects I've included here are fun to make, and at least one of them should suit your tastes.

Pearl Necklace and Earrings Set

Freshwater pearls are dyed in many colors, so you can make many versions of this easy project. You can use freshwater pearls to make jewelry appropriate for a wedding, elegant dinner, or casual evening at the movies. You can also refine and modify the following technique to create many new and fashionable looks. The instructions give measurements to make a 17-inch necklace. Add or reduce wire, as needed, to fit your own length requirements.

Ability Level

Easy (requires that you know how to make a loop—explained in chapter 4).

Time

2 to 2½ hours

Materials

1 spool 24-gauge wire
Wire cutters
File
Round nose pliers
19 3-millimeter brown miracle beads
27 freshwater pearls
Chain nose pliers
Ruler
Black water-soluble ink marker
    (optional, for marking measurements on the wire)
Hook for necklace
Closed earring hook

Making the Necklace

1. Cut a 40-inch length of wire and file the ends smooth.
2. Fold the wire in half, bringing the ends together (see step PN-1).
3. Grip the wire at the fold with round nose pliers and make a loop (see step PN-2).
4. Starting at the loop created in step 3, begin twisting the wires together as you would close a bread wrapper with a twist tie (see step PN-3).
5. After ¼ inch of twisting, slide one of the miracle beads onto one side of the wire (see step PN-4).
6. Twist another ¼ inch and slide a freshwater pearl onto the other side of the wire (see step PN-5).
7. Continue steps 5 and 6 until you have added all 19 miracle beads and 19 freshwater pearls.
8. Continue twisting the wires together until the necklace measures 19 inches from the loop to the loose end.
9. Cut off any wire past ½ inch (see step PN-6).
10. Use the round nose pliers to form a loop in each end of the wire (see step PN-7). Make sure the loops are the same size and are next to each other.
11. Slip the hook over both loops (see step PN-8).
12. Close the loops with the pliers as described in chapter 4.
13. Cut a 30-inch length of wire and file one end smooth.
14. Tightly wrap the filed end around the base of the loop (created in step 3) three times to secure it (see step PN-9).
15. Wrap, loop, and wind this wire around the pearls, beads, and twisted wire of the necklace (see step PN-10). Keep wrapping until you reach the hook.
16. Wrap this wire securely around the base of the hook at least three times to secure it (see step PN-11).
17. Cut off the excess wire about ¼ inch away and file the end until it is smooth.

18. Press the end of this wire around the base of the hook until it lies smooth. Press the wire with the chain nose pliers if necessary.

19. Shape the necklace so it is round.

Making the Earrings

Making the earrings is much like making the necklace, but you'll use less wire and fewer beads.

Step PN-1. Fold the wire in half, bringing the ends together.

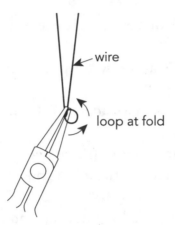

Step PN-2. Grip the wire at the fold with round nose pliers and make a loop.

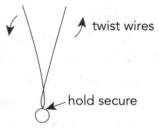

Step PN-3. Starting at the loop created in step 3, begin twisting the wires together as you would close a bread wrapper with a twist tie.

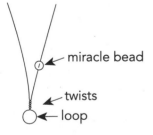

Step PN-4. After ¼ inch of twisting, slide one of the miracle beads onto one side of the wire.

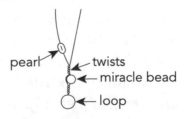

Step PN-5. Twist another ¼ inch and slide a freshwater pearl onto the other side of the wire.

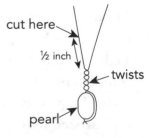

Step PN-6. Cut off any wire past ½ inch.

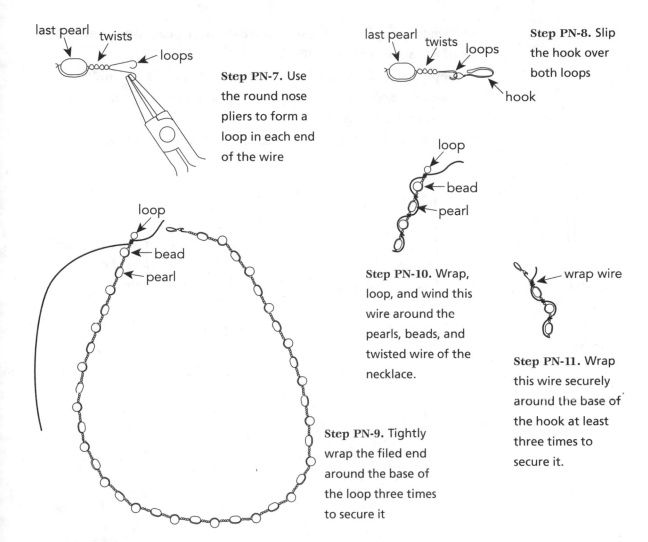

last pearl   twists   loops

Step PN-7. Use the round nose pliers to form a loop in each end of the wire

last pearl   twists   loops

Step PN-8. Slip the hook over both loops

hook

loop

bead

pearl

Step PN-10. Wrap, loop, and wind this wire around the pearls, beads, and twisted wire of the necklace.

wrap wire

Step PN-11. Wrap this wire securely around the base of the hook at least three times to secure it.

loop

bead

pearl

Step PN-9. Tightly wrap the filed end around the base of the loop three times to secure it

1. Cut a 10-inch length of wire.
2. Fold the wire in half, bringing the ends together (see step PE-1).
3. Slide one end through one earring hook (see step PE-2).
4. Make a loop at the fold of the wire, directly above the hook (see step PE-3).
5. Starting at the loop, begin twisting the wires together as you would close a bread wrapper with a twist tie (see step PE-4).

6. Twist three times and slide a freshwater pearl onto one side of the wire (see step PE-5).
7. Repeat step 6 until all three freshwater pearls are added.
8. Use the excess wire to loop, wrap, and wind around the earring (see step PE-6).
9. Repeat steps 1 through 8 to make the other earring.

Step PE-1. Fold the wire in half, bringing the ends together.

Step PE-2. Slide one end through one earring hook.

Step PE-3. Make a loop at the fold of the wire, directly above the hook.

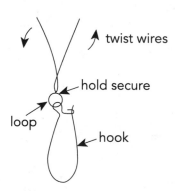

Step PE-4. Starting at the loop, begin twisting the wires together as you would close a bread wrapper with a twist tie.

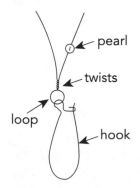

Step PE-5. Twist three times and slide a freshwater pearl onto one side of the wire.

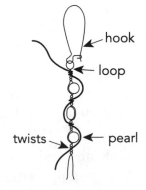

Step PE-6. Use the excess wire to loop, wrap, and wind around the earring.

Illusion-Style Pearl Necklace

These necklaces are lightweight and delicate in appearance, but by using a good brand of wire, such as Soft Flex wire, they are quite strong and resistant to breakage. If you decide to make this style of necklace to sell, you can meet a variety of price points by changing the beads you use. Quick and easy to make, this is a project that will benefit from an assembly line style production of manufacturing, meaning, you can make several copies of the same necklace. The assembly line style of production is following each project step more than once to assemble multiple projects. For example, if you are making ten necklaces, you will complete step 1 ten times, then complete step 2 ten times, and so on. This approach saves time and helps you generally improve your skills as you continuously repeat the same step. Also, as you improve your skills through repetition, it should eventually result in decreasing the time it takes you to complete each step.

Ability Level

Beginner

Time

½ hour

Materials

Wire cutters
Ruler
20 inches gold .019-diameter wire
2 small clamshell knot covers (found in retail bead stores and in catalogs)
2 medium (2 millimeter × 3 millimeter) gold crimp beads
Crimping pliers

14 small (2-millimeter × 2 millimeter) gold crimp beads
Chain nose pliers
Gold barrel-style clasp
7 small-diameter, dyed, freshwater pearls

Instructions

1. Use wire cutters, crimping pliers, and the ruler to cut a 20-inch length of wire.
2. Thread on one clamshell knot cover and one medium crimp bead.
3. Take the end of the wire nearest the crimp bead, and wrap it around the crimp bead until ½ inch extends beyond the crimp bead (see step ISN-1).
4. Use crimping pliers to close the crimp bead, securing the wire (refer to chapter 4).
5. Firmly pull on the wire to ensure that the crimp is secure. If not, repeat the crimping process.
6. Slide the clamshell up to the crimp, making certain that the ½ inch of excess wire extends out through the bottom of the clamshell (see step ISN-2).
7. Gently squeeze the clamshell closed over the crimp with the chain nose pliers (see step ISN-3). Use wire cutters to cut off the excess wire.
8. Put the clamshell hook through the loop on one half of the barrel clasp (see step ISN-4).
9. Use the chain nose pliers to close the hook over the clasp's loop (see step ISN-5).
10. Thread on a crimp bead and position it approximately 1½ inches from the clamshell (see step ISN-6), then secure the crimp bead with your crimping pliers.
11. Thread on a freshwater pearl and another small crimp bead.

12. Grip the crimp bead with the pliers and slide the freshwater pearl and bead right up to the first crimp bead (see step ISN-7). Secure the crimp to complete the step.
13. Continue adding all of the freshwater pearls and small crimp beads, spacing them out along the length of the wire.
14. After all of the freshwater pearls are added, thread on a clamshell, the other medium crimp bead, and the other half of the clasp.
15. Finish the necklace by attaching the other half of the necklace clasp.

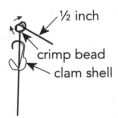

½ inch

crimp bead

clam shell

Step ISN-1. Take the end of the wire nearest the crimp bead, and wrap it around the crimp bead until ½ inch extends beyond the crimp bead.

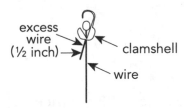

excess wire (½ inch)

clamshell

wire

Step ISN-2. Slide the clamshell up to the crimp, making certain that the ½ inch of excess wire extends out through the bottom of the clamshell

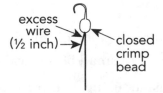

excess wire (½ inch)

closed crimp bead

Step ISN-3. Gently squeeze the clamshell closed over the crimp with the chain nose pliers.

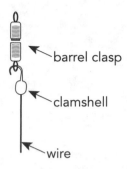

Step ISN-4. Put the clamshell hook through the loop on one half of the barrel clasp.

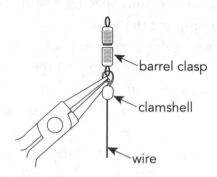

Step ISN-5. Use the chain nose pliers to close the hook over the clasp's loop.

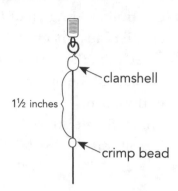

Step ISN-6. Thread on a crimp bead and position it approximately 1½ inches from the clamshell.

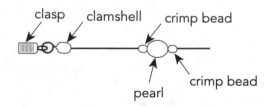

Step ISN-7. Grip the crimp bead with the pliers and slide the freshwater pearl and bead right up to the first crimp bead

Variations

■ Change the look of this delicate necklace with the wide variety of small beads available.

■ Consider using dichroic beads for lots of color, or small, faceted crystals that will catch the light and sparkle when worn.

■ Add or remove wire as needed to fit your measurements or to make a choker.

Spirals and Beads
Necklace and Earrings

This necklace can be put together quickly and easily, once the basic steps are mastered. The spiral cages visually balance the size of the beads. The cages are lightweight and do not contribute much to the weight of the necklace, as the glass dichroic beads are heavy.

Ability Level

Advanced: You must be able to make a loop, and spiral cages with the Spiral Maker. Save this project for a challenge, after you feel more experienced.

Time

Approximately 2 hours

Materials

Wire cutters
1 spool 16-gauge wire (dark blue)
File
Ruler
Black marker
Olympus Spiral Maker (or other spiral maker, if Olympus is not available)
Chain nose pliers
18 3-millimeter black disk beads
11 large glass dichroic beads
Hook clasp and split ring
2 earring findings (posts, wires, or clips)

Making the Necklace

I've broken the instructions down considerably to help you make the project one element at a time.

Making the Wire Cages

1. Use wire cutters to cut ten 8-inch lengths of wire. File the ends smooth.
2. Measure and mark the center of each 8-inch length.
3. Insert the end of one wire into the Spiral Maker. Be sure the wire does not extend beyond the end of the tool.
4. Following the instructions for the tool, wind the wire to the center, creating a flat coil, leaving some unwound wire. Repeat this with the other end. (See figure 10.)
5. Fold the coils closed like a book so they overlap each other and the unwound ends point in opposite directions (see step WC-1).

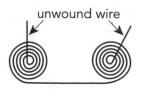

Figure 10. Wire with coils at each end

Step WC-1. Fold the coils like a book so they overlap each other and the unwound ends point in opposite directions.

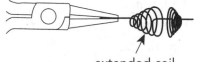

Step WC-2. Grip one unwound end with the chain nose pliers and pull so the coil extends

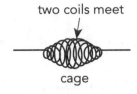

Figure 11. The finished cage, after you complete both sides.

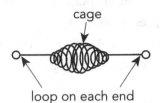

Step WC-3. Make a loop on each end of the cage.

6. Grip one unwound end with the chain nose pliers and pull so the coil extends (see step WC-2). Repeat with the other side until you've created the cage (see figure 11).
7. Make a loop on each end of the cage (see step WC-3).
8. Repeat steps 1 through 7 with the other nine wires.

Making the Bead Segments

1. Cut nine 8-inch lengths of wire and file the ends smooth.
2. Begin by putting a wrapped loop on the end of one wire, as explained in chapter 4 (do not close the loop yet).
3. Slide one loop of one wire cage onto the loop from step 2.
4. Close the loop.
5. Repeat steps 1 through 3 with each piece of wire and each spiral cage.
6. Slide the disk bead, dichroic bead, and second disk bead onto the wire.
7. Make a loop onto the end without the cage, stopping to insert a spiral cage before closing the loop.
8. Repeat step 5, making bead segments and connecting the spiral cage beads.

Making the Clasps

1. Attach the hook clasp to the cage loop at one end of the necklace (see step C-1).
2. Attach the split ring to the other end of the necklace, so the hook is on one end and the split ring is on the other end (see step C-2).
3. Cut off the excess wire and file the end of the remaining wire smooth.

use loop on cage
to attach hook
to necklace

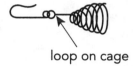

loop on cage

Step C-1. Attach the hook clasp to the cage loop at one end of the necklace.

use split ring
for other part
of clasp

split ring

Step C-2. Attach the split ring to the other end of the necklace, so the hook is on one end and the split ring is on the other end.

Making the Earrings

1. Follow the instructions for making the wire cages, but only put one loop on the cage.
2. Hang one wire cage from the loop on one earring hook.
3. Repeat for the other earring.

Polymer Clay Jewelry

Polymer clay is a relatively new material for the jewelry maker to consider. As artists experiment with polymer clay and share their experiences, this material continues to gain popularity. The vivid colors and the clay's ability to be blended into an unlimited palette of custom colors is only one of the many attractive properties of this medium. Also, polymer clay can be cured at relatively low temperatures (265 to 275 degrees Fahrenheit, depending on the brand) in a common household oven, as opposed to the high temperatures and kiln needed for most other traditional clays. Because polymer clay is still new, it is somewhat difficult to find. Though many national chains, such as Michael's and Wal Mart, carry this clay, it may be easier to find in art and craft stores or on the Internet.

 # Photo Frame Pins

These pins are quick and easy to make and require little clay. They are easily modified by cutting out different patterns. Photo frames are popular and make inexpensive gifts. These pins can be marketed as impulse items in your display or home party, as they can be created with several different "looks," depending on your color choices, to match any home décor or clothing style. Attractive and lightweight, these pins will be an easy addition to your line.

Ability Level

Beginner

Time

30 to 40 minutes after the clay is conditioned

Materials

Polymer clay (translucent and gold)
Rose quartz embossing powder (or color of your choice)
Craft knife
4 index cards

Rolling tool

Ruler

Pencil

Scissors

Striped cane (purchased)

Oven preheated to 265 degrees Fahrenheit

Cyanoacrylate glue

Pinback

Instructions

1. Condition all the clay.
2. Pinch off small pieces of gold clay and roll them into small balls, no larger than ¼ inch in diameter.
3. Cut off half of the translucent clay and form a pancake.
4. Pour a dime-size amount of embossing powder onto the center of the pancake and fold up the edges, sealing the powder inside.
5. Begin kneading the clay and powder together until the powder is evenly dispersed throughout clay. Add more powder if necessary, to ensure that the clay is completely colored by the embossing powder.
6. Cut the powdered clay in half and flatten one half into a pancake.
7. Place the pancake on an index card and use the rolling tool to roll the clay to ⅛-inch thickness.
8. Repeat steps 4 through 7 with the other half of the clay, so you have a front and a back piece.
9. Using the ruler, pencil, and scissors, draw a 1-inch by 1½-inch rectangle in the center of the second index card and cut out the rectangle (see step FP-1). This is the photo opening template for a wallet-sized photo.

10. From the third index card, cut out the outline of the picture frame (create the pattern of your choice), making a template to place onto the clay. You will use this to cut out the photo frame from the clay.

11. Place the outline template from step 10 over one sheet of clay, and use the craft knife to cut out the clay around the outside of the template. This will be your frame front.

12. Repeat step 11 with the second sheet of clay to create a frame back. Flip it over, leaving the clay on the template (for baking purposes).

13. Place the photo opening template from step 9 on the frame front (see step FP-2).

14. Cut out and remove the opening from the clay (see step FP-3).

15. Place the last index card for the photo opening at the top of the frame back you created in step 12, so one end of the index card extends off the edge (see step FP-4).

16. Carefully remove the template from the frame front and place the frame front on the back, over the index card, aligning all edges (see step FP-5).

17. Gently press the three sides not containing the index card together (see step FP-6).

18. Cut thin slices of striped cane. Refer to the project photo in the color insert, or make your own design, and place the cane slices and the gold balls onto the frame front. Press the balls to flatten them slightly.

19. Place the assembled frame (still on the template and with index card inserted) into the preheated oven and bake for 15 minutes.

20. Allow the frame to cool, then gently pull out the index card from the center and peel off the template from the frame back.

> ▼▼▼▼▼▼▼▼▼▼▼▼▼▼▼▼▼▼▼
>
> # Handy Hint
>
> By placing the clay onto the index card, you will be able to manipulate it easily without stretching or pulling it out of shape.
>
> ▲▲▲▲▲▲▲▲▲▲▲▲▲▲▲▲▲▲▲

21. Use cyanoacrylate glue to attach a pinback to the photo frame, near the top back (see step FP-7). This will prevent the frame from tipping forward while worn on clothing.

Variations

■ Use different colors of embossing powder, such as lapis lazuli or malachite, to create uniquely colored clays. Experiment with new metallic glitter and stone-colored polymer clays that can be used to eliminate a step and save time and materials.

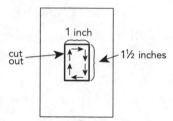

Step FP-1. Using the ruler, pencil, and scissors, draw a 1-inch by 1½-inch rectangle in the center of the second index card and cut out the rectangle.

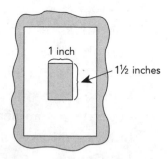

Step FP-2. Place the photo opening template from step 9 on the frame front

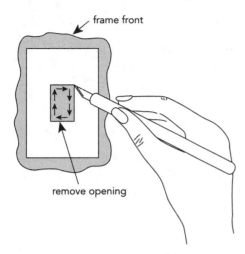

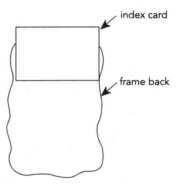

Step FP-3. Cut out and remove the opening from the clay.

Step FP-4. Place the last index card for the photo opening at the top of the frame back you created in step 12, so one end of the index card extends off the edge.

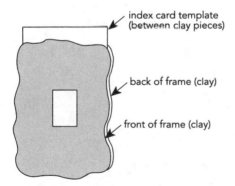

Step FP-5. Carefully remove the template from the frame front and place the frame front on the back, over the index card, aligning all edges

Step FP-6. Gently press the three sides not containing the index card together.

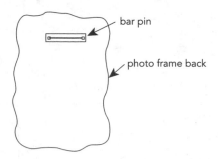

Step FP-7. Use cyanoacrylate glue to attach a pinback to the photo frame, near the top back.

◼ Instead of a pinback, glue a magnet onto the back of the frame.

◼ Change the size to accommodate different-sized photos.

Other polymer clay jewelry ideas include bracelet and earring sets made with caned beads and spacers, key chains made from scrap clay, and single pendants made from assorted clay beads.

Fabric Jewelry

You can create many different styles of fabric jewelry. Simply cut out a printed motif from fabric, or create your own fabric with laces, metallic threads, and other embellishments found in a fabric or quilting shop.

 ## Stitched and Beaded Pin

Customers are constantly looking for unusual items that don't cost a fortune to buy, wear, and enjoy. Using the steps outlined here, you can create the base material for many pins in a short time, then embellish each pin individually, making several different styles. Many of the scraps of fabric and threads you may already have can be incorporated into these projects, reducing your material costs.

Ability Level

Beginner: You need some knowledge of basic sewing machine stitches.

Time

Depending on the number of pins you plan to create and whether you are working assembly line style or making one at a time, the time can vary from 20 minutes to over an hour for an exquisitely beaded pin.

Materials

Assorted fabrics (brightly colored—polyester, cotton prints, challis prints, ultrasuede, felt, or silk. Fabrics that are not appropriate or more difficult to work with include corduroy, high-pile velvets, and slippery fabrics like rayon.)

Fabric scissors

Fiberfill for quilt batting

Straight pins

Sewing machine

Assorted thread (cotton, metallic, quilting)

Iron

Fabric glue

Pinback

Beading needles

Beads (small seed beads, metal charms and stampings, flat decorative beads, or buttons)

Did you know???

Traditionally, pinbacks are glued in position with the clasp end pointing to the right (when looking at it), in order to accommodate a mostly right-handed population.

Instructions

1. Create a 6-inch by 6-inch fabric sandwich by placing a piece of fiberfill or batting between two layers of your chosen fabric (see step SBP-1).

2. Pin the layers together at the edges and use the sewing machine to stitch random lines all over the fabric sandwich, switching threads and changing direction often as you stitch (see step SBP-2). Continue stitching in this manner until the fabric is dense with thread.

3. If you desire a puckered look in your material, use a larger piece of fabric on the top and secure it around the edges. As you sew the fabric, the extra fabric on top will pucker. Press the fabric if you like.

4. Create your own template to use for cutting out the pieces that will become your pins. Experiment with random shapes. If using a patterned fabric, consider cutting out a motif. Cut out a front and back piece of fabric.

5. Cut a second template in the same shape as the template in step 4, but ⅛ inch to ¼ inch smaller.

6. Place the front piece of fabric right side down on your work surface.

7. Cover the smaller template with a thin coating of fabric glue. Place it in the center back of the front piece of fabric and press firmly.

8. Cut a small slit in the upper section of the back piece of fabric to accommodate the pinback (see step SBP-3).

9. Line the larger template up with the back piece of fabric.

10. Using an ink pen, mark through the slit onto the template, to indicate where the pin will go (see step SBP-4).

11. Remove the template from the fabric.

12. Glue the pinback to the line you marked on the template (see step SBP-5).

13. Cover the template with a thin layer of glue and adhere it to the back piece of fabric, making sure to push the pinback up through the slit (see step SBP-6). Allow to dry.

14. Use a beading needle and thread to stitch on any accent beads or fringe as desired.

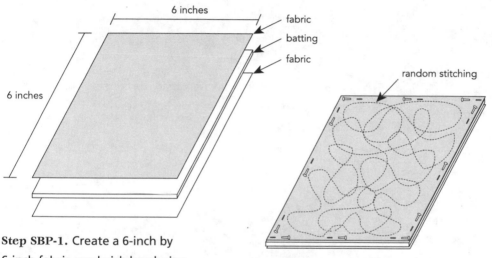

Step SBP-1. Create a 6-inch by 6-inch fabric sandwich by placing a piece of fiberfill or batting between two layers of your chosen fabric.

Step SBP-2. Pin the layers together at the edges and use the sewing machine to stitch random lines all over the fabric sandwich, switching threads and changing direction often as you stitch.

Variations

- Cut out the design from a printed fabric and make a small pillow pin (a small square cut out, stitched to a backing material, and stuffed with polyfil before being stitched closed).

- Create elegantly beaded abstract pins that will accent a blazer or overcoat.

- Design a pin to accent the fabric in a T-shirt or any other item that you can give or sell with the pin as a set.

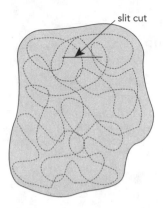

Step SBP-3. Cut a small slit in the upper section of the back piece of fabric to accommodate the pinback.

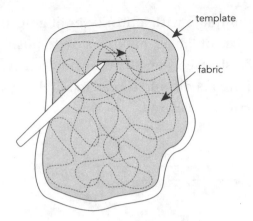

Step SBP-4. Using an ink pen, mark through the slit onto the template, to indicate where the pin will go.

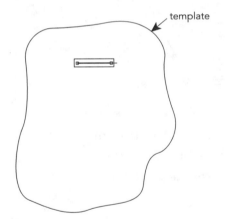

Step SBP-5. Glue the pinback to the line you marked on the template.

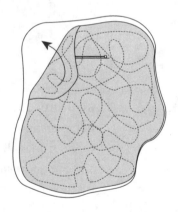

Step SBP-6. Cover the template with a thin layer of glue and adhere it to the back piece of fabric, making sure to push the pinback up through the slit.

Found Object Jewelry

Have you ever lost one earring? Have you had a necklace break, and you just can't find all of the pieces? If you've saved these sorts of items, you can incorporate them into "found object" jewelry. I once found an earring that had been run over in the parking lot of my local mall, yet it still looked interesting, so I kept it and worked it into a pin. I have a friend who goes to yard sales to buy old watches that she takes apart and uses the inner workings to embellish her jewelry. Found object jewelry can be fun, challenging, and cheap because you usually use materials you already have!

 # Puzzle Pin and Earrings Set

Jigsaw puzzles without all of their pieces are great sources of background material for found object jewelry. This project is inexpensive to make; in fact, most of what you will use is found in your home! This quick and easy project is appropriate to sell in markets with low price points—and it's a good assembly line project.

Ability Level

Beginner

Materials

Acrylic paint (gold, metallic copper, and black)
Assorted jigsaw puzzle pieces
Spray webbing (gold)
Low-temperature glue gun
White glue
Mica flakes
1 spool 26-gauge artistic wire (dark blue)
Skewer or knitting needle
Pinback
Post-style earring findings

Time

20 to 30 minutes, including drying time

Making the Pin

1. Paint several puzzle pieces gold and copper and allow them to dry.
2. Arrange the pieces in a pleasing manner so you can start gluing them together. Consider fitting some base pieces together.
3. Once you have a pleasing arrangement, glue the pieces together with a glue gun.
4. Spray lightly with webbing spray and allow the piece to dry.
5. Glue on the mica flakes with white glue (see photo in center of book).
6. Randomly wrap wire around the puzzle pieces.
7. Coil the ends of the wire around a skewer (see photo in center of book) or use a Twist 'n' Curl tool.
8. Glue a pinback on the back of the assembly.

Making the Earrings

1. Repeat steps 1 through 3 from the pin instructions twice to make two earrings.
2. Glue post-style earring findings to the backs of the assemblies.

Variations

- Use small puzzle pieces to form a collage.
- Leave some puzzle pieces unpainted.
- Give pins a seasonal theme by carefully selecting your paint colors and adding charms, buttons, or holiday beads.

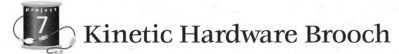 Kinetic Hardware Brooch

This pin is fun to make and fun to wear. People don't expect to see jewelry created from basic hardware store finds. Also, because of the magnet, the elements on the chain can be arranged in an unlimited number of ways, offering a different look and a unique feature for a piece of jewelry.

Ability Level

Beginner

Time

15 to 20 minutes, not including drying time

Materials

3-inch donut magnet
Fine-grade steel wool
Metallic acrylic paint (copper)
1-inch, sponge-style paintbrush
Brush-on sealant
Hot glue gun
Hot glue sticks
1-inch pinback
Beaded chain (commonly used for light pulls)
Wire cutters
Assorted sizes of brass and base metal washers
Assorted rubber o-rings
Metal springs
Beaded chain clasp

Instructions

1. Lightly sand the magnet with steel wool to remove any trace of oil.
2. Paint one side of the magnet with copper paint, and allow the magnet to dry completely. Once you see it is completely

covered without streaks, wash out the paintbrush (you may need to paint more than one coat).

3. When dry, paint on a coat of sealant. Allow the sealant to dry completely and apply a second coat.

4. Using a hot glue gun filled with glue sticks, attach a pinback to the back of the magnet.

5. Cut a 9-inch length of beaded chain with the wire cutters.

6. Thread on an assortment of washers, o-rings, and springs. Be sure that the magnet attracts some of the elements.

7. Insert one end of the chain through the opening of the magnet, and add a clasp to close the chain (see photo in center of book).

Variations

- Change the color of the magnet with paint.

- Add spray webbing or metallic paints to accent the magnet.

- Use beads and wire instead of hardware store items.

chapter 6

Your Crafts Vision

▼▼

JEWELRY IS A SIGNIFICANT PART of our lives. It is one of the most popular gifts people give to family and friends. A gift of jewelry can make any holiday or celebration more memorable. This means that you have a head start when selling your jewelry—your customers are already educated about the meaning and use of your product! As you will learn in the second part of this book, there are dozens of markets for your work and many ways you can sell your hot commodity.

Since you are reading this book, you probably already have an interest in creating jewelry and a desire to make money by selling your work. What are your dreams? How will your talent and creativity play a role in your plans? Do you dream of earning an income from your jewelry? At first, you will have more questions than answers. This book can help you sort out the questions and find the answers. Your decision to sell your creations should be made only after some reflective thought and careful planning. This book is a little a garden. I've planted the seeds of knowledge, technique, traditions, and creativity; now you must do your part to make your garden of ideas grow. However, only you can finish shaping your vision and make it part of your future.

MARIA'S STORY

Maria Filosa is one of the leading designers in the art and craft industry. Her work ranges from kid's crafts to wonderful, one-of-a-kind jewelry pieces. One of her techniques is so clever that it's hard to believe the jewelry was created by combining hot glue and craft foil! And a simple request for an angel brought profits flying in!

Maria explained: "I started to make my special angel pins in 1994 when Tiffany Windsor, a well-know industry TV celebrity, saw my jewelry pieces at a Society of Craft Designer educational seminar. She was opening an angel shop and wanted to know if I could make angels. Well, I hadn't made any angels but I immediately answered her with, 'I'll send you some samples next week!' That was the beginning of a long angel relationship for me. From there, the next event was the *Creating For Life* Auction, which is a big event in the craft industry. I figured angels would be perfect. I sent in fifty-two angels and they all sold in less than 1 hour! From then on, I've sent between 150 and 200 angels to the auction each year. I believe it has come to be a tradition! One simple question had brought about years of angel making and much spiritual healing for myself and others."

But why hot glue as the foundation? "I never really plan to work with any certain material—I really think the material chooses me. It seems to speak to me, not in words but in feelings. I know I'm going to be working with a certain material when I keep going back to it over and over again. I touch it, stare at it, form and re-form it. Although I'd used hot glue for years and years as an adhesive, I'd always been fascinated by the fact that it's liquid and pliable when hot, but when cooled, it's a solid material, so it naturally progressed from there. Meeting another designer, Sharion Cox, also

sparked my interest more because she introduced me to colored hot glue. Being a color
fanatic, I immediately took to it and couldn't
put it down from then on. The foil came in
about a year later. I'd met someone who had
a foil business and she was working with
Sharion. She would drip glue on top of the
foil, let it set up, then make jewelry from it.
I started playing with that for a bit but felt
there was something more to this. One

night about 3:00 A.M., my mind started racing. I kept thinking about the
glue and the foil. I decided to see what would happen if I rolled the glue
out onto the foil, cut out pieces, and layered them. Instead of physically
gluing them together, why couldn't I use the glue that was already attached
to the foil? But how would I make it melt? First I tried the oven. That
worked pretty good but you really had to keep an eye on it and if you are
anything like me, you have the attention span of a flea so I'd frequently
forget I had glue cooking and I'd just wind up with a puddle of mush. I then
decided to try a tool I was using for embossing stamped images. The heat
embossing tool was my ticket to glue jewelry fame. I could control the
amount of heat applied to the piece; even somewhat direct the heat for a
perfect heat fusion."

Maria feels that one of the best things about making jewelry is seeing
the person wear her work. "There is just something so special about angels," she said. Check out this talented jewelry designer's work at her Web
site: www.starchaserdesigns.com.

Everyone has creativity within, and everyone can find a craft they are good at and enjoy doing. The difference between wishing, dreaming, or wanting to do something and actually doing it, is writing and following a plan. In the case of selling jewelry, your written outline will be a statement of your goals and your game plan for accomplishing them. Even if you only want to supplement your hobby or sell your jewelry creations part time, you still need a plan.

Handy Hint

Make a few lists of short- and long-term goals. Break the lists down into smaller, more achievable steps. These lists and goals are your best starting points.

Putting your dreams in writing may seem to take the fun out of using your creativity and skills, but writing a business plan is the most successful and proven way to meet your goals. A plan isn't silly, fruitless, or a waste of valuable time. It's a tool that will help you in all areas of your life, and it's a habit worth acquiring. Before you move on to the following chapters of this book, take the time to think about your dreams and goals. Think about your talents and skills. List all your assets and liabilities. Keep a creativity journal—a notebook in which you write down your dreams, goals, and plans for selling your jewelry. Figure out what questions you need answered. Write down the amount of time that you have available to pursue your dream.

A creativity journal is a wonderful documentation of your dreams. I still have my original 5-year plan. Every once in a while, when I'm feeling stressed or worried about meeting new goals, I take a moment to flip through my old craft and creativity journals. I can hardly believe how far I've come since my first crafting project. My first show was so small you could count the number of exhibitors on two hands. But all my work sold and I felt a strong sense of accomplishment. I had earned money by making items with my own hands! I still wasn't convinced that I could earn a steady income from selling my work, but it was fun to make crafts and I enjoyed the interaction with customers. I signed up for more shows and, to this day, still enjoy the excitement of selling at an outdoor art and craft show. I may have had doubts at the beginning, but today I am more confident than ever that people can make a living selling their creativity. You need to find your niche and then make it grow. There never was, nor is today, any greater thrill for me than to craft a design and watch someone buy it.

I introduced jewelry items almost immediately into my product line. I was making fun jewelry from woodcuts, old buttons and charms, and resin shapes. The pieces were easy to make and I could make a dozen pins or earrings in an hour. The pieces were also easy to package and store between shows, and best of all, the jewelry sold itself! All I had to do was wear a pin on my shirt and tie my hair into a ponytail so my earrings could be seen. Customers admired the jewelry I was wearing and that was a good enough sales pitch to get them to buy a set for themselves!

But, remember I had a plan. I wrote down my goals, and to this day, I still take the time to update and revise my goals. I write down how many jewelry pieces I want to make each week, and how much money I have to spend on supplies and materials. I note how much money I need to earn to make the effort worth my time and investment. Over the years, I haven't reached every goal I've set for myself, and some of my goals have changed, but I have always kept keep track of my goals, reviewed and updated them, and then moved forward.

Who Is Selling Their Jewelry?

Before you begin work on your plan, you might benefit from reading the results of my survey of ten individuals who sell their jewelry creations.

- When asked how long they had been selling their jewelry, I found that two of the individuals in the interview had sold their work for 1 to 2 years, two had sold for 3 to 4 years, three for 3 to 6 years, and three for 10 or more years.

- When asked what mediums they specialized in, the most popular answer was beads, the second most popular answer was wood; then a tie between wire and metal, semiprecious stones and pearls, and fabric and fibers. The least popular mediums were plastics and gold and silver.

- Two members of the group considered jewelry making a source of additional income, working 10 to 20 hours a week, while half of them considered it a part-time job, working 21 to 40 hours a week. The remaining two in the group made jewelry as a full-time occupation, working over 40 hours a week.

- Regarding annual incomes, it was determined that none of the group made less than $3,000 a year. Four members of the group made between $4,000 and $12,000 a year, while half made between $14,000 and $25,000 annually, and one individual made over $35,000 a year making jewelry.

- When asked how many worked from home or off site, results showed that nine members of the group worked primarily from home, while one worked in a rented warehouse.

- The most popular source for selling their crafts was word of mouth to family and friends, craft shows, and Web sites. Other popular sources were craft malls or craft co-ops, sales representatives, and farmer's markets/flea markets. The less popular sources were catalog or mail order and home shows, and no one sold directly to wholesale distributors or at garage sales.

- When asked how much each interviewee charged for his or her items, it was determined that the average fee for a piece of jewelry was $20.00 to $34.99. One person sold for less than $5.00, one sold items between $35.00 and $74.99, two people sold their items between $15.00 and $19.99, one person sold for more than $75.00.

- This group's best-selling items varied. One person said rings, three said earrings, two said necklaces, one said bracelets, and three said brooches or pins.

- When asked what the group considered the best aspect of selling their crafts, two said working for themselves or independence, three said the creativity and new challenges, four said being able to work and still be home with their children, and one person said being able to work with a disability or physical challenge.

Determine Your Goals

The following questionnaire can help you determine your goals and ensure that you are prepared to do what needs to be done to sell your crafts. Use these questions to make lists of your goals, then refine the lists into an effective business plan. Come back to this questionnaire as many times as necessary in the future, as you revise your goals according to your needs.

Your Creative Self

1. List the five reasons you like to be creative.
2. List up to five styles, techniques, or designs in which you feel you excel.
3. List at least five skills, talents, and assets you can bring to this endeavor as an artist.
4. List any weaknesses, liabilities, or obstacles you need to overcome.

5. Do you have the motivation and determination to work on your own? Do you have the time-management skills to schedule your workday and your personal life?

6. Will your family and friends support your efforts?

7. Do you only want to make one-of-a-kind jewelry? Or will you make multiples of a particular design?

8. What jewelry techniques are most interesting or challenging to you?

9. If there were no obstacles in your way, what would your goal be in making jewelry? What obstacles do you see that prevent you from reaching this goal?

10. Are there ways to overcome the obstacles? Is there someone who has the knowledge or skill you need? Where can you learn this knowledge or skill? Is there another direction you can turn and still meet your dream or goal?

Getting Started

1. What is your number one goal? Is there a way you can measure your progress in achieving this goal?

2. How will you define your success? By creative achievement? By the amount of profit? By the freedom of working for yourself? By growth of the market? By the reaction of your family and friends?

3. Do you only plan to earn enough income to support your hobby? Earn extra household income with part-time efforts? Earn extra leisure spending money with part-time efforts? Or do you want to work at jewelry making full time?

4. How much time can you realistically dedicate to your jewelry making?

5. What other responsibilities do you have? Rank these responsibilities in order of importance to you. Rank them in order
   of importance to your family and friends. How do the rank-
   ings compare? How do you feel about the comparison?

Business Basics

1. What are five skills, talents, and assets you can bring to this
   endeavor as a businessperson? List them.

2. Do you want to be a sole proprietor? Form a partnership?
   Incorporate?

3. Do you have starting capital? Can you create a company
   budget?

4. Do you have an accounting system?

5. Do you want employees? If so, will you hire your family or
   friends?

6. Do you want to work from your home?

Day to Day, Year to Year

1. What do you want to accomplish during a day, a week, a
   month, and a year of creating jewelry?

2. Do you have room within your home to dedicate space to
   your work?

3. Will your local area have enough business opportunities to
   help you earn the income you desire? Will you have to market outside your own local area? Do you want to do that?

4. What does your city, county, or state require from you in paperwork or licenses to start a business? Do you understand
   all of the city, county, and state regulations and laws? Do you
   need to consult an attorney?

The Bottom Line

1. How and what business records do you need to keep?

2. How will you price your jewelry? Do you know how similar items are priced in the marketplace? How does your pricing compare?

3. Do you need to consult an accountant?

4. Do you understand all the federal income tax forms required for reporting the extra income? Are you willing to keep all your receipts and invoices filed in a logical order?

5. Do you want to set up a business checking account? Can you keep your personal and business finances separate?

Selling Your Jewelry

1. What makes your jewelry unique? What are the selling points?

2. How should you display your jewelry? Do your pieces need explanations or do they sell on their own merits?

3. Will you need to package your jewelry? Are some pieces fragile, thus requiring special handling?

4. What would you like to name your business? Does the name limit you? Is it self-explanatory? Will your customers remember it?

5. Is there a market, or niche, for your particular jewelry designs?

6. Where can you sell your jewelry in your area? Craft co-op? Craft mall? Art/craft gallery? Annual art/craft shows?

7. Do you want to sell your jewelry directly to the consumer?

8. Do you want to wholesale your work or sell it through a representative?

9. Do you want to sell your jewelry via mail order? If so, do you have space to handle the packaging and shipping supplies needed? How will you cover the costs of shipping and handling?

10. Do you want to sell on the World Wide Web? Will you create and maintain your own Web site or be part of a larger Web site?

Teaching and Demonstrating

1. Do you want to teach others how to make jewelry?

2. Where will you teach? Out of your home? At a retail art or craft store? At a local art museum?

3. Do you want to sell your designs (written instructions) to a magazine? Write a book on jewelry making?

4. How will you keep current on trends, colors, textures, motifs, techniques, lifestyles, and your consumers?

Focus on the Future

1. Where do you want to be a year from now in terms of your dreams, goals, personal life, and business life?

2. Where do you envision your jewelry-making business will be 5 years from now? Ten years from now?

3. How strong is your motivation to build your jewelry making into a business? Are you willing to make sacrifices? Do you have a clear vision of what you hope to accomplish? Can you stay motivated in the face of a setback?

Write Your Plan

Now it's time to focus your drive and ambition. While it's probably impossible to answer every single question in the above

Success in Selling Original Designs

- Make the commitment to become a business. You may choose to start small or part-time, but understand that the goal of a business is to grow and make a profit.

- Write a business plan and keep it with your business records. Your plan should include short- and long-term goals.

- Know your talents and skills. Know your assets and liabilities. The way to succeed is to show off your best.

- Know your markets. Investigate. Place your best work in the markets that will showcase them to best advantage.

- Keep learning. Study classic jewelry designs and the latest trends. Tune in to what kinds of jewelry people are buying and why.

- Keep an updated résumé and a portfolio with pictures of your designs. Don't assume that others know who you are or what you do. A business card in your pocket might mean a future sale.

- Grow your talents and expand your jewelry-making techniques. Experiment and have fun every once in awhile. Change is part of the business. You are not the same person today as you were 5 years ago.

- Share your talents. Volunteer to teach a class in your community. Network with other jewelry designers. Occasionally donate a few pieces of jewelry to support a worthy cause.

- Have faith in your abilities. If you don't believe in yourself, no one else will. Self-promotion is not the same thing as bragging.

- Enjoy your work. Rest often. Daydream every day. And go for it!

questionnaire (and still keep your sanity!), use the answers you did find to form the boundaries of your hopes and dreams. Use your lists to write a more defined plan. For example, from answering these questions, I may realize I only want to support my jewelry-making hobby and I realize I would prefer to do this by teaching instead of selling finished designs. Yet I might also discover I have an interest in having my work published. Now I have two areas of income I want to explore.

Now that you have a plan, Part Two of this book will give you the technical and business information you need to start your jewelry business. You will still have to do your own research and homework. The business world is always changing, growing, and expanding in new ways. Don't be overwhelmed. Your new venture is just beginning.

Part Two

For Profit

Profiting from Your Talent

▼▼

IF YOU HAD TOLD ME 15 years ago that I would be selling my own handmade work to customers all over the United States and that I would end up selling over 1,500 of my designs to magazine editors, book publishers, and television producers, I probably would have laughed and said you needed a reality check. From the very beginning of my creative journey I knew I'd never be the most talented artist or skilled craftsman. I also assumed that only perfect work would be of interest to the public. The only thing I was sure of was that I loved being creative and I loved creating jewelry. It was my enthusiasm and love of art and craft that led to my success.

The advice I now give you (with confidence and pride) is based on my years of hands-on experience. Attitude is everything! If you, too, love working with beads, metals, clays, woods, paints, glues, and jewelry findings, you may have just stumbled upon a way to make your hobby pay for itself. Or you may have found a wonderful way to earn income for yourself and your family. It will be your enthusiasm that turns your talent into cash!

This chapter, and the following chapters in Part Two of this book, will show you how you can profit from your jewelry. You'll discover the many options and possibilities that are available to

135

you. I'll share what I've learned, but remember, your talent is unique, and thus your business will be unique. In addition to reading this book, you'll need to spend time thinking about how to apply all the knowledge it has given you. There is no right or wrong way to explore your choices in jewelry making, but each of us, as professionals, should have short- and long-term goals. Thus, as we strive to reach them, we should stay open to new avenues and feel free to follow new dreams.

I grew up with a strong work ethic and wanted to contribute to my family by earning income. So, when I started selling my work at art and craft shows, my only goal was to make a profit. As I became more established, I dreamed of selling my designs to magazines so I could see them in print. I set a 5-year goal for accomplishing this bit of fame. It took me 7 years before I felt confident enough to submit my jewelry designs to a magazine editor, but I finally did it. And this move opened even more doors for me to sell my creativity and talent. Therefore, my second piece of heartfelt advice is that you sometimes have to risk a piece of yourself in order to reach a goal. Creativity is different from most skills in that it leaves you open to rejection and a feeling of personal failure. There is something a touch frightening about putting your heart and soul into a jewelry design that you will then show to an editor. Even the most professional and well-seasoned artists and craftsmen have their moments of doubt. What if no one likes my work? What if I'm told my jewelry isn't attractive? What if someone laughs at my efforts? Trust me, in most cases this just doesn't happen. And if the worst does happen, you will live through it. The risk is worth the rewards!

Aided by the information and knowledge shared by the authors in this book, you will succeed. And although we might like to take credit for your success, you can take all the credit! Your talent, enthusiasm, and attitude will determine how far you take your business.

Creativity Can Thrive in Business

In addition to earning a profit, I have discovered other benefits from having a career in creativity. What I find appealing about jewelry making is discovering my creativity and the pleasure of using that creativity to make others smile. My dry sense of humor and silly wit can be seen in every jewelry design I make. The compliments I receive from my customers, and even those who are just browsing, continue to tickle my ego and motivate me to create more designs. You'll find the same pleasure and fun in your jewelry making.

Tell the World Your Talents

Many creative souls find the thought of giving or selling their jewelry to family, friends, or strangers (the buying public) a terrifying notion. All artisans put a little bit of themselves into each jewelry creation. The thought that others might not like the result is sometimes enough to start a mild anxiety attack followed by a frantic urge to hide in the hall closet. This book is about jewelry making for fun and for profit. Your profit is not just monetary. You also profit from the process of becoming a salesperson. Many think that selling is the lowliest of occupations, but all of us need persuasive skills throughout our lives. If you want to change a school policy at your child's elementary school, you'll have to sell the school board on your idea. If you want to convince your family to hold the family reunion in Hawaii this year, you'll need to sell each relative on the idea! Each of us faces situations in our everyday lives where selling skills are the key to success. The benefit of learning how to sell is the confidence that you can and will succeed in your business.

Handy Hint

Remain flexible and open to the options that are available to you.

Income with a Byline

1. Make sure your design is original. It should be your own creation that has not previously appeared in print in any form (magazine, book, project sheet, television, and so on).

2. Select a magazine you are familiar with and enjoy. Write to the editor and request the writer's guidelines.

3. Follow the guidelines as you write instructions for your design. Do your best to write according to the magazine's format. Type the instructions, double-spaced.

4. Proofread and edit your copy before submitting it. Also submit a photograph or detailed drawing of your design. Send your design to the magazine's project editor or editor. Expect to wait at least 4 weeks for a response. After 4 weeks, feel free to follow up with a phone call to the editor.

5. If your design is accepted, you will be sent a contract. Read it carefully and don't sign it until you understand the terms and feel comfortable with them. Ask your editor any questions you have and address any concerns, such as more money for your design, or giving the publication first rights only.

6. After signing the contract, be sure to meet your deadlines and supply everything the editor may request, such as a list of supplies needed, how long it takes to make the design, the total cost of the project, and so on.

Few products (including jewelry) sell themselves without a little help from a salesperson. Consumers purchase an item or product either because they need it or because they want it. Jewelry falls into the *want* category. Therefore selling jewelry requires a little sales work on your part.

Fear Not

Making jewelry for your own enjoyment can be stress-free, but selling your pieces is bound to cause some anxiety. Here's a mind-over-emotion exercise that has worked for hundreds of professional

▼▼

7. If your design is rejected, don't take it personally. Different magazines have different needs. Try another magazine.

8. Submitting a design to a book publisher is similar to submitting to a magazine, except that many designs are usually needed. Before you can get a book publisher interested, you need a concept or idea, and up to 36 designs. Book publishers also have writer's guidelines that are available upon request.

9. To locate book publishers, consult your reference librarian. There are several directories with contact information. You can also go to a bookstore, look through the crafting section, and write down the names and addresses of publishers. Searching the Internet is still another way to locate publishers of craft books.

10. Keep current on popular trends, including colors, mediums, techniques, and motifs. Check out craft retailers and shops. Your design will not sell if the required supplies are not readily available to the consumer.

11. Also consider submitting articles on specific jewelry techniques. Editors are always looking for interesting ideas. When submitting your work, keep the magazine's readership and focus in mind.

▲▲

jewelry makers. This technique requires that you continue to use your creativity and imagination even after your jewelry creation is finished. Take a deep breath and exhale slowly. Then close your eyes and pretend that someone else made the piece of jewelry that you want to sell. Mentally list all the reasons why a potential buyer would value and purchase this item. Open your eyes, and write down each positive element of the item. Is the workmanship superior? Does the piece make you smile? Are the colors in fashion? Is the design unique? Can it be worn for multiple occasions? Take your list, which shows the selling points of the design, and turn it into a

1- to 3-minute sales presentation. Practice your presentation in front of a mirror, a family member, and a good friend or two. Get feedback on your presentation, then adjust it until you feel comfortable with it. Congratulations! You've just become a terrific salesperson!

Once you overcome your feelings of anxiety and fear of rejection, you can more clearly see the reasons why a customer might buy your design. Too often, we are our own worst critics, brutally nitpicking and finding fault with our creations. It's easier to come up with a list of values and selling points for a craft when you aren't personally and emotionally involved. Most of us have been taught that it's better to be humble than be perceived as egotistic or boastful. Promoting yourself and your jewelry has little to do with modesty and much to do with recognizing the quality you put into your pieces.

Your Heart in Each Work of Art

A lesson I learned early in my career as a craft professional is that the sale doesn't end when the consumer buys a piece of my work. The creative world is a little different than the rest of the retailing world. Consumers who enjoy wearing handmade jewelry feel that they are also buying a small piece of the personality and character of the artist. It is human nature to want the people you like and love to be successful. In the business world this is called "value added."

Is there a jewelry artist or other craftsperson whose work you admire? I learned early in my selling career that I couldn't take the money I earned selling my jewelry at art and craft shows, then spend it all buying crafts from the other vendors. It was tempting, but as a businessperson, I needed to learn restraint and to be practical. Even so, there was this brilliant jewelry maker who had the most adorable glass blown jewelry I'd ever seen. Granted, I really don't wear that much

Handy Hint

Keep a journal of your creative thoughts and ideas.

jewelry, but I absolutely adored her work. I'd go browsing during my quick breaks from selling, and talk with this artist. She was funny and bright and her great sense of humor was reflected in her jewelry designs. Because I liked her and her jewelry, I wanted her to succeed. And to this day, she is the only vendor I break my NO BUY-ING rule for! Her work is proudly displayed in my jewelry box and I am thrilled to wear it on special occasions.

> ## Did you know???
> The top three reasons people craft are to save money, to make a gift for a friend, and to personalize an item to suit their own tastes.

Your customers will want to get to know you. Share with them who you are and why you craft jewelry, and they will become your biggest supporters. I can't explain the joy I feel when a loyal customer comes running to my booth at a craft show. There is a special bond with a customer who says, "I was looking for you. I always stop at your booth first! What new creation have you made for me this year?" Being a professional in a creative endeavor doesn't allow you to sit quietly in the corner of your display and hope your jewelry sells itself. You must be an active player, sharing your love of creativity, design, and jewelry with your customers.

After you sell your work for a few years, you will get to know your regular customers. When I do the same craft show, in the same town, once a year, customers remember me and make a point to find me the next year. I even started getting requests to sign my pieces. I hadn't signed my pieces because I thought of them as fun jewelry, not heirlooms or valuable collectibles. But many customers told me they were collecting my pieces and that it would mean a lot to them to have my signature on the work. You may not be able to sign all your jewelry pieces, but you can develop a "signature" design. One jewelry artist I know always has a jade frog charm as part of her charm bracelet line. Another jewelry artist always uses clasps with a tiny pearl centered on them.

Avoid Assumptions

Never assume that customers know anything about your work. You might not feel comfortable selling your jewelry at first, but you might feel comfortable explaining how you made a particular piece. The first step in selling is to talk to your customers. Talk about how you selected your supplies. Talk about your metal or wire techniques. Talk about how you carefully select each charm, or how you choose which colors of glass beads to use in a bracelet. It's easy for a potential customer to assume that creating a piece of jewelry is simple. Customers have no way of knowing about the skill that goes into your jewelry unless you explain your process to them. It's also a good idea to memorize and talk about the history, traditions, and other interesting facts connected to the components and techniques you use to make your jewelry.

Many Opportunities Come Your Way

We are often so rushed, that we don't take the time to review all the opportunities that are available to us as outlets for our business. By taking time to read this book, you will gain much of the knowledge needed to explore these options. But keep in mind that no matter how much information you gather, or how many hours you spend reading and studying, the means you use to sell your work will be unique. Explore your options carefully and with an open mind. Will you be bored producing multiples of a particular jewelry design? If so, consider selling the original design with written instructions to a publisher. If you don't want to write, you can become a kit, tool, or product designer in the craft and creative industries. Or maybe you'll choose to teach your techniques and skills. You can expand your business by charging teaching and class fees. Everything you need to know about selling a design for publication, working with craft manufacturers, and setting up jewelry classes is provided in chapter 9.

Professionalism Earns Reputation

The main differences between a professional and a hobbyist are the amount of raw supplies purchased and the number of finished pieces sold in a given year. There are no official studies or surveys in the craft and creative industries that explore the professional jewelry maker in depth. However, established professionals usually purchase their raw supplies wholesale from a distributor or manufacturer, whereas hobbyists usually purchase their raw supplies from retail outlets. Some professional artisans, such as teachers, product or technique demonstrators, and designers, do not purchase large amounts of one kind of raw material. Instead, they use a large variety of materials, making it difficult for them to qualify for the minimum purchasing orders of wholesale supplies. Many manufacturers have set up programs to help teachers, demonstrators, and designers obtain supplies at discount prices. Craft manufacturers also offer endorsement programs that reward the individual, monetarily, for using a specific brand. You might be thinking, "I just want to sell a few pieces of my work. I'm not a professional!" Yes, you are! If you sell your work, you are a member of the ranks of many fine artists, artisans, and craftspeople. The definition of a professional includes more than the number of items you sell or the amount of income you make. It includes attitude, savvy, and selling the best work at the best price with the best customer service. Don't discount your efforts. Take pride in your art.

Declaring yourself a professional jewelry maker isn't the only step required for turning your hobby into a moneymaker. You also have to prepare yourself and your family and friends for the transition. You'll need their support to make a success of your business,

Working with Manufacturers

1. If you've found a product that you love to work with, and your designs are great (if you do say so yourself), you may be able to find work with the product's manufacturer. There is always a need for photographs of finished designs for ads, exhibit displays, and project sheets. Prepare your best designs as finished samples. Workmanship counts.

2. Photograph your work. You don't have to be a professional photographer. Simply use plenty of light (outdoor light is best). Use a gray or light blue sheet or towel as a backdrop for your jewelry. Avoid creases in the backdrop. If your jewelry pieces are small, place a ruler or other object in the photograph to give it perspective. Take several shots from several angles. After developing the film, select one or two of the best shots. Write your name and address on the back of each photo.

3. Write a brief summary of the design piece. Include all the materials used, basic steps, time involved, skill level, and total expense. Include your name and address on the summary. It's also a good idea to title the design.

large or small. Your support group might also include people who have received your designs as gifts. Change on any level is not easy. That same human nature that gives us creativity and enthusiasm is the same human nature that likes to keep the world steady. The same creative soul who feels uneasy about self-promotion and selling is the same person who is working to establish a business or hoping to earn money in order to buy more jewelry-making supplies. It's not easy. It's not simple. And it's not going to happen overnight. You have to work on giving this a consistent, confident message to your family, friends, and community: *I am establishing myself as a business.*

Believe in Yourself

This book gives you the direction and guidance needed to establish your message in a professional manner. I wish I could tell you that

4. Write a cover or query letter to the manufacturer. It's best to take the time to contact the manufacturer in advance of writing, in order to find out who the contact person is for design submission. A design sent to a specific contact person will get a faster response than one sent to a general address.

5. If there is interest in your design, the manufacturer will contact you with a contract. Read it carefully and be sure you fully understand it before signing. This is also the time to ask if the manufacturer has a demonstrator's or designer's program.

6. If your design is rejected, don't take it personally. It might not meet the needs of the manufacturer at the time. Feel free to ask your contact person if the manufacturer is looking for designs and, if so, the types of designs in which the manufacturer is interested. Remember to be polite and professional.

7. Fees paid for designs vary from manufacturer to manufacturer, ranging from $75 to $5000. It depends on how the manufacturer is going to use the design.

jewelry making is considered an important and highly respected profession by all. However, to give you that impression might lead you to stumble. I have a résumé with seven pages of published work, including more than 1,500 designs in print and my own television segment on a national cable network, but when I say I make and sell jewelry, nine out of ten people respond, "How cute. Must be nice to sit home all day making jewelry." If you hear this enough, especially in the patronizing tone often used, you'll feel like throwing a temper tantrum. So much for professionalism. Since we can't allow a customer to see us in a tizzy, we must remain professional in presence and style. I've learned over the years to smile. Then I explain that I have the best of all worlds as a sole proprietor of a small business—I have the freedom of creativity and expression while earning an income from making jewelry. However, what I'd really like to do is invite them over to my office to fill out my state sales tax collection forms which are anything but cute!

To help you believe in yourself as an authentic businessperson, learn what is most important to you. Don't listen to the comments of people who don't understand what you do. Use your goals and your business plan to measure your success. Professional jewelry making, like any creative occupation, will never fit a simple job description. It is an occupation that may perpetually be misunderstood by a society that prefers job descriptions to be black and white.

You are creative enough to come up with your own answers for the questions that are often asked, such as: Do you work? Why are you making so many of those beaded earrings? Do people really buy your necklaces? What do you do for a living? Your attitude toward your efforts will determine how others react to you. If you take yourself seriously, if you approach all challenges as a professional, if you glow with confidence and determination (no one needs to know that you might really be shaking in your boots), the rest of the world will soon follow your lead. There is only one exception: Never take yourself or your business so seriously that you can't have a good laugh every once in a while or that you forget that your work should be a positive influence on your family and community. Sometimes it's tough to keep smiling when facing deadlines, preparing for a big art and craft show, or sending off a design to a new publisher when the last publisher turned you down, but in the long run, that smile will give you the energy to keep trying.

The chapters that follow provide answers to questions about the details of the day-to-day business responsibilities of a craft professional. You will learn the business how-to's that will guide you in making your dreams and goals a reality. You'll also learn how to price and market your jewelry. Enjoy the excitement and challenge of the learning that awaits you.

Pricing Your Jewelry

▼▼

PRICING YOUR WORK CAN BE one of the most difficult aspects of making a profit. Sometimes pricing can seem like pulling a number out of a magician's hat. It's never easy to put a price tag on a manufactured item, let alone an item you made with your own hands.

There are three key factors to consider when pricing your jewelry.

1. Cost of goods
2. Cost of labor
3. Cost of overhead

Cost of Goods

It's easy to overlook small or minuscule supplies that are incorporated into a finished product. Yet, small bits and pieces can add up quickly. The first step in pricing a piece of jewelry is to list all the components of your design. I recommend making this list as you create or assemble an item. Take time to note even the smallest components such as glue, crimp beads, paint, and wire. Create a new list the first several times you make the item. Then combine the lists into one comprehensive list of components and include how much each component costs. Now you have a firm dollar amount that constitutes the "cost of goods" needed for each individual design or product you are going to create to sell.

Cost of Labor

Labor is the dollar amount you pay yourself for your time and effort. Most jewelry makers grossly underestimate the time involved in making a finished design. Time flies when you're having fun and it's easy to forget to keep a time card. I highly recommend timing yourself several times while making a specific item and then average the results to get a true picture of the time you spend creating the design.

▼▼▼▼▼▼▼▼▼▼▼▼▼▼▼▼▼▼▼▼▼

Did you know???

The number one pricing mistake most artists and craftspeople make is underpricing their work.

▲▲▲▲▲▲▲▲▲▲▲▲▲▲▲▲▲▲▲▲▲

Many crafters who sell their work make several components of an item in one sitting, rather than creating one complete item at a time from start to finish. Then they put together several finished items during one work session. This way of crafting is called assembly line or *mass production.* I always laugh at the term mass production when applied to creative businesses, because it makes me think of huge machines pumping out identical parts in quick succession. I have yet to meet a jewelry artist who works like a machine, but mass production is an industry-accepted term and we can work by using an assembly line *process.* A jewelry artist may choose to make a cane for ten sets of earrings in one working session, then cut and create the threading hole and bake the newly created beads in a second session. In a third session, the artist will assemble the beads into ten sets of finished earrings. A final session might be spent carding and packaging the earrings for a show. Whatever method you use, keep track of every minute you spend making your jewelry pieces.

A labor rate can be paid in two ways. The first way is to pay yourself by the hour. Set a rate that you feel is fair and reasonable. Most of us would be tickled to earn $25, $50, or $100 per hour, but a reality check will tell you that your new business can't afford your services! I suggest you pay yourself in 15-minute increments because this makes the math easier than determining the rate to the minute. Round your time up or down as you see fit. As your skills and talents grow, you can increase your labor rate per hour to include your efficiency and acumen. You work for yourself, so avoid caps or ceilings on your income. Consider the national minimum wage as a starting point for your own labor rate.

The second way to pay yourself is by the piece, unit, or finished design. In this case, you set a price for each finished project. You can set a unit rate of $3.00 per earring set or $4.50 per finished necklace. Remember that you are the boss and can always give yourself a merit raise and bonuses!

Selecting the method for pricing your labor is very subjective. Personally, I would rather pay myself by the piece because I am very quick and efficient when crafting. You might prefer to use an hourly rate. Calculate the different ways you can apply a labor rate and see what works best for you and your situation. Labor rates are not written in stone and can be adjusted and reevaluated over time.

Overhead

The final consideration for a pricing formula is referred to as overhead. It's a catchall category for anything outside the cost of goods and labor. You may not think of it, but you probably use electricity as you craft, you occupy space within your home for business rather than personal needs, and most jewelry pieces sold need packaging, price tags, and receipts. You may have supplies that don't directly become part of the item you are selling but that are needed to make the item. Jewelry making includes all kinds of tools, from a dedicated toaster oven for firing polymer clay to needlenose pliers, used to shape wire. Your overhead includes reusable supplies that wear out in less than a year, such as brushes, stencils, needles, molds, and patterns and equipment and depreciable items such as sewing machines, computer or office equipment, cameras, and kilns. There are also expenses for phone, travel, shipping and postage, show fees, display costs, packaging, insurance, and other deductibles used to make your finished product.

You might think that it's not important to consider overhead in your pricing. I had a difficult time doing so. I figured I was going to be home anyway so the electricity needed to run the air conditioning was going to be used whether I crafted or not. But that line of thinking is for the hobbyist. All businesses have overhead, and expenses in overhead are the first ones looked at when a profit isn't being made in a business. If you wish to succeed as a business you must consider overhead when pricing your jewelry.

A Few More Things to Consider

When pricing, you need to understand and have a well-rounded knowledge of how similar items are priced in the marketplace. This research isn't as hard as it seems. Look at catalogs and magazine advertisements for jewelry. Visit a jewelry or gift shop. Browse art and craft shows in your area.

An understanding of your competitors' pricing will give you an idea of what your customers expect to pay. In general, set your prices somewhere in the middle of your competitors' price range. If you underprice, you essentially pay your customers to purchase

Spirals and Beads Necklace and Earrings
Kinetic Hardware Brooch

Pearl Necklace and Earrings Set
Stitched and Beaded Pin

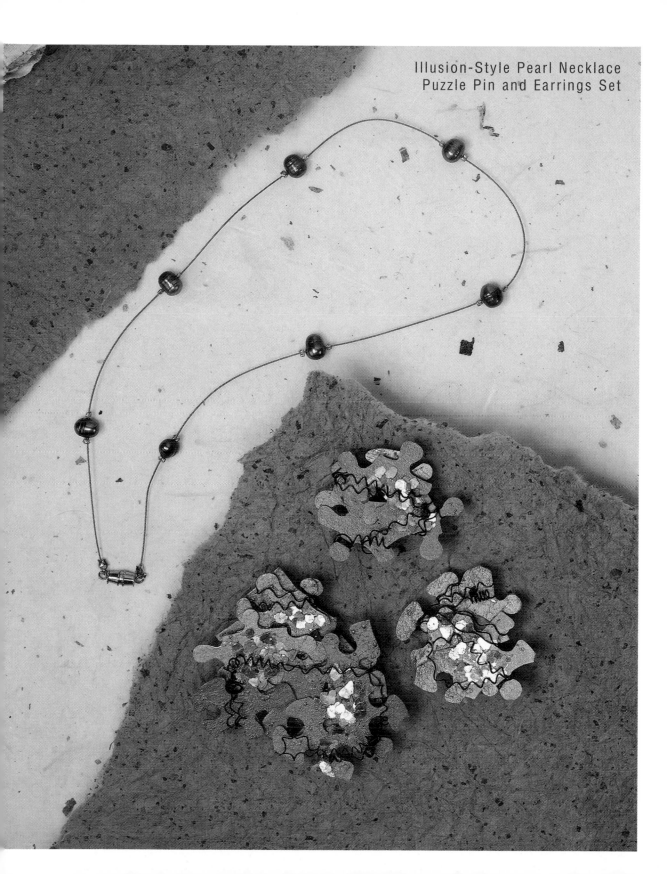

Illusion-Style Pearl Necklace
Puzzle Pin and Earrings Set

Photo Frame Pins

your work. Underpricing also devalues the item in the customer's eyes. If you overprice, you are left with unsold inventory or you have a low turnover rate, causing cash flow problems.

When pricing any piece of jewelry, you must also consider the economy in the area you sell. In Florida, I know that some areas or communities are doing better than others. I live in an area that is deeply affected by the space industry. When times are good, people spend their money freely, but when rumors start flying about budget cuts, I carefully watch the family budget. If I travel to the western coast of Florida, however, where my customers are not as dependent on one industry, I can sell at almost twice my asking price in my home community. Eventually, I decided not to sell directly to my own community because it is not cost-effective. Instead I sold through a local craft co-op that caters to tourists.

Another consideration is that a new design will attract more attention from loyal customers. Loyal customers are usually collecting from a particular artist or craftsperson, and will be inclined to buy a new design. I can increase the retail price of a new item because of the higher demand. Predicting demand is a combination of trusting your gut instincts and throwing caution to the wind. Can you keep up with the demand? Can you keep the item in stock? If you answer "no" to these questions, you should think about raising the price of the piece.

There is no surefire formula for pricing that will work for you and your business all the time. Learn to trust your own judgment. If the market will bear a higher price than you've calculated with a pricing formula, go for it.

Keep turnover in mind when pricing. If you decide to sell at craft shows, home shows, or bazaars, do you want to have to pack up and take home products after each show? Do you want items to sit,

Handy Hint

Do you live in an area that depends on tourist purchases to support the local economy? Do your designs cater to this niche market? You need to consider the answers to these questions when pricing your work.

week after week, at a craft mall, gathering dust? Each time the items are packed and unpacked, there is a risk of damage and loss of product quality. Consider pricing items to move.

I've mentioned getting a feel for how similar items are priced. Now consider how much competition you have in your area. How many other jewelry makers in your area are selling similar designs with respect to motifs, mediums, techniques, style, or form? Look for and keep a running total of how many other artists are working in jewelry and how their items compare to your own inventory. Is your work unique? Does your jewelry stand out, or can you put everyone's work side by side and not see any differences? The only real difference may come down to the price tag. If so, can you still make a profit and stay competitive?

Pricing Formulas

The first way to price is a very basic formula, often referred to as "cost plus markup."

2 to 8 × the cost of goods = retail price

Total all the costs required to make one item and multiply by 2, 3, 4, 5, 6, 7, or 8. Usually, high-supply cost items are multiplied by 2, 3, or 4, and lower-supply cost items are multiplied from 5 up to 8. This is determined by your own judgment, and your personal supply costs. This type of pricing doesn't directly address labor or overhead, but it is great for the hobbyist or part-time jewelry artist. This formula allows for the considerations of supply and demand, area economy, and competitive pricing. Just because you don't add labor and overhead doesn't mean you shouldn't know what those numbers are. The bottom line is to make sure that you are making a profit that includes paying yourself for your time and efforts.

Handy Hint

Review or take some time to read about the theory of supply and demand, which can be found in a basic high school or college economics book.

Example of Pricing a Pair of Earrings.

Cost of Goods:	$3.50
Labor:	$2.50
Total Sum:	$6.00
Overhead (25%):	$1.50
Selling Price:	$7.50

Many professionals would consider this the starting, or wholesale price of the earrings. You will know your area economy the best and know if this price is within range of retail or wholesale pricing. That's why it's so important to do your pricing homework and to know your competitors' pricing too!

Another formula used for pricing is:

(cost of goods + labor) × overhead = retail price

For this formula you will already know your cost of goods (COG) and your labor. You will add your COG and your labor fee. Overhead is normally a percentage calculated from the sum of your COG and labor. This is usually a set percentage. An average percentage for overhead in a jewelry business is 25% to 35% of the sum when adding your cost of goods and labor. I've had feedback over the years from peers and experts that this percentage is much too low, but I stick to my guns. If you allow your overhead costs to exceed 35%, you are not using your overhead items efficiently. Major Fortune 500 companies who find they need to cut costs first look at overhead costs, then the cost of goods, and finally labor costs. Do you want to cut your labor rate? No. Do you want to use inferior or cheaper materials in your piece? No. Then take a serious look at your overhead and don't let it get out of control.

Final Thoughts on Pricing

I've stated before, but it bears repeating, that pricing your work will be one of the most difficult responsibilities you have in your business. I hate to be the bearer of bad news, but this task never really gets any easier for the jewelry artist. Our work is so subjective and why an item catches the eye of a potential buyer can be a mystery. When an item isn't selling we tend to think we've priced it too high. Don't be tempted to use this excuse. It's a negative loop that will leave you frustrated. Instead, do everything you can to be confident and well-versed on pricing your jewelry. In the end, that knowledge will help you sell at the right price.

Being Fair to Yourself and Others

Many years ago, when I first started to exhibit at art and craft shows, I remember being very concerned about having reasonable prices. It was important to me for my items to be affordable to everyone. I still consider this fact when I price my work. Yet, even after a decade of selling crafts, it is still difficult for me to sell to my friends. My first reaction is to give the craft to my friends as a gift. However, I wouldn't be in business very long if I gave my crafts away all the time, so I came up with a compromise. I sell to friends at a discount of 10%. I feel better, and my friends recognize that my crafting is more than a hobby—it's a business.

Fair and reasonable pricing means that you and your customer are satisfied with the final selling price. Do you provide your best work? Do you use quality supplies to make your jewelry? Do you put your love of jewelry design into each piece you create? I know that as you read this you are saying yes. Remember, you deserve fair payment for your work. Don't undervalue your talents and labor.

There may be some items that you enjoy making that are not suitable for selling in the marketplace. You may find that a fair labor cost makes the price of the item too high to sell to the average consumer. Let me give you a personal example. I love to work with paper casting. I can spend hours making the paper, placing it in the molds, allowing the item to dry, painting the piece with colorful paint, adding little details of glitter and lace. Then I apply jewelry findings to create earrings or a brooch. The final price for the jewelry piece is around $15, which means I would price myself out of the market. Therefore, I decided to paper cast for fun, not for profit. Then I got to thinking that maybe I could sell these one-of-a-kind designs to craft magazines. I did, and found that I could make more money selling the design and instructions than I would by selling the finished product.

Art and craft is a sharing, caring activity—we should always strive to introduce new designs to our customers. Yet, we must evaluate how the item is received, how well it is selling, and most importantly, whether we are making a profit. Many professional jewelry makers initially feel a little guilty that they are selling their work. Many would simply like to give their designs to others to share the joy of crafting. But making a profit is not a bad thing. Professional jewelry artists provide products as well as a service. It is only fair that professionals earn a wage or salary and a profit from their business.

Keeping Your Sanity While Making a Profit

Don't let numbers confuse you. I hate math with a passion and calculating formulas gives me a headache. You can ask for help when pricing your jewelry. Ask a friend for his or her opinion of your prices. I stopped pricing my own work several years ago. I was

Use the Right Pricing Tactics

Industry retail studies for pricing indicate that adding cents ending in a 5 or a 9 are the most easily accepted by a consumer. In a random testing, a consumer picked the item priced $5.95 over a similar item priced at $6.00. Consumers even preferred the price of $5.99 over the same item priced just one penny more at $6.00. It may seem deceptive or silly to use this information, but consider the lost sales over what amounts to one penny or five cents. Granted, consumers are savvy and react negatively to being patronized, but I have found that pricing my own work at 25-, 50-, and 75-cent increments instead of the next dollar amount does increase my multiple sales (a customer purchasing more than one of an item).

getting so frustrated and overwhelmed since I make a large variety of items to sell. I asked my husband, Ken, to take over the pricing. I gave him all the information he needed concerning material costs and labor time, and I let him set the overhead percentage.

In some cases, my husband doubled my prices. I was shocked! I told him my customers would flip out over such drastic increases in my pricing. But, I decided to use his pricing at my next show. The worst that could happen is my work would sit in the displays and I'd learn a lesson in pricing. Guess what? My customers didn't blink an eye! It was an unnerving experience to risk being rejected by customers because of pricing, but the risk paid off.

The bottom line is that you must feel comfortable with the price tag you put on your work. It is not a personal rejection if a potential customer does not buy your work. There could be a dozen reasons why a customer did not purchase a design, and maybe none of them has to do with you or your work. Relax. Remember that prices are not set in stone. Feel free to adjust the prices up or down according to your needs and the needs of your customers. The most important part of any pricing formula is that you make a profit that satisfies both you and Uncle Sam.

Pricing For Services

Demonstrating your jewelry-making skills is one way to make money for providing a service rather than a product. You can also teach as a service, which will earn you a fee for your time and efforts. Selling your designs with instructions to magazines and book publishers is also a service, since most of the work involved is in writing the instructions. Demonstrating, teaching, and selling designs are all wonderful ways to earn a living with the art of jewelry, and all three can supplement your income in a part-time fashion.

Demonstrating

In most cases, if you are working with a manufacturer/distributor, the manufacturer/distributor will have standard fees that the company pays a demonstrator. These fees range from an hourly wage to a daily wage. On average, you can expect a manufacturer/distributor to pay $10 to $25 per hour. Before accepting any offer, you should find out everything the fee includes. If travel is expected of you, make sure you can submit a travel expense report to your employer to cover mileage, meals, and lodging, if applicable.

> **Handy Hint**
>
> Don't be afraid to let high-ticket items sit on the shelf. Would you rather give the design away or wait until the right customer comes along who is willing to pay for a quality design?

When I first began attending trade shows, I watched the demonstrators at each booth and said to myself, "That looks easy enough. I bet I could do that job." With that rather cocky attitude I applied to the Hobby Industry Association's (HIA) Certified Professional Demonstrator (CPD) program. All I had to do to become a CPD was read HIA's *Body of Knowledge* for demonstrators and be evaluated by several members of the industry while demonstrating. I thought it was a piece of cake!

I demonstrated for Aleene's Division of Artist because I knew the company's product lines well. I demonstrated for 3 days from 8:00 A.M. to 5:00 P.M. I helped set up the exhibit booth and I helped tear it down. It was the hardest work I'd ever done in my entire life! No one told me my feet could hurt so badly! I passed my review with flying colors to become a CPD. However, I now rarely take demonstrating jobs that are more than a few hours. I'm glad I got the training. It helped me understand how to work with crowds and how to show off and sell a product. I am not cut out to be a demonstrator full time.

I made $75 per day, which worked out to about $8 per hour—more than double the minimum wage at the time. To this day, I've never worked so hard for money! However, the learning experience, meeting so many industry leaders, and the fun of teaching retailers how to use products made the experience priceless. Often you will take on jobs or create designs that you might not get "top dollar" for, but the doors that open to you will eventually lead to larger profits. Make these decisions based on your instincts—they can't be made using pricing formulas. Not every choice you make will work out to be positive, but over time your experiences will be invaluable to your career.

Teaching and Class Fees

Teaching would be a dream if you could just walk into a classroom, teach a class, and walk out to collect a paycheck. But ask any teacher of any subject and you'll find that only in a daydream is teaching that easy. There is a lot of preparation time that goes into a smooth-running class presentation. It's also important that you enjoy working with the public. It's not a job for everyone. Be confident in your people skills before even attempting to teach a class. A great help is to attend several art or craft classes, watch the teachers, and learn first-hand what you liked and disliked. The golden rule is that, as a teacher, your job is to help your students build their skills—not do the work for them.

How much you charge for a class will depend on the length of the class. Most art and craft classes last from 1 to 3 hours. Any longer than that and students will get restless and need breaks. The national averages for class fees vary widely. One factor is your ability and expertise in jewelry making. The bigger your body of work, the more you will be able to charge for your instruction. In general, look for class fees of $10 and under for an hour class and $25 for a class of 2 to 3 hours. If you are going to provide a kit or supply all or some of the supplies and materials

> ### Did you know???
> Some professional demonstrators earn from $25 to $30 per hour for their expertise.

needed for the class, consider charging an additional fee for this service. Point out that all the student needs to bring is a smile when attending your class and that you are saving each student some time and effort by gathering the materials needed. The economy of your teaching area plays a vital role in how you price a class. Check out the class fees of local art and craft shops or other centers that offer classes. I've found that by preparing hour classes that I make more income in the long haul. Make sure each student takes home at least one finished design. And remember, in most cases you will be teaching adults. Adults don't have to go "back to school." Adults decide to spend their valuable time attending a leisure activity class. It's best not to lecture such students, but to make sure they have fun and enjoy the skills you are teaching them.

Publishing Fees

I wish there was an industry standard for what price to ask for a finished jewelry design, sold with written instruction, to a publisher. It would make business so much simpler, but sadly there is no such guide available in the creative industries. It might help to know that an editor is working with a set budget per issue of a magazine. The editor must use this budget not just to gather designs to publish, but also to get the magazine from the drawing board to the printer to the newsstand. An editor must also deliberate on some rather subjective considerations when placing a price value on creative work. Can you compare the time it takes to make a quilt to the time it takes to make a pair of beaded earrings? What fee do you pay for ideas and the execution of those ideas? I remember a conversation I had with a publisher about a new magazine she was in the process of publishing. She just couldn't understand what the difficulty was in taking a few rubberstamps, some ink, some paper, and a few jewelry findings and creating a fun piece of jewelry. She was appalled at the idea that some artists and craftspeople wanted more than $10 or $15 for such a "simple" design. My response was that the artist has invested heavily in the rubberstamps, ink, paper, and jewelry findings. It's not as easy as just sitting down and stamping. One has to consider the current trends, colors, textures, and balance. For every perfect brooch or pin there is a pile of not-so-perfect ones tucked away behind the filing cabinet just waiting for the artist to have a spare moment to fix all the mistakes.

When selling creativity, part of the sale is educating the potential editor or publisher about your work. A soft sell of your skills and abilities is all you need to pitch. A few sentences about your design included in a cover letter to the editor will do. An editor may not be an expert on beading, polymer clay, or wood jewelry, so discussing these things extensively could likely be a waste of time. You need only to sell your technique and your design. Don't get frustrated or discouraged. And never sell a design unless you are happy with the selling price. Nothing eats up creativity quicker than being angry. Nothing sours a working relationship faster than unspoken resentment between two parties. Also understand that you are signing a legal and binding contract with a publisher. Do you sell first rights? All rights? Are you happy with the contact? Don't sign until every last question you have is answered.

Reputation is built one deal at a time. What matters in the end is not how many designs you have sold to how many publishers. What matters is that your work was presented with respect and you were paid well for your abilities. A good reputation will lead to higher fees offered to you. On average, the general consumer magazine editor will pay between $50 to $200 for an original jewelry design. On average, a book publisher will pay around $1,500 to $2,000 for a jewelry book of 20 to 30 designs with a softbound cover, which will retail for $6.95 to $15.99 in an art and craft store. Book (art/craft store quality) publishers may offer a royalty of $0.25 to $0.75 per book sold rather than a flat fee. Consider all the expenses of selling designs for publication including materials, time to write instructions, time to draw illustrations, and the cost to ship materials to the publisher. A survey of designers in the craft industry indicates that most prefer a flat fee over a royalty, except where the design sold is for a tool or a technique. And remember, all fees are negotiable.

> ### Did you know???
>
> You have to plan ahead when submitting a design for magazine publication. Most magazines work 6 months to a year in advance.

What's Needed Next?

You have your pricing all figured out and it's time to sell your work. It may seem out of order to deal with pricing a finished piece before you even know where you are going to sell your work, but without knowing that you will make money selling your jewelry, there is no need for a marketplace for your work. Finding creative markets to sell designs is a lot more fun than figuring out and adding up all the cost of the goods, labor, and overhead! The hard part is over! Turn the page and get ready to go to market!

Selling Your Jewelry

▼▼▼

YOU CAN MAKE THE BEST jewelry in the world, but if you don't have a way to sell it you'll never earn a dime for your efforts or creativity. As a product line, jewelry can fit into almost any marketplace and you can design items to fit anyone's budget. Selling your jewelry doesn't need to be complicated, but you do need to match your jewelry with its best marketplace. You also have to consider the best market for your own needs and business goals.

Jewelry artists have traditionally sold their creations two ways, and these markets are still popular today. The first is to sell from home, directly to family and friends, who in turn, give their purchases as a gifts. A savvy artisan includes at least one business card with each purchase. Over time, clientele grows by word of mouth (which continues to be the best form of advertising for a professional jewelry artist.) If you provide quality products with good customer service, you'll find that nothing beats a personal testimonial or customer recommendation for promoting sales.

The second traditional marketplace for the professional crafter is the art and craft show, which can be a community event, such as a church bazaar, or an elaborate craft show, operated by professional promoters. These shows are often outdoors. The atmosphere ranges from casual flea market to sophisticated gallery. The original outdoor craft show had a festive, carnival feel; service groups would sell hot dogs and popcorn and local talent, such as dancers, singers, and poets, would entertain from morning until closing. Some outdoor shows still maintain this atmosphere.

The appeal of handmade art and craft items has peaks and valleys, just like any other retail product. It may be trite, but everything old is, at some point in time, new again. Since the mid-1980s, there has been a steady trend of consumers wanting to purchase handmade designs. Because of this trend, hundreds of art and craft shows have been organized annually, biannually, quarterly, and even monthly. In any given week, there are at least a dozen craft shows being held somewhere in the United States. People interested in buying jewelry usually want something unique and special, not mainstream or mass-produced. As a jewelry maker you can satisfy this demand by bringing fresh designs to the marketplace.

> ### Did you know???
>
> You have about 6 seconds to catch a potential customer's eye. The colors yellow and red are the top colors the eye is immediately attracted to.

You may decide to sell retail or wholesale. Retail means selling directly to the end consumer. Wholesale means selling to an intermediate buyer. If you decide to sell wholesale, you should really learn as much about it as you can, since it can be more complicated than retail selling. Many professionals boost their year-round income by combining both types of sales; building wholesale accounts during the first and second quarters of the year, and focusing on retail sales during the third and fourth quarters. There are few differences between the two markets, with the exception of pricing and category (trade versus retail). No matter which marketplace you choose, you must find the shows, build your inventory, create a display, and get your jewelry to the customer.

This chapter will take a close look at the many marketing options and venues available to you as a professional artisan. Selecting the right marketplace for you and your designs is just as important as selecting quality supplies or determining the right price for your jewelry pieces. As you read about the markets available to you, ask yourself some serious questions: How involved do you wish to be in the selling of your items? How large a geographical area do you wish to cover? How much inventory can you produce? Can your inventory fill the needs of your marketplace selections?

Retail Craft Shows

In addition to the traditional art and craft shows, retail markets include seasonal boutiques, church and community bazaars, indoor or outdoor swap meets or flea markets, and any other program where you display your work to sell directly to the end user. The outdoor craft show is probably one of the oldest markets in the gift industry, and it started the professional craft and artisan industry as we know it today. Today, many of these shows are also held indoors, in shopping malls and convention centers. Whether shows are held indoors or out, retail craft shows remain one of the most popular and profitable marketplaces for those selling handmade work. It's also the perfect marketplace for selling unique jewelry pieces, as buyers come to art and craft shows to find creative and original handmade work.

If you look around your town or city, you'll probably find that there is at least one retail show going on each month. The show may be outdoors or indoors, with or without a professional promoter. Most shows take place on weekends as 1-, 2-, or 3-day events. There are a few shows that last a week to 2 weeks, usually celebrating an event or festival in a regional area. To participate in a retail show, you need to apply to the show, set up a display to showcase your jewelry, and, in most cases, free up your weekends to participate (most craft shows are scheduled for Saturday and Sunday). A commission is rarely taken from your sales when you sell retail at a craft show.

A craft show provides you with a chance to meet, and learn from, your customers, who can be a great source of information. Talk to browsers about what they are looking for, what colors appeal to them, and what they would like to see on your shelves and tables. Your customers may tell you that necklaces are in demand, or that they are looking for upscale designs for work apparel.

Jewelry styles come and go, but there are some basics that remain constant. Jewelry is made up of necklaces, earrings, brooches, bracelets, and rings. Trends change the materials used, the colors that are popular, or the size of the jewelry pieces. However, wearing jewelry will always be in style and consequently, there will always be a market for it.

Craft shows are perfect selling arenas for wearable art, such as jewelry. You can create interesting displays and build an inventory prior to each show. Most people attending an art and craft show are there to buy, either for themselves or to give their purchases as gifts.

Did you know???

The average retail customer spends an average of 1 hour at an art and craft show. If the show you participate in has 100 exhibitors, you have approximately 6 seconds of that potential buyer's time.

A Traveling Jewelry Show

One disadvantage to outdoor shows is bad weather. Shelters or canopies are a must for the outdoor marketplace. (You can find canopies and other display items advertised in show guides and craft trade journals.) Wind, sun, and rain can take a toll on the best of us. You are essentially a store on wheels, so all the concerns of travel must be considered. Displays must be compact. They should be designed for ease of travel, setup, and breakdown. For each show, pack change boxes, folding chairs, tables, table coverings, and a good attitude. Also think about security, especially for those of you whose jewelry is on the expensive side. For most jewelry makers, the benefits of craft shows far outweigh the negatives.

Craft Show Requirements

One of the first things many new craft professionals want to know is the difference between a juried and a non-juried show. The most basic difference is that acceptance to a non-juried show is based on first come, first served. A potential crafter fills out an application and pays a show fee. Once the spaces are filled, no more applications are taken. Acceptance to a juried show is based on the decision of a show judge or committee. You are required to submit slides or photos of your work or booth. In addition to the application and show fee, you may be required to pay a separate, nonrefundable jurying fee, which pays for the judges' time. The jurying process insures quality of work and, in some cases, limits the number of crafts in a specific medium. For example, a juried show that has a hundred spaces may allow 20% of those spaces to each of five categories, such as jewelry, stained glass, needle arts, ceramics, and mixed mediums. The idea is to keep variety in the show and to spread the competition for the consumer's dollar.

Sometimes people who sell imports are allowed to sell their items at craft shows, which is a deterrent to serious sellers who find it difficult to compete pricewise. (Imports are also referred to as buy/sells.) You may want to inquire upon application as to what type of work or products will be allowed on display during the show.

Finding the Shows

There are some basic requirements in preparing to participate in any show. The first is to locate the shows. Try networking with fellow professionals, calling your local chamber of commerce, or using show guide periodicals. There are many regional show guides, which can be found by searching in the Directory of Periodicals at your local library. *Sunshine Artist Magazine* and American Craft Malls are just two of the companies that list hundreds of craft shows on their Web sites throughout the United States.

See the Resources at the end of the book for detailed information about these and other sources of information. You can also find show guides and other information about craft shows by entering "craft shows" or "craft show list" into any search engine on the World Wide Web.

Not all craft shows are created equal, so it's important to take time to learn as much as possible about a particular show before paying the fee. There are no guarantees that even the most successful craft shows won't have a bad year, but the more you find out about the various shows, the better your odds are at finding ones that are right for your jewelry. See the sidebar, "Basic Information Needed Before Applying to Any Show," on page 170 for some things to consider and some questions to ask the show's contact person.

Once you are accepted to a show, you need to get ready. This can get hectic even for the seasoned professional. If you have never done a show before, it can be downright chaotic. Over the past 15 years I have developed the following checklist, which I use when I pack for each show. I also keep it handy for breaking down the booth to make sure I don't forget to pack each item I brought to the show. (If you use a canopy, use a separate checklist for all items necessary for setup, including all tools required for assembly.)

Basic Items Needed at a Show

- All display items: tables, table covers, shelves, crates, tools needed for assembling the display, chairs, and, if allowed, ice chest/cooler

- Inventory/product (priced, packaged, and ready to display)

- Guest book for building a mailing list

- Cash box, receipt book, plenty of coins and small bills, calculator, charge card imprinter, credit card charge slips, and, if applicable, a state sales tax table

- Pens for writing checks

- Extra price tags

- A mirror for customers to view themselves wearing the jewelry

- Business cards, brochures, signs, or other paper good items

- Special order forms, if applicable

- Copy of your state sales tax license, if applicable, to post in full view of consumers

- A handcart to carry items, if needed

- Items to demonstrate during slow selling times

- Repair kit (to keep in your booth): scissors, glue, tape, jewelry findings, tools, extra beads, and wire

- Snacks and beverages

- Weather gear if outside: visor, hat, change of clothing, sunscreen, and comfortable shoes

- Attitude: positive thinking, high energy, enthusiastic sales presentation, and a smile

Basic Information Needed Before Applying to Any Show

■ What is the show fee and/or the cost of space? (Compare this cost with the cost of other shows.)

■ What is the cost to travel to the show?

■ What are the dates and times of the show?

■ Is this an annual or first-time event?

■ Is it a group, community, or promoter-organized event?

■ Who is the contact person for requesting an application?

■ What is the deadline for submitting applications?

Leave small children, TV, radio, pets, and books at home. Most potential customers find sales help who read during selling hours to be rude and will not ask for help.

If possible, schedule relief times for yourself during the show by asking for help from friends and family. You can pay your relief team an hourly wage, a commission of sales, or a free piece of jewelry. If all else fails, ask your closest neighbor at the show to exchange a break time with you.

A Home Show

Home parties work well for promoting jewelry. A jewelry home show is somewhat like a Tupperware or Mary Kay party. Your customers are mostly women, and what's more fun than sitting around with friends and trying on jewelry? There is an intimacy about jew-

- Are slides or photos required for entry?

- Are there specific categories or mediums allowed?

- How many exhibitors or booths are at the show?

- Is it indoors or outdoors?

- What is the refund or rain date policy?

- Are there specific display requirements for participating?

- What is the booth space size, in exact measurements?

- Are there electrical outlets? If so, is there a charge for electricity?

- What was the attendance at last year's show?

- How is the show promoted and advertised?

elry that makes it special and a home atmosphere reflects that intimacy. The home show takes away all the crowds and noise of the marketplaces that rely on heavy traffic to get sales. At a home show, you can also control the lighting and the ambiance.

There are two ways for a professional jewelry artist to use the home show or home party. The first is to use the home show as the main avenue for selling your jewelry. To earn an income this way, you must book new home shows continually in customers' homes. The second use for the home show is to bring in additional income from your jewelry sales. To do this, you schedule shows in your own home on an annual, biannual, or quarterly basis.

If you use home shows as the main source of income, you must continually and consistently promote your jewelry to increase your sales area. Many professional artisans often hire others to book, prepare, and sell at home shows. They pay the additional sales help a straight fee or a commission, based on total sales. If you use the home show to bring in additional income, you can probably manage an annual or quarterly show without additional sales help.

Whether you use home shows for additional income or as your sole income, contact the city or county where the home show will be held to make sure there are no statutes prohibiting the exchange of money for business reasons within a private home. Every state, city, and county will vary in terms of these statutes. Most municipalities consider annual or quarterly home shows to be similar to garage or estate sales. Most states require that sales tax be collected. Often the city or county's main concern is that the neighborhood is not disturbed by the additional traffic of invited guests. (See chapter 11 for more information about zoning and state sales tax.) Plan ahead for parking, and notify your neighbors when the event will take place. Also keep track of all expenses, including travel and business deductions. Record and file mileage and expenses for each show, and report this information to the IRS.

Advance planning pays off when preparing for a home show. Think about location, date, hours, inventory, invitations, and advertising. Transform a room in the house into a sales showroom. Remove all personal property from the room and set up displays of your work. Set up an area for money exchange and bagging purchases. (When an item is purchased from your display, replace it immediately.) Consider inviting other professionals from noncompeting mediums to join you. This will broaden the appeal, provide others to share expenses, and expand your guest list.

Christmas boutiques are the most popular and successful home shows. Play holiday music, light scented candles, decorate a tree with lights, serve punch and cookies, and hire a babysitter for the

Did you know???

The heaviest sales at craft shows are during the fall and winter seasons, when buyers turn out in force to purchase gifts for Christmas, Mother's Day, and Valentine's Day.

kids so mom or dad can browse without distractions. In the invitation, suggest that customers bring a gift shopping list. Offer free gift-wrapping or supply gift boxes for the jewelry. Have an area of lower-priced jewelry so children can purchase gifts for their parents. Offer a prize, such as an inexpensive necklace or a percentage off an expensive pin, for any buyer who brings a new guest that is added to your mailing list.

Home shows can be fun and enjoyable celebrations of your jewelry, so get creative and show off. If held at the end of your fiscal year, there is the added bonus of reducing your inventory, making it much easier to handle for the tax time ahead of you.

A Few More Thoughts about Shows

If you are prepared, well rested, and enthusiastic about doing a show, the results will be more positive and profitable. Many professional crafters feel they aren't good salespeople. If you feel you are not cut out to sell your own work, hire someone to do it for you. Hiring someone who enjoys selling may be worth the cost if it gives you peace of mind. Remember that everyone has a bad show every once in awhile. Bad weather, poor advertising, and slow regional economics can directly effect your sales. Don't get discouraged. If you do have a bad show, chalk it up to experience and get ready for the next one.

Pay attention to the body language of browsers. If a potential buyer is with a friend, you may need to sell to the friend just as much as to the interested browser. Place your jewelry in the buyer's hand so he or she can touch it and take control of it. Have a mirror available so the buyer can see what the jewelry looks like on him or her. Watch your own body language. Smile and interact with everyone in your booth. Make eye contact and lean closer when you talk to customers. Talk about your craft with pride and enthusiasm, and be sure to ask questions to find out what your customers want. Share what you love about your jewelry pieces. Remember, most buyers aren't just buying your necklaces or earrings; they are buying a small piece of your personality, too.

When you sell your jewelry at art and craft shows, you're in show business! Wear your own jewelry. Demonstrate how to wear special items, such as how to use a brooch to pin a scarf on a jacket. Display jewelry-decorated clothing on pretty hangers, or bead a necklace or twist a wire for the crowd to watch and learn. The art and craft show is the perfect place to develop your showmanship. It's an opportunity to share your love of your art with others. Participating in a show can bring you new markets and customers. So relax and put your best foot forward at all times, even with rude or impatient customers. And trust me, you will meet every kind of temperament and personality while selling at a show. When struggling with a difficult customer, remember that the situation is only temporary. Most of all, enjoy your time with your customers, and take every opportunity to network with your peers. Be courteous not only to your customers, but also to your fellow exhibitors. For example, avoid playing loud music and don't wear strong scents.

Have ample inventory for each show. Don't stay up half the night before a show trying to prepare more inventory, as it is never worth the lost sleep. You are better off feeling rested and refreshed at show time. Arrive early and be prepared to unload your inventory and supplies quickly. Parking is often limited at shows. Usually you will be allowed only a short time to unload and reload near the exhibit area and then you will have to move your vehicle.

It is important to evaluate a show, soon after it is over. Some items to note include total sales; total inventory count, before and after; weather; traffic in the booth; and ease of setting up. The following evaluation form is a sample you can use to fill out after each show. These evaluations are valuable when scheduling future shows.

Sample Show Evaluation

Show Name _____

Sponsor _____

Date of Show _____

Show Fee _____

Location _____

Annual Event? _____ Number of Shows to Date _____

Parking for Vendors: Good   Poor

Parking for Customers: Good   Poor

Customer Turnout: Excellent Good Fair Below Average Poor
Buyers or browsers?

Customers: Men Women Children Teenagers Seniors Other

Publicity: Good   Fair   Poor

Space Provided: Good   Fair   Poor

Is there a better space for increased buyer traffic? _____

Is there a better way to set up your booth for buyer traffic? _____

Space Number _____

Total Exhibitors _____

Direct Competitors _____

Sponsor's Attitude _____

Other Exhibitors' Attitude _____

Shoppers' Attitude _____

Weather and Environmental Conditions _____

Food Available: Good   Poor

Does the sales tax differ from home base? _____

Total Sales _____

Total Expenses _____

Comments _____

_____

_____

_____

_____

Craft Malls

Craft malls, which are found across the country, are like shopping malls that sell arts and crafts. A mall gives you the opportunity to have a mini-store within a larger storefront. Most malls require a signed contract allowing you a set period of time to occupy a set amount of space. A contract of 6 months or 1 year is normal. Craft malls do not require you to spend any time in the mall other than the time you spend stocking your space or changing your display. The display space can vary from a single shelf to large, open floor space. You are responsible for setting the price of items to be sold and for keeping the display stocked. The mall management is responsible for the actual selling, collecting of sales tax, and providing the vendor with a detailed sales report.

Although there is no official directory of craft malls in the United States, many do advertise in show guides and supply source magazines. You can also check your local yellow pages under "Arts and Crafts" to find a craft mall near you. The Professional Crafter Web site is another good resource for finding craft malls (see Resources for Web address).

Exhibiting in a craft mall involves a legal agreement. Before you sign on the dotted line, research the mall where you want to set up shop. I found the following list of questions and considerations at The Professional Crafter Web site. It's a great list of questions for any type of market in which you aren't selling directly to your customer. The list is provided courtesy of Phillip Coomer, the owner of American Craft Malls.

Considerations for Selecting a Craft Mall

APPEARANCE
Does the store look clean?
Are booths straightened?

Are booths well stocked?

Is the front counter cluttered?

Does the store have eye appeal?

SALES STAFF

Does the staff seem helpful?

Did they greet you as you entered the store?

Do they talk to customers?

Are they smiling?

Do they seem positive and easy to talk to?

Can you talk to the manager easily? The owner?

CUSTOMER SERVICE

Do they know the answers to your questions?

Are you able to observe how they handle customer/crafter problems?

If they don't know the answer, will they find out for you?

JURY FOR QUALITY

Does the store allow anything in for sale?

Will it allow imports?

Will it allow factory-made or mass-produced items?

SPACES

Do they have a complete floor plan with sizes and space names marked?

Is there more than one size of booth?

Can you change booths—upsize or downsize—without penalty?

Do traffic patterns take customers to your booth?

SIGNAGE

Can the store and sign be seen easily from the main road?

Can you tell it's a craft mall?

Is the sign lit at night?

LOCATION

Is the location in a high traffic area?

What is the demographic profile of the area around the store?

Are there plenty of cars in the parking lot?

Are there complementary businesses nearby, such as antique malls or women's stores?

HOURS

Are they open 7 days a week?

Are they closed more than 4 or 5 days of the year?

Are they open during the standard retail hours of the rest of the shopping center?

Are they open when it will be convenient for you to stock your shelves?

CRAFTER RESOURCES

Do they have a resource center?

Do they keep you informed of trends?

CRAFTER DEVELOPMENT

Will they help you with display? Pricing? New ideas?

LEGAL

Do they inform you of legal requirements? Licenses?

Will they help protect your copyrights?

Do they allow others to violate copyrights in the store?

INFORMATION

Do they produce an informative newsletter?

Are the newsletter articles interesting?

Will they tell you sales levels for the store?

Do they keep you informed of store events?

Do they advise you of or show you specific advertising?

Do they constantly have promotional events going on?

Are the ads for your individual store?

Do the ads affect the area immediately around the store?
Do the ads look great? Good? Boring?

SALES

Does the store allow layaways on any item?
Will the store coordinate special orders, or is the store hands-off?
Does the store protect you from check and credit card fraud?
Does the store accept major credit cards?
Can you check sales for all of the stores within the chain at your store?

REMOTE SERVICE

Does the mall provide a remote service for out-of-state or out-of-city vendors?
Will the mall accept shipments of crafts?
Will your products be set up and displayed with care?
Is there an additional fee charged for the remote service?
How many remote vendors are in the mall?

TERMS OF THE CONTRACT

Read all contracts carefully because of the legal commitments.
Understand exactly what is expected of you as a vendor.
Understand what you expect from the mall management.
How long must you agree to display your goods in the contact? Six months? A year?
Read the contract several times and ask questions.
Get an opinion from a lawyer on the contract.

PAYMENT AND MONEY

Do they pay frequently? Every 2 weeks? End of the month?
Is the time short from closeout of sales to "check in the mail?"
Can you pick up your check? Is direct deposit available?
Can you call any time to get a summary of your sales?

COSTS

Do they pay sales taxes or do you?

Do they take a commission? If so, how much?

Is the space fee or booth fee above or below average?

Does a space at the front counter cost as much as one in the back of the store?

When are space or booth fees due? Can you pay at the store?

SECURITY

How do they prevent shoplifting?

If they have an electronic system, what do tags cost?

Can the tags be concealed?

Do they check containers on the way out?

SALES AND MERCHANDISING

Does the manager or staff have a booth at the store?

Can you pick your crafter number or is one assigned to you?

Do you have to buy their tags?

Are you required to bar code?

Are you required to work at the store?

Are you allowed to decorate your booth?

THE BUSINESS

Has the store been around for a long time? Will they be around tomorrow?

Who is the competition?

Do they consistently pay on time?

Do they have more than one location?

Can you get discounts?

What are the benefits of a remote program?

Do they have regular sales?

Do they have crafter gatherings regularly?

Are they a credible risk? What makes them one?

What are other crafters saying?

Have you checked for complaints against the company?
Do they compete in any way with crafters?

Craft Cooperative

The main difference between a cooperative (co-op) and a craft mall is that in a co-op situation the individuals who make up the co-op have "ownership" of it. A craft mall is operated by an owner or manager in conjunction with a paid sales staff. In a co-op, each vendor is expected to spend a certain amount of time working in the shop as a member of the sales staff. Another difference between a craft mall and a cooperative is that a co-op is normally juried. You submit finished samples of your work for review by a committee of co-op members. The work is judged on quality of work and originality. In most cases, a competitor of a current co-op member will not be allowed in the co-op. One of the great advantages to a co-op is that it limits the number of arts or crafts in different media.

You may also have a bigger voice in the management and policies of a co-op. Because you have control over the look of your display, you can change the theme and motifs frequently to keep regular customers interested. Low-ticket items (from $5 to $15) sell quickest and will more than likely cover rent and commission expenses. Make unique hang tags and keep a good supply of business cards in your display. It is also an excellent idea to post a brief bio and photo of yourself within your display to give customers a chance to find out more about you, even when you are not there. If you have the option to work in the shop once or twice a month, take advantage of the opportunity. Working on site will keep you in contact with your buyers, show you how a business with a storefront operates, and allow you to add inventory to your display. The same set of questions listed under Craft Malls can be applied to cooperatives.

TRACIA'S STORY

Over 20 years ago, Tracia Ledford Williams of Orlando, Florida picked up a paint brush and fell in love with decorative painting. She has sold her finished work for 15 years now, selling to gift shops, selling wholesale through a sales representative, and selling directly to consumers at art and craft shows throughout Florida. In 1995, Tracia decided to put her designs into pattern packets. "My wood cut-out jewelry designs were the easiest projects I had, so I launched my design career with them," said Tracia. "I picked my top five best sellers from my retail sales and just went for it. The toughest aspect was getting distribution for the pattern packets, but selling directly to wood cut-out distributors solved that. Those companies already had a distribution plan in place. I didn't have to start from scratch trying to build a reputation with retailers across the United States. The positive feedback I got from my customers really helped inspire me to concentrate on pattern packets.

"I also sell jewelry designs to magazines for publication, but the best satisfaction comes from publishing my own patterns. I plan my instructions and illustrations. I have friends proofread and carefully follow the steps to make sure that anyone who buys my patterns will be purchasing the best instructions possible. Then I get a lot of help from my printer who spends some time helping [me] understand how to layout the pages. I hire a professional photographer to take studio shoots of each finished piece and pay for the negatives of the best shots. I then order photos in bulk from

Consignment

Consignment sales are different from those of a craft mall or co-op. In simple terms, you allow a retailer to display your jewelry, and

a local photo developer. I could have the photos printed, but I prefer to use a real photo. Color, and seeing the finished item is very important to decorative painters. The final step is assembling all the parts into a plastic hang bag—the best packaging for pattern packets. I hire the kids in the neighborhood to assemble and package the patterns. The teenagers love the easy work and making some spending money.

"Part of my promotion of my jewelry designs is to make sure I keep up with the consumer magazines. I decided early on that my focus was decorative painting although I have had some of my designs transferred into fabric, too. I think it's important to understand what one's creative strengths are and to develop those talents and skills to the max! Whenever I sell an individual design to a magazine I make sure I'm allowed to include my company contact information. That way more consumers find out about all my designs that are available in patterns.

"The best part of jewelry design for me is that I can really experiment with color and form. It is so easy to create fun and fanciful jewelry pieces with all the great wood cut-outs available so readily at most craft shops. And who can't use just one more great jewelry accessory?"

when a sale is made, you are paid. As a jewelry artist you will find that most upscale galleries and boutiques work on a consignment basis. In most cases, the retailer adds a percentage to the price of an item to make the shop's profit. The retail shop doesn't claim

Business Credentials

There are a few items you should have to support your work in any marketplace. This paperwork helps to establish you as a legitimate business in the eyes of your customers, suppliers, and business community. This is just a brief checklist. For detailed information on each subject, see chapter 11.

■ State, city, or county business licenses, if applicable.

■ Résumé: List name; contact address; contact numbers such as phone, fax, and e-mail; photo of self and of work; past shows and other markets; and company mission statement. This is your advertisement—your foot in the door to introduce yourself to potential buyers.

■ Portfolio: Picture book of your work, accomplishments, awards, and items for sale. Photos do not need to be professionally done. Clear photographs that show your jewelry pieces from different angles will work. Include measurements if the photos do not show the item's proportions.

■ Business cards: Make your card unique to your company. Include your business name, your name, contact address, and phone number. If you have an e-mail address or Web site, list it on your business card and on all other business materials.

ownership of the jewelry, but it should be responsible for damage or theft. At all times during a consignment agreement, the professional holds all ownership rights to the product. Yet, the artisan usually has no control over the final selling price, how the work will be displayed, or how well the items will be explained or highlighted. This category of sales is one of the most controversial, with horror stories of shops closing overnight and wonderful stories of very successful sales. Do your homework. Talk to other consignees within the shop.

There are good reasons to sell your jewelry on consignment. First, it is better to have your pieces on display somewhere rather than just stored in inventory. Second, consignment has no up-front investment, in terms of rent, time, and expenditures. Third, in

- Letterhead: Should match the business card. This is a must for all business and professional correspondence.

- Business checking account: There is no business without one. It is highly recommended that you also have a business savings account. For small-business matters, consult your accountant, lawyer, bank, or savings institution. Do not use a personal saving or checking account for business. Never borrow out of the business for personal use unless it is a true emergency.

- Copy of resale or tax collection certificate. If your state collects sales tax, keep a copy of the original on hand at all times when selling or making a sales presentation.

- Copy of a supplier invoice and a copy of a customer invoice. This is a basic requirement at most trade shows and provides credit information to a supplier of your raw goods.

many cases, a shop may eventually buy your jewelry outright if it is selling well. Make sure there is a contract that states what is expected of both parties, even if you must write the contract yourself. Frequent calls to the shop should allow you to make sure you have enough inventory on the shelves to make this market worth the effort. Always tag the product with your business name, to develop a following in the shop.

Using the Internet

The Web may be the greatest business tool a jewelry artist has in the current business market because it offers marketing alternatives.

Participating in a new craft mall can be a gamble if the management team lacks business savvy. (More than 50% of craft malls close their doors before their first anniversary.) Our communities can get over-run with craft show after craft show that saturate the local market and compete for the same gift dollar. Artisans and craftspeople are increasingly competing against imports of cheap junk jewelry mass produced in countries that pay employees pennies for labor. These items are sold so cheaply that the artist is tempted to buy the imports and sell them rather than put labor into original handcrafted items. How do we stay current and compete with an ever-increasing consumer base? Check out a cyber craft show on the Web and see how other jewelry artists are selling their work—this will help you find a way to sell your jewelry online.

Research the Internet, as you would any potential marketplace. Take time to find and view established Web sites, as each has a unique way of presenting its offerings. Some sites have up to 1,000 visitors a day from all over the globe. To become part of a Web site showcase or gallery, you will have two investments: programming time to set up your page at the site, which is normally an hourly charge, and a rental fee per month to maintain the page. Shop around because pricing for both programming and Web site page rental varies greatly. It also is very helpful if you have an e-mail ad-dress for inquiries, which means you must be somewhat Internet wise—a task that really is not that difficult or time consuming. To participate with electronic mail, your business must have a com-puter, modem, and online service. To sell on the Internet, you do not need to access the Internet, but the more involved you are with your selling tools the better informed you will be.

Many jewelry makers have been very successful online. Many use the Internet as a tool to expand customer base, build a mailing list, and increase yearly sales. Catalogs, new product information, and newsletters can all be sent very inexpensively via electronic

Internet Auctions

Professional jewelry artisans are raving about the profits being made by selling their pieces at Internet Auction Web sites. Most feel there is little investment to reach the incredible audience that a successful Web site can pull in. So how do you get a piece of the action? It's a simple process and, after a bit of research, you may be saying, "Going, going, gone!"

1. Check out some of the auction sites. You want to see if the site has an area where jewelry is being sold. Take a look at what jewelry is being offered at the auction. Check out quality, pricing, and the history of the buyers.

2. Review the cyber paperwork needed to register at the site. Most auction sites will take a set percentage of the selling price. Always double check, but most sites do not charge if the item doesn't sell.

3. You'll be setting a starting bid and you can also enter a minimum bid. The minimum bid means you will not sell the item for less than a set price so that you don't end up giving your jewelry away.

4. Make sure you understand who pays for the shipping. In most cases the bidder pays the shipping, but you are responsible to make sure it is shipped properly and in a timely fashion.

5. A few sites to take a look at are: ebay.com, yahoo.com, and auctionwatch.com.

mail. It is also an excellent idea to participate in Bulletin Board Services (areas where notes are posted, usually within an online service) and newsgroups (notes posted from all over the world about specific topics, such as polymer clay, beading, wiring, or jewelry fashion). Some commercial Bulletin Board Services allow you to sell products directly through the board. The most successful craft professionals keep an eye on the future, so stay aware of new marketplaces and marketing tools and take risks every once in a while. The Internet is the future. Whether you network with fellow

Selling Your Work on the Web

Phillip Coomer of Craftmark recommends several key tips for placing your work on the Web.

1. Be a part of a large site. It's tempting to want your own domain, but to key into buyers you need to be a part of a larger site. At a larger site, your buyer finds you more quickly and more easily.

2. Be creative and change your site periodically. Add different products to sell.

3. Be ready for orders. Think out payment plans and shipping needs in advance.

4. Check out other vendors and sites. Be different. Stand out.

5. Ask about how the site advertises. Ask about the marketing plans for the site.

6. Do your research and study the contracts. Be aware of what you are being offered in services. Find out if each service is an additional charge or part of the monthly fee.

7. Because you are on the World Wide Web, your customer may not be using American currency. Therefore, consider money exchanges and services fees.

8. Keywords are important for search engines. What keywords will help your customer find you? Search engines use words, not graphics, so be descriptive of your product even if you have excellent graphics. Tell your buyer exactly what they are buying (list materials used and dimensions).

professionals or sell your jewelry pieces, keep up to date on what's happening on the Web.

Selling Your Designs for Publication

Before selling your jewelry designs to publishers, it is important to understand what is considered an original design. Every professional artisan must be very careful not to infringe on the copyrights of another individual or publisher. For years, I've heard the rumor that if you change 10% of a design or three parts of a design, you may claim it as your own. As is the case with most rumors, however, there is no foundation for this thinking. An original design is one you create on your own merits or skills. Motifs may be used by many. For example, many people use roses, hearts, or angels in their original designs. But you may not directly copy the style of another person or business. Details about copyrights can be found in chapter 11.

Many talented people have created soft sculpture dolls; however, no one may copy the Cabbage Patch Kids. If you use the designs of others to build your talents, you may not sell that work as your own design to a publisher. A copyright for your designs will be filed with the necessary paperwork at the Library of Congress. There is a small fee for filing. You own the copyright to your work the minute you create it; however, to protect your rights, it is best to consult a lawyer and file the appropriate forms with the government. There are publishers who do allow a restricted use of their designs and patterns to the professional jewelry artist. However, this doesn't include commercial use, only the limited production of handmade items. A wonderful example of this is the use of rubberstamps in designs. If you were to use a manufacturer's rubberstamp to create a greeting card, you can sell this finished product in a limited number (this number varies from manufacturer to manufacturer). You are also allowed to sell the finished card and written instructions for making it to a publisher. But, as is always the case, there are some exceptions. It's best to stay away from licensed designs, such as Disney or Marvel Comics. It's also a good idea to ask the manufacturer for permission to use the stamped image. Be familiar with copyright laws, both as a hobbyist and as a professional, because there may come a time when you will want to copyright a design or group of designs. One of the reasons I'm so adamant about professionals knowing the law is that litigated disputes over copyrights and infringements are becoming commonplace. The only way to protect your interests and have a hope of winning is to be well documented and prepared. There are several ways to document and keep records of your jewelry designs. Take photographs of each new design you create. It's easy to forget just how much you have created over time. As a professional, I usually sell a finished item to the public for at least 1 to 3 years before I attempt to sell the work and written instructions to a publisher. You might also create an item that you may not want to sell but that is perfect for publication. When writing project instructions, use the photographs to jog your memory. Digital cameras are now at affordable prices and can be a great investment if you decided that selling designs is where you will concentrate most of your efforts. Or you may send the photographs to an editor for consideration. It's also important to keep a work journal with notes about supplies used on different items. Most jewelry designers use journals to track productivity and as handy references for future projects. Tracia Ledford Williams, a decorative painter and teacher who loves creating one of a kind jewelry pieces, highly recommends keeping a design journal. "I've been painting for over 20 years, and even in the beginning I wrote comments and notes to myself in a spiral notebook. Just a few years ago, I decided to publish my own line of pattern packets. I used my journals to create the packets. It saved me time and effort. I didn't have to start from scratch!"

Before deciding to publish your jewelry designs, take an honest look at your ability to communicate. Designing for publication takes practice, discipline, and patience. Writing may not be your forte, but you will have to develop those skills if you want to publish your designs. A healthy self-esteem comes in handy, as even the best designers receive rejection letters. If you'd like to see your name in print and get paid for the effort, follow these basic steps.

Handy Hint

Don't give up if a publisher or editor sends you a rejection slip. Persistence does pay off!

1. Find a publisher who matches your style or work. The easiest way is to select your favorite craft magazine. If your design is quick or easy to do, submit your work to a publication such as *Quick and Easy Crafts Magazine*. But if your design is a complicated metalsmithing necklace, you might want to consider another publication, such as *Bead & Button*. Take a look at all the art, craft, jewelry, and home decor magazines. You can also go to the reference section of any library and use a periodical guide, which lists magazines by category.

2. Write a brief letter to the editor asking for the magazine's writer's guidelines. Even if you are submitting to two magazines published by the same company, be sure to get writer's guidelines for each publication. The name of the editor and the magazine's address are usually listed near the front of the magazine. Also, ask for a copy of the magazine's editorial calendar, which shows what the magazine will be looking for in future issues and includes deadline information. It's too late to submit a design for Mother's Day in March or a Thanksgiving design in October. Most designs are needed 6 months to a year before the publication date of the magazine.

3. Send a query letter to the editor describing your design and include a sketch or clear photograph of your jewelry pieces.

4. Allow time for the editor to review your submission. If you haven't heard after 4 to 6 weeks, follow up with a phone call or letter.

5. If your design is accepted, find out about your deadlines. If you haven't written instructions for the design, do so immediately. Ship the design sample and instructions to the editor.

6. You will be signing a contract, so be sure to read and understand it thoroughly. If you don't understand the details of the

contract, ask questions. Most contracts specify that all rights belong to the publisher, but you can always negotiate this. Don't be intimidated by legal language.

7. If your jewelry design is rejected, don't take it personally. It may not fit the magazine's current needs, so try a different magazine.

Teaching or Demonstrating

The final marketplace to be discussed in this chapter is teaching and demonstrating your skills to others. Teaching can be a wonderful outlet, once you've mastered jewelry-making techniques and have developed a body of work. You may find that friends and family ask you to make pieces for them or show them how to make jewelry themselves. I found this to be true when I developed my wearable art skills, and I began teaching in small groups as a means to share what I had learned to several friends at once, rather than showing them, one-on-one, several times over. Standing before a group of people to explain and demonstrate basic techniques is great motivation for developing and perfecting your own skills. Many successful jewelry designers have developed their teaching skills and now earn money by traveling around the country, teaching others.

You can begin teaching as a volunteer, build a reputation, and become a paid teacher or demonstrator. Teaching requires a class plan. You will have to create a project; write an outline for the class, including step-by-step instructions; prepare a list of class materials each student must bring; and coordinate how the lesson will flow. Ask yourself how much time you will need to teach your class, and determine whether students will leave with a finished project.

Preparation is the key to teaching success. Check out the location of the class. Is there enough space to move about safely while teaching? Does the room have everything you need, such as running water and good lighting? How many students can fit in the room without crowding? What do you have to bring to the classroom (glue guns, needlenose pliers, table protection, jewelry findings, bead holders, and so on)? What will the storeowner or organizer provide? The classroom may not be perfect. Some of the problems will be solved easily while others might have to be worked around by making adjustments to your lesson plan.

Learn as much as you can about your students. What is the age group and gender? Are the students beginners with no knowledge of even the basics of jewelry making? Although you can, to a certain degree, set the standard for the students you want to teach, be prepared for anything.

The final consideration for you is the cost of the class. Determining the price of your class or demonstration is like pricing your jewelry pieces. Research the going rate of other teacher's fees and determine what the regional economy can afford. You can set a flat fee or you can charge by the hour. Whichever you choose, consider the cost of preparing samples of goods used during the class, of transportation to and from the class, and of your time spent in class. Keep in mind that some stores and organizations charge a room fee to the teacher or ask for a percentage of the class fee. Carefully write down all your expenses. You may not make money the first time you teach the class, but remember that a good class can be taught many, many times even in the same regional area. Make sure that your bottom line is in the black, not in the red.

> **Handy Hint**
>
> Begin your teaching career by teaching friends and family— they're the most forgiving group. They will also be your greatest cheerleaders!

The more experience you get as a teacher, the higher your class fee can be. When I started teaching, my class fee was about $10 per hour of teaching. I often supplied my own materials for students to use in class. I still supply materials for my classes, but my average class fee is now $20 per hour of class. At trade shows, I can earn up

Take a Class—or Be a Teacher

Many classes are available in crafting. You might want to get involved as a volunteer or even as a teacher. The following are locations and organizations that may already have classes or may be willing to sponsor one.

Adult education programs

Art supply stores

After-school child care

Book stores

Churches

City parks

City recreational centers

Civic club lunches or meetings

Community colleges

Community festivals

Craft retail stores

Craft shows

Cultural associations

Day care

Elementary schools

Family gatherings/reunions

Hardware/do-it-yourself shops

High schools

Home show or home party

Libraries

Local chapters of associations

Middle schools

Museums

Nursing homes

Scouting groups

Senior centers

Trade schools

Trade shows

Universities

to $200 for an hour class, because the planning and preparation time is much more intense than for a local class. In addition to being paid a fee, teaching is a great means to sell your finished pieces—your students may wish to purchase some of your pieces for themselves, or to use as gifts. Demonstrating doesn't need as much detail as teaching because you will only be showing others how to make a particular piece of jewelry. The audience learns from you and takes the information home to make the item. The most successful demonstrators often supply a handout or flyer that lists the supplies needed to create whatever they are demonstrating.

Most demonstrations are set up at a table where you can stand or sit while demonstrating. If your demonstration goes on for hours, be sure to take breaks. As a demonstrator, you may be paid an hourly rate or a flat day rate or whatever you set up with the organizer of the demonstration. The fee usually does not include setup or breakdown time, but you may arrange to have reimbursement for travel expenses. The industry average is about $60 for a 4- to 5-hour day. Never assume anything about what is expected of you as a demonstrator. Ask questions, and better yet, get all agreements in writing.

Whether approaching a store or organization as a teacher or a demonstrator, it's important that you provide a résumé and a portfolio. A portfolio is a visual display of your work that can be as simple as a three-ring binder or as elaborate as a professional portfolio case (which you can find at office supply or art stores). The portfolio can include illustrations, drawings, published work, awards, personal and work references, and photos. The objective of the résumé and portfolio is to show the potential client that you are professional, motivated, prepared, and ready to take on any assignment given to you. Be creative, but be honest.

Displaying Your Work

I recommend that you visit several trade or retail shows before preparing for your first jewelry display. Look at the different products, displays, props, and pricing. Note what attracts your eye and what brings you into a booth. Record your reaction to prices and salespeople. Depending on what you want your display to accomplish, you can use anything from a simple setup of a table and chair to an elaborate system of shelves, tables, signs, and props.

Visit every jewelry shop you can locate. Make notes of how these stores display pieces of jewelry. Jot down what colors the displays use for background or draping. Are any props used to display the jewelry? Department stores often have jewelry displays that you can use as inspiration when creating your own displays.

Use the time you have to catch your customers' eye wisely by putting together an eye-catching display of your work. The average retail customer spends less than 30 minutes shopping in a retail gift shop, like a craft mall or co-op. So, you only have about 6 seconds to grab the attention of that buyer. But this time, you aren't even there to help promote your craft. Therefore you must have a display that serves as a top-notch sales force.

There are several components to an eye-catching display. Your display should have a general or specific theme that pulls your work together. The theme can be based on your craft. For example, if you sew or quilt your jewelry, sprinkle sewing-related notions, such as buttons, spools of thread, pincushions, and thimbles throughout your booth. If you paint your jewelry, you might want to incorporate a variety of brushes, colors of paint, or a palette in your display. The small touches are what bring continuity to your visual presentation. Many artisans use seasonal or holiday themes to create a buying mood—colored lights, garlands of evergreen or fall leaves, or bright spring flowers.

Props can be more than just decoration. They can also be demonstrations of your craft. Use a rotating rack to display earrings and necklaces. Use a real jewelry box to display pieces. Though you can lay some pieces flat on a table, it's better to give the display texture and detail by adding things like gift-wrapped boxes, bricks, peach crates, terra-cotta pots, or plastic or ceramic risers. Display expensive pieces in a locked case to avoid smudges and marks from people continuously handling them.

Use color to carry a theme. Color catches the eye. The right color selections will accent and complement your work. Choose an accent color that enhances and brings attention to, rather than de-tracts from or overwhelms, your pieces. Experiment with color choices. Your work should pop from the display rather than fade into it. Use contrasting colors for your table covers so that your jewelry pieces do not blend into the tables or shelves. Colors can set a mood. Bright bold colors are fes-tive. Pastel, soft colors are comforting. Country colors with gray undertones are rustic and relaxing. Black and white is stark but builds confidence. Red or yellow means caution, slow down, and yield. Color is also important in the packaging you use, especially when this packaging is placed against the backdrop of your display. Don't get lazy or careless when selecting your color choices.

> **Handy Hint**
>
> Learn to trust your own fashion judgment. If you love jewelry, you'll notice what styles of jewelry are popular with the current fashion trends.

Signs within displays are important for explaining certain crafts. Your customer may not know that the item that looks like an ornate chopstick is really used as a hair bobble. Maybe you have created a necklace that has a different pendent for each holiday season. Does your customer know that? Easy-to-read, concise, printed signs can help the uneducated buyer. Small signs can also be used to remind buyers of upcoming holidays or events such as Valentine's Day, Secretary's Day, and so on. Pointing out this information can add more sales to your day. When making signs, follow retail guidelines: Never use more than three to four words per line and use no more than three lines per sign.

Another element of your display is the lighting. There should be enough light within your display to show clearly the details and quality of your jewelry pieces. Avoid shadows. For indoor shows, you may have to invest in spotlights for times when your pieces are placed in a darker corner of the room. For outdoor shows, lighting is rarely a problem. Be sure to use a canopy that enhances, rather than distorts, the true colors of your jewelry. Most jewelry artists use off-white or beige canopy tops, which offer the least amount of light distortion and which allow natural sunlight to enhance the color of their items.

Last but not least, give the buyer plenty of room to move within and around your display. Keep traffic flow in mind when designing your booth. Use a U- or L-shape layout of tables. Most booth spaces are approximately 10 × 10 feet, so make efficient use of every available nook and cranny within your display. Also remember that you will transport, set up, and break down your display many, many times, so you don't want a huge display to deal with. It's best to try to make your display-booth parts only one-quarter of your available transportation space in a vehicle or small enough to avoid unnecessary expenses when shipping.

Conclusion

There are so many different markets for your jewelry creations that an entire book could be written about each one. This chapter has highlighted only a few of the most popular and easy-to-access markets. There are many more, including selling directly to a retailer, organizing a craft fair, selling on TV shopping channels, using direct mail, showing at galleries, or opening a storefront. If zoning allows, you can even open a shop in your home, or dedicate space within your home as a permanent display of your jewelry when customers call for an appointment to view your designs. There are many considerations to this option. You will have to set store hours when you will be onsite.

Part of growing a jewelry business is to keep searching for new and exciting areas to promote and sell your unique designs. Sometimes this growth means taking a risk, but most markets can be researched first with the help of the Small Business Administration or other business-consulting firms. Have a firm idea of how you expect to be paid for your jewelry. In most cases, at any type of craft show, you will be dealing with cash, check, or charge customers. If you decide to accept credit cards, you must contact a bank or a financial institution that works with small businesses or non-storefronts. Carefully research and compare start-up investments and charges. Read chapter 11 for details about how to research credit-card services and banks.

Talk with other professionals who accept credit cards. Ask your local bank for advice on accepting personal checks before you make your first sale. Most banks have a checklist of what information you must record in case the check bounces.

I hope you feel the same excitement that I do when thinking about the different markets that sell jewelry. I've watched the markets change and grow over the years, but there is always a market for high-quality, handmade jewelry. You may decide to sell your jewelry only in one craft mall or you may choose to use a combination of craft shows, direct-mail catalogs, and a Web site to reach your customers. There is no right or wrong market for the professional. Your market choices should complement your goals. As your business grows, your interests and goals may change, too. The marketplace is flexible enough to bend and turn with your business needs. So the next step is to let your customers know where to find you, which leads us to my first love—advertising! Chapter 10 gives you a head start at getting the word out about you, your business, and your jewelry.

Marketing Your Jewelry

Advertising and Publicity

▼▼

YOU CAN PLACE YOUR JEWELRY in the best marketplace, but if your buyers don't know where to find you and what you have to offer, your jewelry will sit in inventory, gathering dust.

You need to continually advertise your jewelry to your target market of buyers and publicize your crafts business to the general public. This chapter is all about the many ways you can do that.

Here's My Card

A very basic tool for advertising is a business card. There are three essential elements to this card. The first is your business name. While you can use your own name as your business name, I strongly recommend using a name that truly symbolizes your business. It should be a name that's easy to remember, easy to spell, and should communicate your expertise to the customer. Use your business name on all your printed materials, such as brochures, letterhead, and invoices (and on your Web site, if you have one).

When I started to sell my work to the public, I used *By Maria* as my company name. Fewer than 2 years later, I felt that this name

Creating Your Business Cards

A business card should include:

Company name

Contact person within the company

Phone number

Mailing address

Company logo or appropriate clip art

And, if applicable:

Fax number

E-mail address

Web site address

didn't reflect my work and that my customers didn't remember it. Around that time, I was getting a new dining room set from the Virginia House furniture manufacturing company. I liked that company name because it sounded strong and solid. The name also sounded prestigious to me in that it resounded with a feeling of success and prosperity. Although you might not guess it was a furniture manufacturer by the name, it was a name you could trust—easy to remember and easy to spell—in short, it was memorable. Thus, *Nerius House* was born. Since I didn't want to limit my possibilities (I've always thought in the big picture), I added *& Companies* to my business name. Once I began to use *Nerius House & Co.* on my business cards and letterhead, consumer recognition doubled. A company name gives clout and identity to the business. It's a small, but serious part of your work. If your jewelry is sophisticated and high end, your company name should reflect this message. If your jewelry is fun and funky, and designed with humor, then consider a name that will ring of festivity.

The final chapter of this book details some of the rules and regulations for selecting a business name. For example, you can't simply add *incorporated, limited,* or other legal terms unless you take the legal steps to use such terms. Keep in mind that a fictitious name is not a trademarked name, nor does it give you sole rights to use the name. Your state may require you to file a fictitious name statement so the community will know that you "do business as" (dba) or you are "also know as" (aka). It's important that you be well versed in the legalities required by your city, county, and state.

Did you know???

More than forty-five million Americans work full time from home businesses and home offices.

The second element of a business card is your contact information. This should include your name (unless you want someone else to be the contact person for your company) and an address for correspondence. Use your home address or rent a post office box. Depending on how convenient it is to rent a post office box in your community, I strongly recommend considering this additional expense. From my own experience, there are sometimes misunderstandings with a customer who assumes you own a retail storefront. I've had people stop by while in the neighborhood, which can be an inconvenience. Many businesses use a post office box for privacy, even though most creative professionals are home-based.

Contact information should also include a phone number. Since you are a business, it is best if you don't allow children to answer the phone during set business hours (for example, 8:00 A.M. to 5:00 P.M.). Use an answering machine during the day if you don't want interruptions while you work. Although your customers might find it charming to hear your child's voice yelling for you, a supplier or other business associate might not be so thrilled. One of the down sides of being in business is that at all times you must be professional and businesslike in your work. Other important contact information to include, if applicable, are an e-mail address, a Web site address, business hours, job title, and selling slogan or trademark.

The final ingredient of a business card is a logo. Many professionals use copyright-free clip art. If you have artistic ability, create your own logo. In designing mine, I turned to a graphic artist recommended by my printing company. Just like your business name, your logo should convey a strong image of what you do. My original logo was a clip art doll. At the time I was solely a doll maker and felt that the clip art would help people remember what I do. Once I started making enough money to budget for a graphic artist, I hired one to create an illustration of my own unique doll, with wild jute hair and a simple, sweet face. I was thrilled with the image and used it immediately on all my business papers, from business cards to letterhead to invoices. My callbacks from customers increased 200% that year! The most amazing thing to me is that, even to this day, I have customers who pull out my well-worn business card from their wallets and say, "Remember when I first bought a doll from you?" Since then I've changed much of my company's product line to include items like soap, rubberstamp collage, and jewelry, but I'm keeping my doll logo because my customers quickly recognize it.

My friend Nancee started her business by selling handmade baskets. Her company name, Creative Hands, was displayed with a clip-art graphic of a woven basket. Two years later, her baskets were not selling well, so Nancee started making brooches from plastic materials. Buyers went crazy for her brooches, but she never got any callbacks from her customers, and she couldn't figure out why. Finally, at a craft show, a repeat customer came into her booth and said she'd been trying to locate Nancee to buy more brooches. The customer had Nancee's business card in her hand, but she never called because she couldn't remember Nancee's name, and the card threw her off because it had a basket on it. Nancee immediately hired a graphic artist to create a new logo of one of her best-selling jewelry pieces. The new logo did the trick, increasing customer awareness of her jewelry line.

You may not feel that a logo or graphic is right for your jewelry line or business. In that case, you can get a similar effect by carefully selecting the font or type style of the lettering used on your business cards. Ask your printer for some help in this area. Most printers have dozens of examples of business cards they have done over the years. Ask to take a look. There are many wonderful new fonts that express emotion, personality, and character. The font you choose should be used on all of your printed materials. It will make an impression and help identify your jewelry business to your customer base.

> ### Handy Hint
>
> Make sure you ask new customers how they found out about you and your company. This will help you spend your advertising budget more effectively and reach your target audience.

Repetition of your logo and identifying type faces will help people remember your information. Reinforce your name, company name, and contact information whenever possible. Tag all your designs and products with this basic contact information. Insert a business flyer in all the designs you bag, ship, or package. Take every opportunity to promote and advertise your talents, skills, products, and designs.

Always have several business cards with you. Then you are always ready to tell someone new about your work and your business. Handing them a business card reinforces your message.

Local Press Pays Off

We've all heard the saying, "There's no such thing as a free lunch." Yet, there can be some free promotion available to you. The first area to explore is that of the press release (see sidebar, Sample Press

Release, on page 207). This is a simple document written to tell the world of your business, your talents, or any other newsworthy event that happens to your company. You submit a press release to any media in your area or community.

Take a good look at your local newspaper. Is there a section dedicated to business? Are there regular weekly feature articles on businesses or activities in your neighborhood or local area? If you can't find such sections, then call the newspaper and ask. Call local radio and television stations, as well, and ask them the same questions. You might be surprised at how eager your local media is to spotlight hometown talent. Think of a press release as good free advertising for your business. It's a part of your advertising plan that will never make a hole in your advertising budget. You never know who might be reading the newspaper or watching a television spot. An hour spent polishing a press release could lead to new work and new customers.

Include all contact information in the release, so the person receiving it can call for confirmation or to ask questions. Use simple language and be brief. A concise, interesting press release will be published and read more often than a complicated, novel-length one.

Don't be afraid to follow up a press release with a phone call to the media contact. Allow 1 to 2 weeks for the press release to be received and read. See the sample press release on page 207.

You might be surprised at the local reaction to a press release printed in your regional area. I usually get 15 to 30 calls after a press release has run in my local paper. Half the calls are from friends and customers, letting me know that I made the paper! But the other half is from new contacts interested in my work.

Let Your Customers Help You Sell

Satisfied customers who give you word-of-mouth advertising are a good source of new clientele. Word of mouth is mostly based on

Sample Press Release

Here's an example of a press release. Note the following key points of information: Heading (immediate release or stated date for release of information), contact information, body of release, and end of release (with ##END##, the standard symbol that ends text).

For Immediate Release
November 2, 2000
Contact:
Maria Nerius
Nerius House & Co.
Phone: (321) 951-3929
Fax: (407) 725-0792
E-mail: Mnerius@aol.com
Web site: www.procrafter.com

Nerius House celebrates its 15th anniversary by adding a limited edition bracelet to its product line. Established in 1984, Nerius House has manufactured quality handmade goods ranging from folk dolls to wood jewelry for every season.

"There has been a strong consumer demand for a collectible in our product line and Nerius House owes its success to its customers. We pay attention to consumer comments and look for any opportunity to meet our customers' needs," said Nerius. "The bracelet is made up of wood charms that represent each year of business for Nerius House."

Maria Nerius is available for interviews and demonstrations. The anniversary bracelet is part of the company's product line called Hello Dolly and is available at the American Craft Malls or can be ordered at the company's Web site, www.procrafter.com.

##END##

how good your customer service is and how happy your customers are with your products, so treat your customers with respect and give them a smile, and they will tell others about your company. Also use customer incentives. Consider giving a 5 to 10% discount on a purchase for every new customer that a loyal customer brings in. Or offer a discount for every $100 purchase. Give a free gift, such as a simple necklace or other low-ticket item to customers after they have made six or ten purchases. These are small but effective incentives that spread goodwill between you and your customer base.

Placing Local Ads

You might consider placing a small ad in a local newspaper to advertise a show you will be participating in or to advertise your business. Many shows and events have flyers or programs that are handed out to the attendees. This is also a great place to advertise.

Keep Promoting Yourself and Your Jewelry

No matter what you call it—bio sheet, publicity release, self-promotion brochure, or bragging papers—everyone in a creative business needs to write a 100- to 300-word document describing who they are and what they do. This document should be attached to press releases, new customer contacts, supplier credit forms, and any other business materials to let the other person know what your company is about. This very important tool can help open doors to you and get others to take notice of your efforts. The bio sheet is a form of introduction. A real bonus is to include a photo of yourself with your

Keeping Your Customers Close

Keep a mailing list of all your customers. To gather names for the list, use a guest book or sign-up sheet wherever you sell your work. Mail a postcard to alert customers of upcoming events, such as an open house, a craft show, or when you add new designs to your line. Offer a small discount or special gift if the customer brings the postcard back to you. I keep a list of all customers who spend more than $100 on a purchase, and I mail a note shortly after the purchase, thanking them for their business. This small task has paid for itself many times over by keeping my loyal customers happy and coming back for more.

designs. You can ask your local printer how to incorporate a photo into a one-page bio sheet, or you can make your own on a computer if you have access to a scanner. The cost of producing a bio sheet will pay off in customer recognition of your business, yourself, and your designs.

Self-promotion was discussed in chapter 7, but some points bear repeating. None of us wants to become a big-headed, egotistical lout, but in order to survive in a very competitive world, we must let others know what we are doing. It is not easy to sit down and come up with a few hundred words that describe you and your business, but writing your bio sheet is an effective way to promote yourself to others. The bio sheet can also help you focus on your goals. It may seem morbid, but I think of my bio sheet as my own eulogy— one that I get to write! If you find yourself struggling to find the right words, write your bio sheet in the third person, as if you were writing about someone you admire. Make your bio sheet interesting by adding the flair, creativity, and imagination of your own personality to the facts.

Mission Statement

A great way to write a bio sheet is to open with a mission statement. In one or two sentences, write your goals or hopes for your jewelry business. This concise statement will lead into the other tidbits and facts included in your bio sheet. Can you guess which companies might have the following mission statements? (I made up four of these examples with a sense of humor, but the message gets across. One mission statement is real and used by Nerius House & Co.)

1. Make a statement with our fashion jewelry.

2. Our name rings a bell!

3. Santa would be proud. Our earrings are made by the happiest elves south of the North Pole.

4. Crafting can express the care and love of our community. And the world is our community. Let us be the first to make a difference.

5. No celebration goes unnoticed for it is our goal to make a memory with a heirloom your grandmother would love.

    A. Nerius House & Co.

    B. Grandma's Brooches

    C. Liberty Rings & Things

    D. Jewelry Factory in Nosnow, Alaska

    E. Runway Model Toe Rings Company

Answers: 1-E; 2-C; 3-D; 4-A; 5-B

Some Final Thoughts about Jewelry Making

Jewelry and the making of jewelry are a big part of my genuine enjoyment in crafting. I consider my jewelry pieces the bread and butter of my business. Even at the worst shows, I've always sold enough jewelry to make my expenses and have enough money to buy gas to get home! Jewelry, whether made of pure gold or Kool-Aid-dyed macaroni can become priceless and treasured pieces of family traditions and celebrations. I have a hunch I fell in love with jewelry when Santa Claus left a yummy candy necklace in my Christmas stocking when I was five. I ate that sweet treat, one candy bead at a time, and the necklace may have ended up as a sticky elastic band, but I can still taste the fun and joy that first piece of jewelry gave me. I hope the information I have shared in this book will give you the same thrill and pleasure.

I believe that you will succeed in any goal you set for yourself. You may decide that all you really want to do is become your best at beading or making polymer canes. You may choose to design jewelry and sell the instructions to magazines. You may end up as a world-renowned jewelry artist! Whatever path you take, never forget why you started making jewelry to begin with. Never forget the excitement of completing a set of earrings. Never forget the smile your friend gave to you when you gifted her with a necklace you made with your own hands. Never forget that the real goal of art and craft is joy—that wonderful feeling of creativity!

Chapter 11 will fill in all the legal details and final business information you need to succeed in selling your jewelry for a profit. The Resource section of this book is filled with more information for you to use in your hobby or business. It includes lists of

Public Relations

It's free advertising! Advertising your business may be hard on your budget, but there are some simple and free ways to publicize your work and business.

- Teach a craft to a scouting group. There are plenty of parents involved who are potential customers.

- Offer to set up a display of your work at a school's teachers' lounge. Teachers have little time to shop the craft shows and malls, so bring your jewelry to them. Small items are best for this group.

- Get involved with a fundraiser.

- When exciting events happen within your business (for example, getting a new wholesale account, donating to a fundraiser, winning a ribbon at a show, adding a new craft mall), write a press release for the newspaper.

- A press release is simple. Type your name, company name, address, and phone number across the top of a sheet of paper. Just below this, type "FOR IMMEDIATE RELEASE." Then write the information for the press (see the sidebar, Sample Press

suppliers, Web sites, and recommended books and magazines. It is very important to continue learning and gathering knowledge about your techniques, designs, and business practices. Change is a part of the crafting world, with new trends forming even as you read these words. Colors, textures, themes, motifs, and styles come and go over the years. However, the basics, as outlined and explained in this book, will never be dated. Keep this book handy in your work area or office. When you find your niche, when you discover that perfect something that makes your life better and brighter and bolder, then you've found what it is you were meant to do in this world. Artists, artisans, and craftspeople make the world more colorful with rainbows of creativity. Whether you plan to enjoy jewelry making as a hobby or as a part-time or full-time occupation, I wish

Release, on page 207). Send the press release to the community, local, or business section editor, unless the newspaper indicates otherwise. Have plenty of inexpensive black-and-white or color photographs of yourself and your work to send out with press releases.

- Contact a local television station and volunteer to go on air to talk about crafting, demo a simple craft, or show samples of your work.

- Join any local guild, crafting group, or art association. Network and be an active member in order to learn of opportunities that might be happening. Join national guilds, societies, and associations. Keep on top of trends, events, and activities.

- If you are involved in a charitable activity involving crafting or if you make a very unique item, contact a craft magazine. Many consumer craft magazines have regular columns featuring crafters. Many also spotlight individual artists. Write your story and send it in. Many cover pieces are from individual artists and craftspeople. Send in a clear photo or slide of your work.

you success and satisfaction in your talents and skills. Remember to share these skills and talents with others so the traditions and heritage of jewelry making will pass on to the next generation. Take time every once in a while to teach and help others be creative.

My part in this book became a reality thanks to my family and friends, who patiently helped me collect and assemble all my information without losing my writing style or voice. Your family and friends will also be significant to your success. I know I don't have to remind you, but make sure you let your loved ones know how much you value them. You should always have time to make a piece of jewelry as a gift to yourself or for someone you love. Without a doubt, our family, friends, and customers are the gems of life!

A Mini-Course in Crafts-Business Basics

by Barbara Brabec

▼▼

THIS SECTION OF THE BOOK will familiarize you with important areas of legal and financial concern and enable you to ask the right questions if and when it is necessary to consult with an attorney, accountant, or other business adviser. Although the tax and legal information included here has been carefully researched by the author and is accurate to the best of her knowledge, it is not the business of either the author or publisher to render professional services in the area of business law, taxes, or accounting. Readers should therefore use their own good judgment in determining when the services of a lawyer or other professional would be appropriate to their needs.

Information presented applies specifically to businesses in the United States. However, because many U.S. and Canadian laws are similar, Canadian readers can certainly use the following information as a start-up business plan and guide to questions they need to ask their own local, provincial, or federal authorities.

Contents

7. Insurance Tips

Homeowner's or Renter's Insurance
Liability Insurance
Insurance on Crafts Merchandise
Auto Insurance

8. Important Regulations Affecting Artists and Craftspeople

Consumer Safety Laws
Labels Required by Law
The Bedding and Upholstered Furniture Law
FTC Rule for Mail-Order Sellers

9. Protecting Your Intellectual Property

Perspective on Patents
What a Trademark Protects
What Copyrights Protect
Copyright Registration Tips
Respecting the Copyrights of Others
Using Commercial Patterns and Designs

10. To Keep Growing, Keep Learning

Motivational Tips

A "Things to Do" Checklist with Related Resources

■ Business Start-Up Checklist
■ Government Agencies
■ Craft and Home-Business Organizations
■ Recommended Crafts-Business Periodicals
■ Other Services and Suppliers
■ Recommended Business Books
■ Helpful Library Directories

1. Starting Right

In preceding chapters of this book, you learned the techniques of a particular art or craft and realized its potential for profit. You learned what kinds of products are likely to sell, how to price them, and how and where you might sell them.

Now that you've seen how much fun a crafts business can be (and how profitable it might be if you were to get serious about selling what you make!) you need to learn about some of the "nitty-gritty stuff" that goes hand in hand with even the smallest business based at home. It's easy to start selling what you make and it's satisfying when you earn enough money to make your hobby self-supporting. Many crafters go this far and no further, which is fine. But even a hobby seller must be concerned about taxes and local, state, and federal laws. And if your goal is to build a part- or full-time business at home, you must pay even greater attention to the topics discussed in this section of the book.

Everyone loves to make money . . . but actually starting a business frightens some people because they don't understand what's involved. It's easy to come up with excuses for why we don't do certain things in life; close inspection of those excuses usually boils down to fear of the unknown. We get the shivers when we step out of our comfort zone and try something we've never done before. The simple solution to this problem lies in having the right information at the right time. As someone once said, "Knowledge is the antidote to fear."

The quickest and surest way to dispel fear is to inform yourself about the topics that frighten you. With knowledge comes a sense of power, and that power enables you to move. Whether your goal is merely to earn extra income from your craft hobby or launch a genuine home-based business, reading the following information will help you get started on the right legal foot, avoid financial pitfalls, and move forward with confidence.

When you're ready to learn more about art or crafts marketing or the operation of a home-based crafts business, a visit to your library or bookstore will turn up many interesting titles. In addition to the special resources listed by this book's author, you will find my list of recommended business books, organizations, periodicals, and other helpful resources later in this chapter. This information is arranged in a checklist you can use as a plan to get your business up and running.

Before you read my Mini-Course in Crafts-Business Basics, be assured that I understand where you're coming from because I was once there myself.

For a while I sold my craft work, and this experience led me to write my first book, *Creative Cash.* Now, 20 years later, this crafts-business classic ("my baby") has reached its sixth edition. Few of those who are totally involved in a crafts business today started out with a business in mind. Like me, most began as hobbyists looking for something interesting to do in their spare time, and one thing naturally led to another. I never imagined those many years ago

Social Security Taxes

When your crafts-business earnings are more than $400 (net), you must file a Self-Employment Tax form (Schedule SE) and pay into your personal Social Security account. This could be quite beneficial for individuals who have some previous work experience but have been out of the workplace for a while. Your re-entry into the business world as a self-employed worker, and the additional contributions to your Social Security account, could result in increased benefits on retirement.

Because so many senior citizens are starting home-based businesses these days, it should be noted that there is a limit on the amount seniors age 62 to 65 can earn before losing Social Security benefits. This dollar limit increases every year, however, and once you are past the age of 65, you can earn any amount of income and still receive full benefits. Contact your nearest Social Security office for details.

when I got serious about my craft hobby that I was putting myself on the road to a full-time career as a crafts writer, publisher, author, and speaker. Because I and thousands of others have progressed from hobbyists to professionals, I won't be at all surprised if someday you, too, have a similar adventure.

2. Taxes and Record Keeping

"Ambition in America is still rewarded . . . with high taxes," the comics quip. Don't you long for the good old days when Uncle Sam lived within his income and without most of yours?

Seriously, taxes are one of the first things you must be concerned about as a new business owner, no matter how small your endeavor. This section offers a brief overview of your tax responsibilities as a sole proprietor.

Is Your Activity a "Hobby" or a "Business"?

Whether you are selling what you make only to get the cost of your supplies back or actually trying to build a profitable business, you need to understand the legal difference between a profitable hobby and a business, and how each is related to your annual tax return.

The IRS defines a hobby as "an activity engaged in primarily for pleasure, not for profit." Making a profit from a hobby does not automatically place you "in business" in the eyes of the Internal Revenue Service, but the activity will be *presumed* to have been engaged in for profit if it results in a profit in at least 3 out of 5 years. Or, to put it another way, a "hobby business" automatically becomes a "real business" in the eyes of the IRS at the point where you can state that you are (1) trying to make a profit, (2) making regular business transactions, and (3) have made a profit 3 out of 5 years.

As you know, all income must be reported on your annual tax return. How it's reported, however, has everything to do with the amount of taxes you must pay on this income. If hobby income is less than $400, it must be entered on the 1040 tax form, with taxes payable accordingly. If the amount is greater than this, you must file a Schedule C form with your 1040 tax form. This is to your advantage, however, because taxes are due only on your *net profit.* Because you can deduct expenses up to the amount of your hobby income, there may be little or no tax at all on your hobby income.

Self-Employment Taxes

Whereas a hobby cannot show a loss on a Schedule C form, a business can. Business owners must pay not only state and federal income taxes on their profits, but self-employment taxes as well. (See sidebar, Social Security Taxes, page 219.) Because self-employed people pay Social Security taxes at twice the level of regular, salaried workers, you should strive to lower your annual gross profit figure on the Schedule C form through every legal means possible. One way to do this is through careful record keeping of all expenses related to the operation of your business. To quote IRS publications, expenses are deductible if they are "ordinary, necessary, and somehow connected with the operation and potential profit of your business." In addition to being able to deduct all expenses related to the making and selling of their products, business owners can also depreciate the cost of tools and equipment, deduct the overhead costs of operating a home-based office or studio (called the Home Office Deduction), and hire their spouse or children.

> ***Avoid this pitfall:*** Many new businesses that end up with a nice net profit on their first year's Schedule C tax form find themselves in financial trouble when tax time rolls around because they did not make estimated quarterly tax payments throughout the year. Aside from the penalties for underpayment of taxes, it's

a terrible blow to suddenly realize that you've spent all your business profits and now have no money left for taxes. Be sure to discuss this matter with a tax adviser or accountant when you begin your business.

Given the complexity of our tax laws and the fact that they are changing all the time, a detailed discussion of all the tax deductions currently available to small-business owners cannot be included in a book of this nature. Learning, however, is as easy as reading a book such as *Small Time Operator* by Bernard Kamoroff (my favorite tax and accounting guide), visiting the IRS Web site, or consulting your regular tax adviser.

You can also get answers to specific tax questions 24 hours a day by calling the National Association of Enrolled Agents (NAEA). Enrolled agents (EAs) are licensed by the Treasury Department to represent taxpayers before the IRS. Their rates for doing tax returns are often less than those you would pay for an accountant or CPA.

Keeping Tax Records

Once you're in business, you must keep accurate records of all income and expenses, but the IRS does not require any special kind of bookkeeping system. Its primary concern is that you use a system that clearly and accurately shows true income and expenses. For the sole proprietor, a simple system consisting of a checkbook, a cash receipts journal, a cash disbursements ledger, and a petty cash fund is quite adequate. Post expenses and income regularly to avoid year-end pile-up and panic.

If you plan to keep manual records, check your local office supply store or catalogs for the *Dome* series of record-keeping books, or use the handy ledger sheets and worksheets included in *Small Time Operator*. (This classic tax and accounting guide by CPA Bernard Kamoroff includes details on how to keep good records and prepare financial reports.) If you have a computer, there are a number of accounting software programs available, such as Intuit's Quicken, MYOB (Mind Your Own Business) Accounting, and Intuit's

An important concept to remember is that even the smallest business is entitled to deduct expenses related to its business, and the same tax-saving strategies used by "the big guys" can be used by small-business owners. Your business may be small now or still in the dreaming stage, but it could be larger next year and surprisingly profitable a few years from now. Therefore it is in your best interest to always prepare for growth, profit, and taxes by learning all you can about the tax laws and deductions applicable to your business. (See the sidebar, Keeping Tax Records on page 222.)

Sales Tax Is Serious Business

If you live in a state that has a sales tax (all but five states do), and sell products directly to consumers, you are required by law to register with your state's Department of Revenue (Sales Tax division) for a resale tax number. The fee for this in most states ranges from $5 to $25, with some states requiring a bond or deposit of up to $150.

QuickBooks, the latter of which is one of the most popular and best bookkeeping systems for small businesses. The great advantage of computerized accounting is that financial statements can be created at the press of a key after accounting entries have been made.

Regardless of which system you use, always get a receipt for everything and file receipts in a monthly envelope. If you don't want to establish a petty cash fund, spindle all of your cash receipts, tally them at month's end, and reimburse your personal outlay of cash with a check written on your business account. On your checkbook stub, document the individual purchases covered by this check.

At year's end, bundle your monthly tax receipt envelopes and file them for future reference, if needed. Because the IRS can audit a return for up to 3 years after a tax return has been filed, all accounting and tax records should be kept at least this long, but 6 years is better. Personally, I believe you should keep all your tax returns, journals, and ledgers throughout the life of your business.

Depending on where you live, this tax number may also be called a Retailer's Occupation Tax Registration Number, resale license, or use tax permit. Also, depending on where you live, the place you must call to obtain this number will have different names. In California, for example, you would contact the State Board of Equalization; in Texas, it's called the State Comptroller's Office. Within your state's revenue department, the tax division may have a name such as sales and use tax division or department of taxation and finance. Generally speaking, if you check your telephone book under "Government," and look for whatever listing comes closest to "Revenue," you can find the right office.

If your state has no sales tax, you will still need a reseller's permit or tax exemption certificate to buy supplies and materials at wholesale prices from manufacturers, wholesalers, or distributors. Note that this tax number is only for supplies and materials used to make your products, not for things purchased at the retail level or for general office supplies.

Once registered with the state, you will begin to collect and remit sales and use tax (monthly, quarterly, or annually, as determined by your state) on all *taxable sales*. This does not mean *all* of your gross income. Different states tax different things. Some states put a sales tax on certain services, but generally you will never have to pay sales tax on income from articles sold to magazines, on teaching or consulting fees, or subscription income (if you happen to publish a newsletter). In addition, sales taxes are not applicable to:

- **Items sold on consignment through a charitable organization, shop, or other retail outlet, including craft malls and rent-a-space shops (because the party who sells directly to the consumer is the one who must collect and pay sales tax).**

- **Products you wholesale to others who will be reselling them to consumers. (Be sure to get their tax-exemption ID number for your own files, however, in case you are ever questioned as to why you did not collect taxes on those sales.)**

As you sell throughout the year, your record-keeping system must be set up so you can tell which income is taxable and which is tax-exempt for reporting on your sales tax return.

Collecting Sales Tax at Craft Shows

States are getting very aggressive about collecting sales tax, and agents are showing up everywhere these days, especially at the larger craft fairs, festivals, and small-business conferences. As I was writing this chapter, a posting on the Internet stated that in New Jersey the sales tax department is routinely contacting show promoters about a month before the show date to get the names and addresses of exhibitors. It is expected that other states will soon be following suit. For this reason, you should always take your resale or tax collection certificate with you to shows.

Although you must always collect sales tax at a show when you sell in a state that has a sales tax, how and when the tax is paid to the state can vary. When selling at shows in other states, you may find that the show promoter has obtained an umbrella sales tax certificate, in which case vendors would be asked to give management a check for sales tax at the end of the show for turning over to a tax agent. Or you may have to obtain a temporary sales tax certificate for a show, as advised by the show promoter. Some sellers who regularly do shows in two or three states say it's easier to get a tax ID number from each state and file an annual return instead of doing taxes on a show-by-show basis. (See sidebar, Including Tax in the Retail Price, page 226.)

Collecting Sales Tax at a Holiday Boutique

If you're involved in a holiday boutique where several sellers are offering goods to the public, each individual seller will be responsible for collecting and remitting his or her own sales tax. (This means someone has to keep very good records during the sale so each seller receives a record of the sale and the amount of tax on that sale.) A reader who regularly has home boutiques told me that in her community she must also post a sign at her "cash station" stating that sales tax is being collected on all sales, just as craft-fair sellers must do in some states. Again, it's important that you get complete details from your own state about its sales tax policies.

> ***Avoid this pitfall:*** Individuals who are selling "just for the fun of it" may think they don't have to collect sales taxes, but this is not true. As an official in my state's Department of Revenue told me, "Everyone who sells anything to consumers must collect sales tax. If you hold yourself out as a seller of merchandise, then you're subject to tax, even if you sell only a couple of times a year." The financial penalties for violating this state law can be severe. In Illinois, for example, lawbreakers are subject to a penalty of 20% over and above any normal tax obligation, and could receive for each offense (meaning each return not filed)

Including Tax in the Retail Price

Is it okay to incorporate the amount of sales tax into the retail price of items being sold directly to consumers? It's best to check with your individual state because each state's sales tax law is different.

Crafters like to use round-figure prices at fairs because this encourages cash sales and eliminates the need for taking coins to make change. Some crafters tell their customers that sales tax has been included in their rounded-off prices, but you should not do this until you check with your state. In some states, this is illegal; in others, you may find that you are required to inform your customers, by means of a sign, that sales tax has been included in your price. You may also have to print this information on customer receipts as well.

If you make such a statement and collect taxes on cash sales, be sure to report those cash sales as taxable income and remit the tax money to the state accordingly. Failure

from 1 to 6 months in prison and a fine of $5,000. As you can see, the collection of sales tax is serious business.

Collecting Tax on Internet Sales

Anything you sell that is taxable in your state is also taxable on the Internet. This is simply another method of selling, like craft fairs or mail-order sales. You don't have to break out Internet sales separately; simply include them in your total taxable sales.

3. The Legal Forms of Business

Every business must take one of four legal forms:

Sole Proprietorship
Partnership
LLC (Limited Liability Company)
Corporation

to do this would be a violation of the law, and it's easy to get caught these days when sales tax agents are showing up at craft fairs across the country.

Even if rounding off the price and including the tax within that figure turns out to be legal in your state, it will definitely complicate your bookkeeping. For example, if you normally sell an item for $5 or some other round figure, you must have a firm retail price on which to calculate sales tax to begin with. Adding tax to a round figure makes it uneven. Then you must either raise or lower the price, and if you lower it, what you're really doing is paying the sales tax for your customer out of your profits. This is no way to do business.

I suggest that you set your retail prices based on the pricing formulas given in this book, calculate the sales tax accordingly, and give your customers change if they pay in cash. You will be perceived as a professional when you operate this way, whereas crafters who insist always on "cash only" sales are sending signals to buyers that they don't intend to report this income to tax authorities.

As a hobby seller, you automatically become a sole proprietor when you start selling what you make. Although most professional crafters remain sole proprietors throughout the life of their business, some do form craft partnerships or corporations when their business begins to generate serious money, or if it happens to involve other members of their family. You don't need a lawyer to start a sole proprietorship, but it would be folly to enter into a partnership, LLC, or corporation, without legal guidance. Here is a brief look at the main advantages and disadvantages of each type of legal business structure.

Sole Proprietorship

No legal formalities are involved in starting or ending a sole proprietorship. You're your own boss here, and the business starts when you say it does and ends automatically when you stop running it. As discussed earlier, income is reported annually on a Schedule C form and taxed at the personal level. The sole proprietor is fully liable for all business debts and actions. In the event of a lawsuit, personal assets are not protected.

Partnership

There are two kinds of partnerships: general and limited.

A *general partnership* is easy to start, with no federal requirements involved. Income is taxed at the personal level and the partnership ends as soon as either partner withdraws from the business. Liability is unlimited. The most financially dangerous thing about a partnership is that the debts incurred by one partner must be assumed by all other partners. Before signing a partnership agreement, make sure the tax obligations of your partner are current.

In a *limited partnership,* the business is run by general partners and financed by silent (limited) partners who have no liability beyond an investment of money in the business. This kind of partnership is more complicated to establish, has special tax withholding regulations, and requires the filing of a legal contract with the state.

> ***Avoid this pitfall:*** Partnerships between friends often end the friendship when disagreements over business policies occur. Don't form a partnership with anyone without planning in advance how the partnership will eventually be dissolved, and spell out all the details in a written agreement. What will happen if either partner dies, wants out of the business, or wants to buy out the other partner? Also ask your attorney about the advisability of having partnership insurance, to protect against the complications that would arise if one of the partners becomes ill, incapacitated, or dies. For an additional perspective on the pros and cons of partnerships, read the book *The Perils of Partners* (see page 291 for inforamtion).

The Limited Legal Protection of a Corporation

Business novices often think that by incorporating their business they can protect their personal assets in the event of a lawsuit. This is true if you have employees who do something wrong and cause your business to be sued. As the business owner, however, if you personally do something wrong and are sued as a result, you might in some cases be held legally responsible, and the "corporation door" will offer no legal protection for your personal assets.

Or, as CPA Bernard Kamoroff explains in *Small Time Operator,* "A corporation will not shield you from personal liability that you normally should be responsible for, such as not having car insurance or acting with gross negligence. If you plan to incorporate solely or primarily with the intention of limiting your legal liability, I suggest you find out first exactly how limited the liability really is for your particular venture. Hire a knowledgeable lawyer to give you a written opinion." (See section 7, Insurance Tips.)

LLC (Limited Liability Company)

This legal form of business reportedly combines the best attributes of other small-business forms while offering a better tax advantage than a limited partnership. It also affords personal liability protection similar to that of a corporation. To date, few craft businesses appear to be using this business form.

Corporation

A corporation is the most complicated and expensive legal form of business and not recommended for any business whose earnings are less than $25,000 a year. If and when your business reaches this point, you should study some books on this topic to fully understand the pros and cons of a corporation. Also consult an accountant or attorney for guidance on the type of corporation you should select—a "C" (general corporation) or an "S" (subchapter S corporation).

The main disadvantage of incorporation for the small-business owner is that profits are taxed twice: first as corporate income and again when they are distributed to the owner-shareholders as dividends. For this reason, many small businesses elect to incorporate as subchapter S corporations, which allows profits to be taxed at owners' regular individual rates. (See sidebar, The Limited Legal Protection of a Corporation, on page 229.)

4. Local and State Laws and Regulations

This section will acquaint you with laws and regulations that affect the average art or crafts business based at home. If you've unknowingly broken one of these laws, don't panic. It may not be as bad as you think. It is often possible to get back on the straight and narrow merely by filling out a required form or by paying a small fee of some kind. What's important is that you take steps now to comply with the laws that pertain to your particular business. Often, the fear of being caught when you're breaking a law is much worse than doing whatever needs to be done to set the matter straight. In the end, it's usually what you don't know that is most likely to cause legal or financial problems, so never hesitate to ask questions about things you don't understand.

Even when you think you know the answers, it can pay to "act dumb." It is said that Napoleon used to attend meetings and pretend to know nothing about a topic, asking many probing questions. By feigning ignorance, he was able to draw valuable information and insight out of everyone around him. This strategy is often used by today's small-business owners, too.

Business Name Registration

If you're a sole proprietor doing business under any name other than your own full name, you are required by law to register it on both the local and state level. In this case, you are said to be using an "assumed," "fictitious," or "trade" name. Registration enables authorities to connect an assumed name to an individual who can be held responsible for the actions of a business. If you're doing business under your own name, such as Kay Jones, you don't have to register your business name on either the local or state level. If your name is part of a longer name, however (for example, Kay Jones Designs), you should check to see if your county or state requires registration.

Local Registration

To register your name, contact your city or county clerk, who will explain what you need to do to officially register your business on

Picking a Good Business Name

If you haven't done it already, think up a great name for your new business. You want something that will be memorable—catchy, but not too cute. Many crafters select a simple name that is attached to their first name, such as "Mary's Quilts" or "Tom's Woodcrafts." This is fine for a hobby business, but if your goal is to build a full-time business at home, you may wish to choose a more professional-sounding name that omits your personal name. If a name sounds like a hobby business, you may have difficulty getting wholesale suppliers to take you seriously. A more professional name may also enable you to get higher prices for your products. For example, the above names might be changed to "Quilted Treasures" or "Wooden Wonders."

Don't print business cards or stationery until you find out if someone else is already using the name you've chosen. To find out if the name has already been registered, you

the local level. At the same time, ask if you need any special municipal or county licenses or permits to operate within the law. (See the next section, Licenses and Permits.) This office can also tell you how and where to write to register your name at the state level. If you've been operating under an assumed name for a while and are worried because you didn't register the name earlier, just register it now, as if the business were new.

Registration involves filling out a simple form and paying a small fee, usually around $10 to $25. At the time you register, you will get details about a classified ad you must run in a general-circulation newspaper in your county. This will notify the public at large that you are now operating a business under an assumed name. (If you don't want your neighbors to know what you're doing, simply run the ad in a newspaper somewhere else in the county.) After publication of this ad, you will receive a Fictitious Name Statement that you must send to the county clerk, who in turn will file it with your registration form to make your business completely legit-

can perform a trademark search through a search company or hire an attorney who specializes in trademark law to conduct the search for you. And if you are planning to eventually set up a Web site, you might want to do a search to see if that domain name is still available on the Internet. Go to www.networksolutions.com to do this search. Business names have to be registered on the Internet, too, and they can be "parked" for a fee until you're ready to design your Web site.

It's great if your business name and Web site name can be the same, but this is not always possible. A crafter told me recently she had to come up with 25 names before she found a domain name that hadn't already been taken. (Web entrepreneurs are grabbing every good name they can find. Imagine my surprise when I did a search and found that two different individuals had set up Web sites using the titles of my two best-known books, *Creative Cash* and *Homemade Money*.)

imate. This name statement or certificate may also be referred to as your DBA ("doing business as") form. In some areas, you cannot open a business checking account if you don't have this form to show your bank.

> ***Avoid this pitfall:*** Failure to register your business name may result in your losing it—after you've spent a considerable amount of money on business cards, stationery, advertising, and so on. If someone sees your name, likes it, and finds on checking that it hasn't been registered, they can simply register the name and force you to stop using it.

State Registration

Once you've registered locally, contact your secretary of state to register your business name with the state. This will prevent its use by a corporate entity. At the same time, find out if you must obtain any kind of state license. Generally, home-based crafts businesses will not need a license from the state, but there are always exceptions. An artist who built an open-to-the-public art studio on his property reported that the fine in his state for operating this kind of business without a license was $50 a day. In short, it always pays to ask questions to make sure you're operating legally and safely.

Federal Registration

The only way to protect a name on the federal level is with a trademark, discussed in section 9.

Licenses and Permits

A "license" is a certificate granted by a municipal or county agency that gives you permission to engage in a business occupation. A "permit" is similar, except that it is granted by local authorities. Until recently, few crafts businesses had to have a license or permit of any kind, but a growing number of communities now have new laws on their books that require home-based business owners to obtain a "home occupation permit." Annual fees for such permits may range from $15 to $200 a year. For details about the law in your particular community or county, call your city or county clerk (depending on whether you live within or outside city limits).

Use of Personal Phone for Business

Although every business writer stresses the importance of having a business telephone number, craftspeople generally ignore this advice and do business on their home telephone. Although it's okay to use a home phone to make outgoing business calls, you cannot advertise a home telephone number as your business phone number without being in violation of local telephone regulations. That means you cannot legally put your home telephone number on a business card or business stationery or advertise it on your Web site.

That said, let me also state that most craftspeople totally ignore this law and do it anyway. (I don't know what the penalty for breaking this law is in your state; you'll have to call your telephone company for that information and decide if this is something you want to do.) Some phone companies might give you a slap on the wrist and tell you to stop, while others might start charging you business line telephone rates if they discover you are advertising your personal phone number.

The primary reason to have a separate phone line for your business is that it enables you to freely advertise your telephone number to solicit new business and invite credit card sales, custom order inquiries, and the like. Further, you can deduct 100% of the costs of a business telephone line on your Schedule C tax form, while deductions for the business use of a home phone are severely limited. (Discuss this with your accountant.)

If you plan to connect to the Internet or install a fax machine, you will definitely need a second line to handle the load, but most crafters simply add an additional personal line instead of a business line. Once on the Internet, you may have even less need for a business phone than before because you can simply invite contact from buyers by advertising your e-mail address. (Always include your e-mail and Internet addresses on your business cards and stationery.)

If your primary selling methods are going to be consignment shops, craft fairs, or craft malls, a business phone number would be necessary only if you are inviting orders by phone. If you present a holiday boutique or open house once or twice a year, there should be no problem with putting your home phone number on promotional flyers because you are, in fact, inviting people to your home and not your business (similar to running a classified ad for a garage sale).

If and when you decide a separate line for your business is necessary, you may find it is not as costly as you think. Telephone companies today are very aware of the number of people who are working at home, and they have come up with a variety of affordable packages and second-line options, any one of which might be perfect for your crafts-business needs. Give your telephone company a call and see what's available.

Zoning Regulations

Before you start any kind of home-based business, check your home's zoning regulations. You can find a copy at your library or at city hall. Find out what zone you're in and then read the information under "Home Occupations." Be sure to read the fine print and note the penalty for violating a zoning ordinance. In most cases, someone who is caught violating zoning laws will be asked to cease and desist and a penalty is incurred only if this order is ignored. In other cases, however, willful violation could incur a hefty fine.

Zoning laws differ from one community to another, with some of them being terribly outdated (actually written back in horse-and-buggy days). In some communities, zoning officials simply "look the other way" where zoning violations are concerned because it's easier to do this than change the law. In other places, however, zoning regulations have recently been revised in light of the growing number of individuals working at home, and these changes have not always been to the benefit of home-based workers or self-employed individuals. Often there are restrictions as to (1) the amount of space in one's home a business may occupy (impossible to enforce, in my opinion), (2) the number of people (customers, students) who can come to your home each day, (3) the use of non-family employees, and so on. If you find you cannot advertise your home as a place of business, this problem can be easily solved by renting a P.O. box or using a commercial mailbox service as your business address.

Although I'm not suggesting that you violate your zoning law, I will tell you that many individuals who have found zoning to be a problem do ignore this law, particularly when they have a quiet business that is unlikely to create problems in their community.

Zoning officials don't go around checking for people who are violating the law; rather, they tend to act on complaints they have received about a certain activity that is creating problems for others. Thus, the best way to avoid zoning problems is to keep a low profile by not broadcasting your home-based business to neighbors. More important, never annoy them with activities that emit fumes or odors, create parking problems, or make noise of any kind.

Although neighbors may grudgingly put up with a noisy hobby activity (such as sawing in the garage), they are not likely to tolerate the same noise or disturbance if they know it's related to a home-based business. Likewise, they won't mind if you have a garage sale every year, but if people are coming to your home every year to buy from your home shop, open house, home parties, or holiday boutiques, you could be asking for trouble if the zoning laws don't favor this kind of activity.

> *Avoid this pitfall:* If you're planning to hold a holiday boutique or home party, check with zoning officials first. (If they don't know what a holiday boutique is, tell them it's a temporary sales event, like a garage sale.) Generally, the main concerns will be that you do not post illegal signs, tie up traffic, or otherwise annoy your neighbors. In some areas, however, zoning regulations strictly prohibit (1) traffic into one's home for any commercial reason; (2) the exchange of money in a home for business reasons; or (3) the transfer of merchandise within the home (affecting party plan sellers, in particular). Some sellers have found the solution to all three of these problems as simple as letting people place orders for merchandise that will be delivered later, with payment collected at time of delivery.

5. General Business and Financial Information

This section offers introductory guidelines on essential business basics for beginners. Once your business is up and running, however, you need to read other crafts-business books to get detailed information on the following topics and many others related to the successful growth and development of a home-based art or crafts business.

Making a Simple Business Plan

As baseball star Yogi Berra once said, "If you don't know where you are going, you might not get there." That's why you need a plan.

Like a road map, a business plan helps you get from here to there. It doesn't have to be fancy, but it does have to be in written form. A good business plan will save you time and money while helping you stay focused and on track to meet your goals. The kind of business plan a craftsperson makes will naturally be less complicated than the business plan of a major manufacturing company, but the elements are basically the same and should include:

- *History*—how and why you started your business
- *Business description*—what you do, what products you make, why they are special
- *Management information*—your business background or experience and the legal form your business will take
- *Manufacturing and production*—how and where products will be produced and who will make them; how and where supplies and materials will be obtained, and their estimated costs; labor costs (yours or other helpers); and overhead costs involved in the making of products
- *Financial plan*—estimated sales and expense figures for 1 year
- *Market research findings*—a description of your market (fairs, shops, mail order, Internet, and so on), your customers, and your competition
- *Marketing plan*—how you are going to sell your products and the anticipated cost of your marketing (commissions, advertising, craft fair displays, and so on)

If this all seems a bit much for a small crafts business, start managing your time by using a daily calendar/planner and start a

Get a Safety Deposit Box

The longer you are in business, the more important it will be to safeguard your most valuable business records. When you work at home, there is always the possibility of fire or damage from some natural disaster, be it a tornado, earthquake, hurricane, or flood. You will worry less if you keep your most valuable business papers, records, computer disks, and so forth off-premises, along with other items that would be difficult or impossible to replace. Some particulars I have always kept in my business safety deposit box include master software disks and computer back-up disks; original copies of my designs and patterns, business contracts, copyrights, insurance policies, and a photographic record of all items insured on our homeowner's policy. Remember: Insurance is worthless if you cannot prove what you owned in the first place.

notebook you can fill with your creative and marketing ideas, plans, and business goals. In it, write a simple mission statement that answers the following questions:

- What is my primary mission or goal in starting a business?
- What is my financial goal for this year?
- What am I going to do to get the sales I need this year to meet my financial goal?

The most important thing is that you start putting your dreams, goals, and business plans on paper so you can review them regularly. It's always easier to see where you're going if you know where you've been.

When You Need an Attorney

Many business beginners think they have to hire a lawyer the minute they start a business, but that would be a terrible waste of money if you're just starting a simple art or crafts business at home, operating as a sole proprietor. Sure, a lawyer will be delighted to hold your hand and give you the same advice I'm giving you here (while charging you $150 an hour or more for his or her time). With this book in hand, you can easily take care of all the "legal details" of a small-business start-up. The day may come, however, when you do need legal counsel, such as when you:

Form a Partnership or Corporation

As stated earlier, an attorney's guidance is necessary in the formation of a partnership. Although many people have incorporated without a lawyer using a good how-to book on the topic, I wouldn't recommend doing this because there are so many details involved, not to mention different types of corporate entities.

Defend an Infringement of a Copyright or Trademark

You don't need an attorney to get a simple copyright, but if someone infringes on one of your copyrights, you will probably need legal help to stop the infringer from profiting from your creativity. You can file your own trademark application (if you are exceedingly careful about following instructions), but it would be difficult to protect your trademark without legal help if someone tries to steal it. In both cases, you would need an attorney who specializes in copyright, patent, and trademark law. (If you ever need a good attorney who understands the plight of artists and crafters, contact me by e-mail at barbara@crafter.com and I'll refer you to the attorney who has been helpful to me in protecting my common-law trademark to *Homemade Money*, my home-business classic. The sixth edition of this book includes the details of my trademark infringement story.)

Negotiate a Contract

Many craft hobbyists of my acquaintance have gone on to write books and sell their original designs to manufacturers, suddenly finding themselves with a contract in hand that contains a lot of confusing legal jargon. When hiring an attorney to check any kind of contract, make sure he or she has experience in the particular field involved. For example, a lawyer specializing in real estate isn't going to know a thing about the inner workings of a book publishing company and how the omission or inclusion of a particular clause or phrase might impact the author's royalties or make it difficult to get publishing rights back when the book goes out of print. Although I have no experience in the licensing industry, I presume the same thing holds true here. What I do know for sure is that the problem with most contracts is not so much what's *in* them, as what *isn't*. Thus you need to be sure the attorney you hire for specialized contract work has done this kind of work for other clients.

Hire Independent Contractors

If you ever grow your business to the point where you need to hire workers and are wondering whether you have to hire employees or can use independent contractors instead, I suggest you seek counsel from an attorney who specializes in labor law. This topic is very complex and beyond the scope of this beginner's guide, but I do want you to know that the IRS has been on a campaign for the past several years to abolish independent contractors altogether. Many small businesses have suffered great financial loss in back taxes and penalties because they followed the advice of an accountant or regular attorney who didn't fully understand the technicalities of this matter.

If and when you do need a lawyer for general business purposes, ask friends for a reference, and check with your bank, too, because bank representatives will probably know most of the attorneys with private practices in your area. Note that membership in some small-business organizations will also give you access to affordable prepaid legal services. If you ever need serious legal help but have no funds to pay for it, contact the Volunteer Lawyers for the Arts.

Why You Need a Business Checking Account

Many business beginners use their personal checking account to conduct the transactions of their business, *but you must not do this* because the IRS does not allow commingling of business and personal income. If you are operating as a business, reporting income on a Schedule C form and taking deductions accordingly, the lack of a separate checking account for your business would surely result in an IRS ruling that your endeavor was a hobby and not a business. That, in turn, would cost you all the deductions previously taken on earlier tax returns and you'd end up with a very large tax bill. Don't you agree that the cost of a separate checking account is a small price to pay to protect all your tax deductions?

You do not necessarily need one of the more expensive business checking accounts; you just need a *separate account* through which you run all business income and expenditures. Your business name does not have to be on these checks so long as only your name (not your spouse's) is listed as account holder. You can save money on your checking account by first calling several banks and savings and loan institutions and comparing the charges they set for imprinted checks, deposits, checks written, bounced checks, and other services. Before you open your account, be sure to ask if the bank can set you up to take credit cards (merchant account) at some point in the future.

> *Avoid this pitfall:* Some banks charge extra for each out-of-state check that is deposited, an expense that is prohibitively expensive for active mail-order businesses. For that reason, I have always maintained a business checking account in a savings and loan association, which has no service charges of any kind (except for bad checks). S&L's also pay interest on the amount in a checking account, whereas a bank may not. The main disadvantage of doing your business checking through an S&L is that they do not offer credit card services or give business loans. At the

point where I found I needed the latter two services for my publishing business, I had to open a second account with a local bank.

Accepting Credit Cards

Most of us today take credit cards for granted and expect to be able to use them for most everything we buy. It's nice to be able to offer credit card services to your craft fair customers, but it is costly and thus not recommended for beginning craft sellers. If you get into selling at craft fairs on a regular basis, however, at some point you may find you are losing sales because you don't have "merchant status" (the ability to accept credit cards as payment).

Some craftspeople have reported a considerable jump in sales once they started taking credit cards. That's because some people who buy with plastic may buy two or three items instead of one, or may be willing to pay a higher price for something if they can charge it. Thus, the higher your prices, the more likely you are to lose sales if you can't accept credit cards. As one jewelry maker told me, "I always seem to get the customers who have run out of cash and left their checkbook at home. But even when they have a check, I feel uncomfortable taking a check for $100 or more."

This section discusses the various routes you can travel to get merchant status. You will have to do considerable research to find out which method is best for you. All will be costly, and you must have sufficient sales, or the expectation of increased sales, to consider taking credit cards in the first place. Understand, too, that taking credit cards in person (called face-to-face transactions where you have the card in front of you) is different from accepting credit cards by phone, by mail, or through a Web site (called non–face-to-face transactions). Each method of selling is treated differently by bankcard providers.

> ***Avoid this pitfall:*** If you are relatively new at selling, and uncertain about whether you will be taking credit cards for a long time, do not sign a leasing arrangement for credit card processing equipment. Instead, leave yourself an escape route by opting for a rental agreement you can get out of with a month's notice, such as that offered by some banks and organizations discussed below.

Merchant Status from Your Bank

When you're ready to accept credit cards, start with the bank where you have your business checking account. Where you bank, and where you live, has everything to do with whether you can get merchant status from your bank. Home-business owners in small towns often have less trouble than do those in large cities. One crafter told me Bank of America gave her merchant status with no problem, but some banks simply refuse to deal with anyone who doesn't operate out of a storefront. Most banks now insist that credit card sales be transmitted electronically, but a few still offer manual printers and allow merchants to send in their sales slips by mail. You will be given details about this at the time you apply for merchant status. All banks will require proof that you have a running business and will want to see your financial statements.

Merchant Status Through a Crafts Organization

If you are refused by your bank because your business is home based or just too new, getting bankcard services through a crafts or home-business organization is the next best way to go. Because such organizations have a large membership, they have some negotiating power with the credit card companies and often get special deals for their members. As a member of such an organization, the chances are about 95% that you will automatically be accepted into its bankcard program, even if you are a brand-new business owner.

One organization I can recommend to beginning sellers is the National Craft Association. Managing Director Barbara Arena tells me that 60% of all new NCA members now take the MasterCard/VISA services offered by her organization. "Crafters who are unsure about whether they want to take credit cards over a long period of time have the option of renting equipment," says Barbara. "This enables them to get out of the program with a month's notice. NCA members can operate on a software basis through their personal computer (taking their laptop computer to shows and calling in sales on their cell phone) or use a swipe machine. Under NCA's program, crafters can also accept credit card sales on their Internet site."

Merchant Status from Credit Card Companies

If you've been in business for a while, you may find you can get merchant status directly from American Express or Novus Services, Inc., the umbrella company that handles the Discover, Bravo, and Private Issue credit cards. American Express says that in some cases it can grant merchant status immediately on receipt of some key information given on the phone. As for Novus, many crafters have told me how easy it was to get merchant status from this company. Novus says it needs only your social security number and information to check your credit rating. If Novus accepts you, it can also get you set up to take VISA and MasterCard as well, if you meet the special acceptance qualifications of these two credit card companies. (Usually, they require you to be in business for at least 2 years.)

Merchant Status from an Independent Service Organization Provider (ISO)

ISOs act as agents for banks that authorize credit cards, promoting their services by direct mail, through magazine advertising, telemarketing, and on the Internet. Most of these bankcard providers are operating under a network marketing program (one agent representing one agent representing another, and so on). They are everywhere on the Internet, sending unsolicited e-mail messages to Web site owners. In addition to offering the merchant account service itself, many are also trying to get other Web site owners to promote the same service in exchange for some kind of referral fee. I do not recommend that you get merchant status through an ISO because I've heard too many horror stories about them. If you want to explore this option on the Internet, however, use your browser's search button and type "credit cards + merchant" to get a list of such sellers.

In general, ISOs may offer low discount rates but will sock it to you with inflated equipment costs, a high application fee, and extra fees for installation, programming, and site inspection. You will also have to sign an unbreakable 3- or 4-year lease for the electronic equipment.

> *Avoid this pitfall:* Some people on the Internet may offer to process your credit card sales through their individual merchant account, but this is illegal as it violates credit card company rules. And if you were to offer to do this for someone else, your account would be terminated. In short, if you do not ship the goods, you can't process the sale.

As you can see, you must really do your homework where bankcard services are concerned. In checking out the services offered by any of the providers noted here, ask plenty of questions. Make up a chart that lets you compare what each one charges for application and service fees, monthly charges, equipment costs, software, discount rates, and transaction fees.

Transaction fees can range from $0.20 to $0.80 per ticket, with discount rates running anywhere from 1.67 to 5%. Higher rates are usually attached to non–face-to-face credit card transactions, paper transaction systems, or a low volume of sales. Any rate higher than

5% should be a danger signal because you could be dealing with an unscrupulous seller or some kind of illegal third-party processing program.

I'm told that a good credit card processor today may cost around $800, yet some card service providers are charging two or three times that amount in their leasing arrangements. I once got a quote from a major ISO and found it would have cost me $40 a month to lease the terminal—$1,920 over a period of 4 years—or I could buy it for just $1,000. In checking with my bank, I learned I could get the same equipment and the software to run it for just $350!

In summary, if you're a nervous beginner, the safest way to break into taking credit cards is to work with a bank or organization that offers equipment on a month-by-month rental arrangement. Once you've had some experience in taking credit card payments, you can review your situation and decide whether you want to move into a leasing arrangement or buy equipment outright.

6. Minimizing the Financial Risks of Selling

This book contains an informative chapter on how and where to sell your crafts, but I thought it would be helpful for you to have added perspective on the business management end of selling through various outlets, and some things you can do to protect yourself from financial loss and legal hassles.

You must accept the fact that all businesses occasionally suffer financial losses of one kind or another. That's simply the nature of business. Selling automatically carries a certain degree of risk in that we can never be absolutely sure that we're going to be paid for anything until we actually have payment in hand. Checks may bounce, wholesale buyers may refuse to pay their invoices, and consignment shops can close unexpectedly without returning merchandise to crafters. In the past few years, a surprising number of craft mall owners have stolen out of town in the middle of the night, taking with them all the money due their vendors, and sometimes the vendors' merchandise as well. (This topic is beyond the scope of this book, but if you'd like more information on it, see my *Creative Cash* book or visit my Web site at www.barbarabrabec.com.)

Now, I don't want you to feel uneasy about selling or be suspicious of every buyer who comes your way, because that would take all the fun out of selling. But I *do* want you to know that bad things sometimes happen to good craftspeople who have not done their homework (by reading this book, you are doing *your* homework). If you will follow the cautionary guidelines discussed in this section, you can avoid some common selling pitfalls and minimize your financial risk to the point where it will be negligible.

Selling to Consignment Shops

Never consign more merchandise to one shop than you can afford to lose, and do not send new items to a shop until you see that payments are being made regularly according to your written consignment agreement. It should cover the topics of:

- Insurance (see Insurance Tips, section 7)
- Pricing (make sure the shop cannot raise or lower your retail price without your permission)
- Sales commission (40% is standard; don't work with shop owners who ask for more than this. It makes more sense to wholesale products at 50% and get payment in 30 days)
- Payment dates
- Display of merchandise

■ Return of unsold merchandise (some shops have a clause stating that if unsold merchandise is not claimed within 30 to 60 days after a notice has been sent, the shop can dispose of it any way it wishes)

Above all, make sure your agreement includes the name and phone number of the shop's owner (not just the manager). If a shop fails and you decide to take legal action, you want to be sure your lawyer can track down the owner. (See sidebar, State Consignment Laws, below.)

Selling to Craft Malls

Shortly after the craft mall concept was introduced to the crafts community in 1988 by Rufus Coomer, entrepreneurs who understood the profit potential of such a business began to open malls all over the country. But there were no guidebooks and everyone was flying by the seat of his or her pants, making up operating rules along the way. Many mall owners, inexperienced in retailing, have

State Consignment Laws

Technically, consigned goods remain the property of the seller until they are sold. When a shop goes out of business, however, consigned merchandise may be seized by creditors in spite of what your consignment agreement may state. You may have some legal protection here, however, if you live in a state that has a consignment law designed to protect artists and craftspeople in such instances. Such laws exist in the states of CA, CO, CT, IL, IA, KY, MA, NH, NM, NY, OR, TX, WA, and WI. Call your secretary of state to confirm this or, if your state isn't listed here, ask whether this law is now on the books. Be sure to get full details about the kind of protection afforded by this law because some states have different definitions for what constitutes "art" or "crafts."

since gone out of business, often leaving crafters holding the bag. The risks of selling through such well-known chain stores as Coomer's or American Craft Malls are minimal, and many independently owned malls have also established excellent reputations in the industry. What you need to be especially concerned about here are new malls opened by individuals who have no track record in this industry.

I'm not telling you *not* to set up a booth in a new mall in your area—it might prove to be a terrific outlet for you—but I am cautioning you to keep a sharp eye on the mall and how it's being operated. Warning signs of a mall in trouble include:

- **Less than 75% occupancy**
- **Little or no ongoing advertising**
- **Not many shoppers**
- **Crafters pulling out (usually a sign of too few sales)**
- **Poor accounting of sales**
- **Late payments**

If a mall is in trouble, it stands to reason that the logical time for it to close is right after the biggest selling season of the year, namely Christmas. Interestingly, this is when most of the shady mall owners have stolen out of town with crafters' Christmas sales in their pockets. As stated in my *Creative Cash* book:

> If it's nearing Christmastime, and you're getting uncomfortable vibes about the financial condition of a mall you're in, it might be smart to remove the bulk of your merchandise— especially expensive items—just before it closes for the holidays. You can always restock after the first of the year if everything looks rosy.

Avoiding Bad Checks

At a craft fair or other event where you're selling directly to the public, if the buyer doesn't have cash and you don't accept credit cards, your only option is to accept a check. Few crafters have bad check problems for sales held in the home (holiday boutique, open house, party plan, and such), but bad checks at craft fairs are always possible. Here are several things you can do to avoid accepting a bad check:

- Always ask to see a driver's license and look carefully at the picture on it. Write the license number on the check.

- If the sale is for a large amount, you can ask to see a credit card for added identification, but writing down the number will do no good because you cannot legally cover a bad check with a customer's credit card. (The customer has a legal right to refuse to let you copy the number as well.)

- Look closely at the check itself. Is there a name and address printed on it? If not, ask the customer to write in this information by hand, along with his or her phone number.

- Look at the sides of the check. If at least one side is not perforated, it could be a phony check.

- Look at the check number in the upper right-hand corner. Most banks who issue personalized checks begin the numbering system with 101 when a customer reorders new checks. The Small Business Administration says to be more cautious with low sequence numbers because there seems to be a higher number of these checks that are returned.

- Check the routing number in the lower left-hand corner and note the ink. If it looks shiny, wet your finger and see if the ink rubs off. That's a sure sign of a phony check because good checks are printed with magnetic ink that does not reflect light.

Collecting on a Bad Check

No matter how careful you are, sooner or later, you will get stuck with a bad check. It may bounce for one of three reasons:

> Nonsufficient funds (NSF)
> Account closed
> No account (evidence of fraud)

I've accepted tens of thousands of checks from mail-order buyers through the years and have rarely had a bad check I couldn't collect with a simple phone call asking the party to honor his or her obligation to me. People often move and close out accounts before all checks have cleared, or they add or subtract wrong, causing their account to be overdrawn. Typically, they are embarrassed to have caused a problem like this.

When the problem is more difficult than this, your bank can help. Check to learn its policy regarding bounced checks. Some automatically put checks through a second time. If a check bounces at this point, you may ask the bank to collect the check for you. The check needs to be substantial, however, because the bank fee may be $15 or more if they are successful in collecting the money.

If you have accepted a check for a substantial amount of money and believe there is evidence of fraud, you may wish to do one of the following:

- Notify your district attorney's office
- Contact your sheriff or police department
  (because it is a crime to write a bad check)
- Try to collect through small claims court

For more detailed information on all of these topics, see *The Crafts Business Answer Book & Resource Guide* (see page 292 for information).

7. Insurance Tips

As soon as you start even the smallest business at home, you need to give special attention to insurance. This section offers an introductory overview of insurance concerns of primary interest to crafts-business owners.

Homeowner's or Renter's Insurance

Anything in the home being used to generate income is considered to be business-related and thus exempt from coverage on a personal policy. Thus your homeowner's or renter's insurance policy will not cover business equipment, office furniture, supplies, or inventory of finished goods unless you obtain a special rider. Such a rider, called a "Business Pursuits Endorsement" by some companies, is inexpensive and offers considerable protection. Your insurance agent will be happy to give you details.

As your business grows and you have an ever-larger inventory of supplies, materials, tools, and finished merchandise, you may find it necessary to buy a special in-home business policy that offers broader protection. Such policies may be purchased directly from insurance companies or through craft and home-business organizations that offer special insurance programs to their members.

Avoid this pitfall: If you have an expensive computer system, costly tools, equipment, or office furnishings, the coverage

Insuring Your Art or Crafts Collection

The replacement cost insurance you may have on your personal household possessions does not extend to "fine art," which includes such things as paintings, antiques, pictures, tapestries, statuary, and other articles that cannot be replaced with new articles. If you have a large collection of art, crafts, memorabilia, or collector's items, and its value is more than $1,500, you may wish to have your collection appraised so it can be protected with a separate all-risk endorsement to your homeowner's policy called a "fine arts floater."

afforded by a simple business rider to your homeowner's policy may be insufficient for your needs. Although you may have replacement-value insurance on all your personal possessions, anything used for business purposes would be exempt from such coverage. In other words, the value of everything covered by the rider would be figured on a depreciable basis instead of what it would cost to replace it. (See also sidebar, Insuring Your Art or Crafts Collection, on page 253.)

Liability Insurance

There are two kinds of liability insurance. *Product* liability insurance protects you against lawsuits by consumers who have been injured while using one of your products. *Personal* liability insurance protects you against claims made by individuals who have suffered bodily injury while on your premises (either your home or the place where you are doing business, such as in your booth at a craft fair).

Your homeowner's or renter's insurance policy will include some personal liability protection, but if someone were to suffer bodily injury while on your premises for *business* reasons, that coverage might not apply. Your need for personal liability insurance will be greater if you plan to regularly present home parties, holiday boutiques, or open house sales in your home where many people might be coming and going throughout the year. If you sell at craft fairs, you would also be liable for damages if someone were to fall and be injured in your booth or if something in your booth falls and injures another person. For this reason, some craft fair promoters now require all vendors to have personal liability insurance.

As for product liability insurance, whether you need it depends largely on the type of products you make for sale, how careful you are to make sure those products are safe, and how and where you sell them. Examples of some crafts that have caused injury to consumers and resulted in court claims in the past are stuffed toys with wire or pins that children have swallowed; items made of yarn or fiber that burned rapidly; handmade furniture that collapsed when someone put an ordinary amount of weight on it; jewelry with sharp points or other features that cut the wearer, and so on. Clearly, the best way to avoid injury to consumers is to make certain your products have no health hazards and are safe to use. (See discussion of Consumer Safety Laws in section 8.)

Few artists and craftspeople who sell on a part-time basis feel they can afford product liability insurance, but many full-time craft professionals, particularly those who sell their work wholesale, find it a necessary expense. In fact, many wholesale buyers refuse to buy from suppliers that do not carry product liability insurance.

I believe the least expensive way to obtain both personal and product liability insurance is with one of the comprehensive in-home or crafts-business policies offered by a crafts- or home-business organization. Such policies generally offer $1 million of both personal and product liability coverage. (See A "Things to Do" Checklist with Related Resources on page 282 and the Resources section for some organizations you can contact for more information. Also check with your insurance agent about the benefits of an umbrella policy for extra liability insurance.)

Insurance on Crafts Merchandise

As a seller of art or crafts merchandise, you are responsible for insuring your own products against loss. If you plan to sell at craft fairs, in craft malls, rent-a-space shops, or consignment shops, you may want to buy an insurance policy that protects your merchandise both at home or away. Note that while craft shops and malls generally have fire insurance covering the building and its fixtures, this coverage cannot be extended to merchandise offered for sale because it is not the property of the shop owner. (Exception: Shops and malls in shopping centers are mandated by law to buy fire insurance on their contents whether they own the merchandise or not.)

This kind of insurance is usually part of the home- or crafts-business insurance policies mentioned earlier.

Auto Insurance

Be sure to talk to the agent who handles your car insurance and explain that you may occasionally use your car for business purposes. Normally, a policy issued for a car that's used only for pleasure or driving to and from work may not provide complete coverage for an accident that occurs during business use of the car, particularly if the insured is to blame for the accident. For example, if you were delivering a load of crafts to a shop or on your way to a craft fair and had an accident, would your business destination and the "commercial merchandise" in your car negate your coverage in any way? Where insurance is concerned, the more questions you ask, the better you'll feel about the policies you have.

8. Important Regulations Affecting Artists and Craftspeople

Government agencies have a number of regulations that artists and craftspeople must know about. Generally, they relate to consumer safety, the labeling of certain products, and trade practices. Following are regulations of primary interest to readers of books in Prima's FOR FUN & PROFIT series. If you find a law or regulation related to your particular art or craft interest, be sure to request additional information from the government agency named there.

Consumer Safety Laws

All product sellers must pay attention to the Consumer Product Safety Act, which protects the public against unreasonable risks of injury associated with consumer products. The Consumer Product

Safety Commission (CPSC) is particularly active in the area of toys and consumer goods designed for children. All sellers of handmade products must be doubly careful about the materials they use for children's products because consumer lawsuits are common where products for children are concerned. To avoid this problem, simply comply with the consumer safety laws applicable to your specific art or craft.

Toy Safety Concerns

To meet CPSC's guidelines for safety, make sure any toys you make for sale are:

- Too large to be swallowed
- Not apt to break easily or leave jagged edges
- Free of sharp edges or points
- Not put together with easily exposed pins, wires, or nails
- Nontoxic, nonflammable, and nonpoisonous

The Use of Paints, Varnishes, and Other Finishes

Since all paint sold for household use must meet the Consumer Product Safety Act's requirement for minimum amounts of lead, these paints are deemed to be safe for use on products made for children, such as toys and furniture. Always check, however, to make sure the label bears a nontoxic notation. Specialty paints must carry a warning on the label about lead count, but "artist's paints" are curiously exempt from CPS's lead-in-paint ban and are not required to bear a warning label of any kind. Thus you should *never* use such paints on products intended for use by children unless the label specifically states they are *nontoxic* (lead-free). Acrylics and other water-based paints, of course, are nontoxic and completely safe for use on toys and other products made for children. If you plan to use a finishing coat, make sure it is nontoxic as well.

Fabric Flammability Concerns

The Flammable Fabrics Act is applicable only to those who sell products made of fabric, particularly products for children. It prohibits the movement in interstate commerce of articles of wearing apparel and fabrics that are so highly flammable as to be dangerous when worn by individuals, and for other purposes. Most fabrics comply with this act, but if you plan to sell children's clothes or toys, you may wish to take an extra step to be doubly sure the fabric you are using is safe. This is particularly important if you plan to wholesale your products. What you should do is ask your fabric supplier for a *guarantee of compliance with the Flammability Act*. This guarantee is generally passed along to the buyer by a statement on the invoice that reads "continuing guarantee under the Flammable Fabrics Act." If you do not find such a statement on your invoice, you should ask the fabric manufacturer, wholesaler, or distributor to furnish you with their "statement of compliance" with the flammability standards. The CPSC can also tell you if a particular manufacturer has filed a continuing guarantee under the Flammable Fabrics Act.

Labels Required by Law

The following information applies only to crafters who use textiles, fabrics, fibers, or yarn products to make wearing apparel, decorative accessories, household furnishings, soft toys, or any product made of wool.

Different government agencies require the attachment of certain tags or labels to products sold in the consumer marketplace, whether manufactured in quantity or handmade for limited sale. You don't have to be too concerned about these laws if you sell only at local fairs, church bazaars, and home boutiques. As soon as you get out into the general consumer marketplace, however—doing large craft fairs, selling through consignment shops, craft malls, or wholesaling to shops—it would be wise to comply with all the federal labeling laws. Actually, these laws are quite easy to comply with because the required labels are readily available at inexpensive prices, and you can even make your own if you wish. Here is what the federal government wants you to tell your buyers on a tag or label:

- *What's in a product, and who has made it.* The Textile Fiber Products Identification Act (monitored both by the Bureau of Consumer Protection and the Federal Trade Commission) requires that a special label or hangtag be attached to all textile wearing apparel and household furnishings, with the exception of wall hangings. "Textiles" include products made of any fiber, yarn, or fabric, including garments and decorative accessories, quilts, pillows, placemats, stuffed toys, rugs, and so on. The tag or label must include (1) the name of the manufacturer and (2) the generic names and percentages of all fibers in the product in amounts of 5% or more, listed in order of predominance by weight.

- *How to take care of products.* Care Labeling Laws are part of the Textile Fiber Products Identification Act, details about which are available from the FTC. If you make wearing apparel or household furnishings of any kind using textiles, suede, or leather, you must attach a permanent label that explains how to take care of the item. This label must indicate whether the item is to be dry-cleaned or washed. If it is washable, you must indicate whether in hot or cold water, whether bleach may or may not be used, and the temperature at which it may be ironed.

- *Details about products made of wool.* If a product contains wool, the FTC requires additional identification under a separate law known as the Wool Products Labeling Act of 1939. FTC rules require that the labels of all wool or textile products clearly indicate when imported ingredients are used. Thus, the label for a skirt knitted in the United States from wool yarn imported from England would read, "Made in the USA from imported products" or similar wordage.

If the wool yarn was spun in the United States, a product made from that yarn would simply need a tag or label stating it was "Made in the USA" or "Crafted in USA" or some similarly clear terminology.

The Bedding and Upholstered Furniture Law

This is a peculiar state labeling law that affects sellers of items that have a concealed filling. It requires the purchase of a license, and products must have a tag that bears the manufacturer's registry number.

A Proper Copyright Notice

Although a copyright notice is not required by law, you are encouraged to put a copyright notice on every original thing you create. Adding the copyright notice does not obligate you to formally register your copyright, but it does serve to warn others that your work is legally protected and makes it difficult for anyone to claim they have "accidentally stolen" your work. (Those who actually do violate a copyright because they don't understand the law are called "innocent infringers" by the Copyright Office.)

A proper copyright notice includes three things:

1. The word *copyright,* its abbreviation, *copr.,* or the copyright symbol, ©

2. The year of first publication of the work (when it was first shown or sold to the public)

3. The name of the copyright owner. Example: © 2000 by Barbara Brabec. (When the words *All Rights Reserved* are added to the copyright notation, it means that copyright protection has been extended to include all of the Western Hemisphere.)

The copyright notice should be positioned in a place where it can easily be seen. It can be stamped, cast, engraved, painted, printed, wood-burned, or simply written by hand in permanent ink. In the case of fiber crafts, you can attach an inexpensive label with the copyright notice and your business name and logo (or any other information you wish to put on the label).

Bedding laws have long been a thorn in the side of crafters because they make no distinction between the large manufacturing company that makes mattresses and pillows, and the individual craft producer who sells only handmade items. "Concealed filling" items include not just bedding and upholstery, but handmade pillows and quilts. In some states, dolls, teddy bears, and stuffed soft sculpture items are also required to have a tag.

Fortunately, only 29 states now have this law on the books, and even if your state is one of them, the law may be arbitrarily enforced. (One exception is the state of Pennsylvania, which is reportedly sending officials to craft shows to inspect merchandise to see if it is properly labeled.) The only penalty that appears to be connected with a violation of this law in any state is removal of merchandise from store shelves or craft fair exhibits. That being the case, many crafters choose to ignore this law until they are challenged. If you learn you must comply with this law, you will be required to obtain a state license that will cost between $25 and $100, and you will have to order special "bedding stamps" that can be attached to your products. For more information on this complex topic, see *The Crafts Business Answer Book & Resource Guide.*

FTC Rule for Mail-Order Sellers

Even the smallest home-based business needs to be familiar with Federal Trade Commission (FTC) rules and regulations. A variety of free booklets are available to business owners on topics related to advertising, mail-order marketing, and product labeling (as discussed earlier). In particular, crafters who sell by mail need to pay attention to the FTC's Thirty-Day Mail-Order Rule, which states that one must ship customer orders within 30 days of receiving payment for the order. This rule is strictly enforced, with severe financial penalties for each violation.

Unless you specifically state in your advertising literature how long delivery will take, customers will expect to receive the product within 30 days after you get their order. If you cannot meet this shipping date, you must notify the customer accordingly, enclosing a postage-paid reply card or envelope, and giving them the option to cancel the order if they wish. Now you know why so many catalog sellers state, "Allow 6 weeks for delivery." This lets them off the hook in case there are unforeseen delays in getting the order delivered.

9. Protecting Your Intellectual Property

"Intellectual property," says Attorney Stephen Elias in his book, *Patent, Copyright & Trademark,* "is a product of the human intellect that has commercial value."

This section offers a brief overview of how to protect your intellectual property through patents and trademarks, with a longer discussion of copyright law, which is of the greatest concern to individuals who sell what they make. Because it is easy to get patents, trademarks, and copyrights mixed up, let me briefly define them for you:

- A *patent* is a grant issued by the government that gives an inventor the right to exclude all others from making, using, or selling an invention within the United States and its territories and possessions.

- A *trademark* is used by a manufacturer or merchant to identify his or her goods and distinguish them from those manufactured or sold by others.

- A *copyright* protects the rights of creators of intellectual property in five main categories (described in this section).

Perspective on Patents

A patent may be granted to anyone who invents or discovers a new and useful process, machine, manufacture, or composition of matter, or any new and useful improvement thereof. Any new, original, and ornamental design for an article of manufacture can also be patented. The problem with patents is that they can cost as much as $5,000 or more to obtain, and, once you've got one, they still require periodic maintenance through the U.S. Patent and Trademark Office. To contact this office, you can use the following Web sites: www.uspto.com or www.lcweb.loc.gov.

Ironically, a patent doesn't even give one the right to sell a product. It merely excludes anyone else from making, using, or selling your invention. Many business novices who have gone to the trouble to patent a product end up wasting a lot of time and money because a patent is useless if it isn't backed with the right manufacturing, distribution, and advertising programs. As inventor Jeremy Gorman states in *Homemade Money,* "Ninety-seven percent of the U.S. patents issued never earn enough money to pay the patenting fee. They just go on a plaque on the wall or in a desk drawer to impress the grandchildren 50 years later."

What a Trademark Protects

Trademarks were established to prevent one company from trading on the good name and reputation of another. The primary function of a trademark is to indicate origin, but in some cases it also serves as a guarantee of quality.

You cannot adopt any trademark that is so similar to another that it is likely to confuse buyers, nor can you trademark generic or descriptive names in the public domain. If, however, you come up with a particular word, name, symbol, or device to identify and distinguish your products from others, you may protect that mark by trademark provided another company is not already using a similar mark. Brand names, trade names, slogans, and phrases may also qualify for trademark protection.

Many individual crafters have successfully registered their own trademarks using a how-to book on the topic, but some would say never to try this without the help of a trademark attorney. It depends on how much you love detail and how well you can follow directions. Any mistake on the application form could cause it to be rejected, and you would lose the application fee in the process. If this is something you're interested in, and you have designed a mark you want to protect, you should first do a trademark search to see if someone else is already using it. Trademark searches can be done using library directories, an online computer service (check with your library), through private trademark search firms, or directly on the Internet through the Patent and Trademark Office's online search service (see A "Things to Do" Checklist with Related Resources on page 282). All of these searches together could still be inconclusive, however, because many companies have a stash of trademarks in reserve waiting for just the right product. These "non-published" trademarks are in a special file that only an attorney or trademark search service could find for you.

Selling How-To Projects to Magazines

If you want to sell an article, poem, or how-to project to a magazine, you need not copyright the material first because copyright protection exists from the moment you create that work. Your primary consideration here is whether you will sell "all rights" or only "first rights" to the magazine.

The sale of first rights means you are giving a publication permission to print your article, poem, or how-to project once, for a specific sum of money. After publication, you then have the right to resell that material or profit from it in other ways. Although it is always desirable to sell only "first rights," some magazines do not offer this choice.

If you sell all rights, you will automatically lose ownership of the copyright to your material and you can no longer profit from that work. Professional designers often refuse to work this way because they know they can realize greater profits by publishing their own pattern packets or design leaflets and wholesaling them to shops.

Like copyrights, trademarks have their own symbol, which looks like this: ®. This symbol can be used only after the trademark has been formally registered through the U.S. Patent and Trademark Office. Business owners often use the superscript initials ™ with a mark to indicate they've claimed a logo or some other mark, but this offers no legal protection. While this does not guarantee trademark protection, it does give notice to the public that you are claiming this name as your trademark. However, after you've used a mark for some time, you do gain a certain amount of common-law protection for that mark. I have, in fact, gained common-law protection for the name of my *Homemade Money* book and successfully defended it against use by another individual in my field because this title has become so closely associated with my name in the home-business community.

Whether you ever formally register a trademark or not will have much to do with your long-range business plans, how you feel about protecting your creativity, and what it would do to your business if someone stole your mark and registered it in his or her own name. Once you've designed a trademark you feel is worth protecting, get additional information from the Patent and Trademark Office and read a book or two on the topic to decide whether this is something you wish to pursue. (See A "Things to Do" Checklist with Related Resources on page 282.)

What Copyrights Protect

As a serious student of the copyright law, I've pored through the hard-to-interpret copyright manual, read dozens of related articles and books, and discussed this subject at length with designers, writers, teachers, editors, and publishers. I must emphasize, however, that I am no expert on this topic, and the following information does not constitute legal advice. It is merely offered as a general guide to a very complex legal topic you may wish to research further on your own at some point. In a book of this nature, addressed to hob-byists and beginning crafts-business owners, a discussion of copy-rights must be limited to three basic topics:

- What copyrights do and do not protect
- How to register a copyright and protect your legal rights
- How to avoid infringing on the rights of other copyright holders

One of the first things you should do now is send for the free booklets offered by the Copyright Office (see A "Things to Do" Checklist with Related Resources on page 282). Various free circu-lars explain copyright basics, the forms involved in registering a copyright, and how to submit a copyright application and register a

Protecting Your Copyrights

If someone ever copies one of your copyrighted works, and you have registered that work with the Copyright Office, you should defend it as far as you are financially able to do so. If you think you're dealing with an innocent infringer—another crafter, perhaps, who has probably not profited much (if at all) from your work—a strongly worded letter on your business stationery (with a copy to an attorney, if you have one) might do the trick. Simply inform the copyright infringer that you are the legal owner of the work and the only one who has the right to profit from it. Tell the infringer that he or she must immediately cease using your copyrighted work, and ask for a confir-mation by return mail.

If you think you have lost some money or incurred other damages, consult with a copyright attorney before contacting the infringer to see how you can best protect your rights and recoup any financial losses you may have suffered. This is particu-larly important if the infringer appears to be a successful business or corporation. Although you may have no intention of ever going to court on this matter, the copy-right infringer won't know that, and one letter from a competent attorney might immediately resolve the matter at very little cost to you.

copyright. They also discuss what you cannot copyright. Rather than duplicate all the free information you can get from the Copyright Office with a letter or phone call, I will only briefly touch on these topics and focus instead on addressing some of the particular copyright questions crafters have asked me in the past.

Things You Can Copyright

Some people mistakenly believe that copyright protection extends only to printed works, but that is not true. The purpose of the copyright law is to protect any creator from anyone who would use the creator's work for his or her own profit. Under current copyright law, claims are now registered in seven classes, five of which pertain to crafts:

1. *Serials* (Form SE)—periodicals, newspapers, magazines, bulletins, newsletters, annuals, journals, and proceedings of societies.
2. *Text* (Form TX)—books, directories, and other written works, including the how-to instructions for a crafts project. (You could copyright a letter to your mother if you wanted to— or your best display ad copy, or any other written words that represent income potential.)
3. *Visual Arts* (Form VA)—pictorial, graphic, or sculptural works, including fine, graphic, and applied art; photographs, charts; technical drawings; diagrams; and models. (Also included in this category are "works of artistic craftsmanship insofar as their form but not their mechanical or utilitarian aspects are concerned.")
4. *Performing Arts* (Form PA)—musical works and accompanying words, dramatic works, pantomimes, choreographic works, motion pictures, and other audiovisual works.
5. *Sound Recordings* (Form SR)—musical, spoken, or other sounds, including any audio- or videotapes you might create.

Things You Cannot Copyright

You can't copyright ideas or procedures for doing, making, or building things, but the *expression* of an idea fixed in a tangible medium may be copyrightable—such as a book explaining a new system or technique. Brand names, trade names, slogans, and phrases cannot be copyrighted, either, although they might be entitled to protection under trademark laws.

The design on a craft object can be copyrighted, but only if it can be identified separately from the object itself. Objects themselves (a decorated coffee mug, a box, a tote bag) cannot be copyrighted.

Copyright Registration Tips

First, understand that you do not have to formally copyright anything because copyright protection exists from the moment a work is created, whether you add a copyright notice or not.

So why file at all? The answer is simple: If you don't file the form and pay the fee (currently $30), you'll never be able to take anyone to court for stealing your work. Therefore, in each instance where copyright protection is considered, you need to decide how important your work is to you in terms of dollars and cents, and ask yourself whether you value it enough to pay to protect it. Would you actually be willing to pay court costs to defend your copyright, should someone steal it from you? If you never intend to go to court, there's little use in officially registering a copyright; but because it costs you nothing to add a copyright notice to your work, you are foolish not to do this. (See sidebar, Protecting Your Copyrights, on page 266.)

If you do decide to file a copyright application, contact the Copyright Office and request the appropriate forms. When you file the copyright application form (which is easy to complete), you must include with it two copies of the work. Ordinarily, two actual copies of copyrighted items must be deposited, but certain items are exempt from deposit requirements, including all three-dimensional sculptural works and any works published only as reproduced in or on jewelry, dolls, toys, games, plaques, floor coverings, textile and other fabrics, packaging materials, or any useful article. In these cases, two photographs or drawings of the item are sufficient.

Note that the Copyright Office does not compare deposit copies to determine whether works submitted for registration are similar to any material already copyrighted. It is the sender's responsibility to determine the originality of what's being copyrighted. (See discussion of "original" in the next section, under Respecting the Copyrights of Others.)

Mandatory Deposit Requirements

Although you do not have to officially register a copyright claim, it *is* mandatory to deposit two copies of all "published works" for the collections of the Library of Congress within 3 months after publication. Failure to make the deposit may subject the copyright owner to fines and other monetary liabilities, but it does not affect copyright protection. No special form is required for this mandatory deposit.

Note that the term *published works* pertains not just to the publication of printed matter, but to the public display of any item. Thus you "publish" your originally designed craftwork when you first show it at a craft fair, in a shop, on your Web site, or any other public place.

Respecting the Copyrights of Others

Just as there are several things you must do to protect your "intellectual creations," there are several things you must not do if you wish to avoid legal problems with other copyright holders.

Copyright infringement occurs whenever anyone violates the exclusive rights covered by copyright. If and when a copyright case goes to court, the copyright holder who has been infringed on must

Changing Things

Many crafters have mistakenly been led to believe that they can copy the work of others if they simply change this or that so their creation doesn't look exactly like the one they have copied. But many copyright court cases have hinged on someone taking "a substantial part" of someone else's design and claiming it as their own. If your "original creation" bears even the slightest resemblance to the product you've copied—and you are caught selling it in the commercial marketplace—there could be legal problems.

Crafters often combine the parts of two or three patterns in an attempt to come up with their own original patterns, but often this only compounds the possible copyright problems. Let's imagine you're making a doll. You might take the head from one pattern, the arms and legs from another, and the unique facial features from another. You may think you have developed an original creation (and perhaps an original pattern

prove that his or her work is the original creation and that the two works are so similar that the alleged infringer must have copied it. This is not always an easy matter, for *original* is a difficult word to define. Even the Copyright Office has trouble here, which is why so many cases that go to court end up setting precedents.

In any copyright case, there will be discussions about "substantial similarity," instances where two people actually have created the same thing simultaneously, loss of profits, or damage to one's business or reputation. If you were found guilty of copyright infringement, at the very least you would probably be ordered to pay to the original creator all profits derived from the sale of the copyrighted work to date. You would also have to agree to refund any orders you might receive for the work in the future. In some copyright cases where the original creator has experienced considerable financial loss, penalties for copyright infringement have been as high as $100,000. As you can see, this is not a matter to take lightly.

you might sell), but you haven't. Because the original designer of any of the features you've copied might recognize her work in your "original creation" or published pattern, the designer could come after you for infringing on "a substantial part" of his or her design. In this case, all you've done is multiply your possibilities for a legal confrontation with three copyright holders.

"But I can't create my own original designs and patterns!" you moan. Many who have said this in the past were mistaken. With time and practice, most crafters are able to develop products that are original in design, and I believe you can do this, too. Meanwhile, check out Dover Publications' *Pictorial Archive* series of books (see A "Things to Do" Checklist with Related Resources). Here you will find thousands of copyright-free designs and motifs you can use on your craft work or in needlework projects. And don't forget the wealth of design material in museums and old books that have fallen into the public domain. (See sidebar, What's in the Public Domain? on page 274.)

This is a complex topic beyond the scope of this book, but any book on copyright law will provide additional information if you should ever need it. What's important here is that you fully understand the importance of being careful to respect the legal rights of others. As a crafts-business owner, you could possibly infringe on someone else's designs when you (1) quote someone in an article, periodical, or book you've written; (2) photocopy copyrighted materials; or (3) share information on the Internet. Following is a brief discussion of these topics.

1. **Be careful when quoting from a published source.** If you're writing an article or book and wish to quote someone's words from any published source (book, magazine, Internet, and so on), you should always obtain written permission first. Granted, minor quotations from published sources are okay when they fall under the Copyright Office's Fair Use Doctrine, but unless you completely understand this doctrine, you should protect yourself by

obtaining permission before you quote anyone in one of your own written works. It is not necessarily the quantity of the quote, but the value of the quoted material to the copyright owner.

In particular, never *ever* use a published poem in one of your written works without written permission. To the poet, this is a "whole work," much the same as a book is a whole work to an author. Although the use of one or two lines of a poem, or a paragraph from a book, may be considered "fair use," many publishers now require written permission even for this short reproduction of a copyrighted work.

2. **Photocopying can be dangerous.** Teachers often photocopy large sections of a book (sometimes whole books) for distribution to their students, but this is a flagrant violation of the copyright law. Some publishers may grant photocopying of part of a work if it is to be used only once as a teaching aid, but written permission must always be obtained first.

   It is also a violation of the copyright law to photocopy patterns for sale or trade because such use denies the creator the profit from a copy that might have been sold.

3. **Don't share copyrighted information on the Internet.** People everywhere are lifting material from *Reader's Digest* and other copyrighted publications and "sharing" them on the Internet through e-mail messages, bulletin boards, and the like. *This is a very dangerous thing to do.* "But I didn't see a copyright notice," you might say, or "It indicated the author was anonymous." What you must remember is that *everything* gains copyright protection the moment it is created, whether a copyright notice is attached to it or not. Many "anonymous" items on the Internet are actually copyrighted poems and articles put there by someone who not only

violated the copyright law but compounded the matter by failing to give credit to the original creator.

If you were to pick up one of those "anonymous" pieces of information and put it in an article or book of your own, the original copyright owner, upon seeing his or her work in your publication, would have good grounds for a lawsuit. Remember, pleading ignorance of the law is never a good excuse.

Clearly there is no financial gain to be realized by violating the rights of a copyright holder when it means that any day you might be contacted by a lawyer and threatened with a lawsuit. As stated in my *Crafts Business Answer Book & Resource Guide:*

> The best way to avoid copyright infringement problems is to follow the "Golden Rule" proposed by a United States Supreme Court justice: "Take not from others to such an extent and in such a manner that you would be resentful if they so took from you."

Using Commercial Patterns and Designs

Beginning crafters who lack design skills commonly make products for sale using commercial patterns, designs in books, or how-to instructions for projects found in magazines. The problem here is that all of these things are published for the general consumer market and offered for *personal use* only. Because they are all protected by copyright, that means only the copyright holder has the right to profit from their use.

That said, let me ease your mind by saying that the sale of products made from copyrighted patterns, designs, and magazine how-to projects is probably not going to cause any problems *as long as sales are limited, and they yield a profit only to you, the crafter.* That means no sales through shops of any kind where a sales commission or profit is received by a third party, and absolutely no wholesaling of such products.

It's not that designers and publishers are concerned about your sale of a few craft or needlework items to friends and local buyers; what they are fighting to protect with the legality of copyrights is their right to sell their own designs or finished products in the commercial marketplace. You may find that some patterns, designs, or projects state "no mass-production." You are not mass-producing if you make a dozen handcrafted items for sale at a craft fair or holiday boutique, but you would definitely be considered a mass-producer if you made dozens, or hundreds, for sale in shops.

Consignment sales fall into a kind of gray area that requires some common-sense judgment on your part. This is neither wholesaling nor selling direct to consumers. One publisher might con-

What's in the Public Domain?

For all works created after January 1, 1978, the copyright lasts for the life of the author or creator plus 50 years after his or her death. For works created before 1978, there are different terms, which you can obtain from any book in your library on copyright law.

Once material falls into the public domain, it can never be copyrighted again. As a general rule, anything with a copyright date more than 75 years ago is probably in the public domain, but you can never be sure without doing a thorough search. Some characters in old books—such as Beatrix Potter's *Peter Rabbit*—are now protected under the trademark law as business logos. For more information on this, ask the Copyright Office to send you its circular "How to Investigate the Copyright Status of a Work."

Early American craft and needlework patterns of all kinds are in the public domain because they were created before the copyright law was a reality. Such old patterns may

sider such sales a violation of a copyright while another might not. Whenever specific guidelines for the use of a pattern, design, or how-to project are not given, the only way to know for sure if you are operating on safe legal ground is to write to the publisher and get written permission on where you can sell reproductions of the item in question.

Now let's take a closer look at the individual types of patterns, designs, and how-to projects you might consider using once you enter the crafts marketplace.

Craft, Toy, and Garment Patterns

Today, the consumer has access to thousands of sewing patterns plus toy, craft, needlework, and woodworking patterns of every kind and description found in books, magazines, and design or project leaflets. Whether you can use such patterns for commercial use

show up in books and magazines that are copyrighted, but the copyright in this case extends only to the book or magazine itself and the way in which a pattern has been presented to readers, along with the way in which the how-to-make instructions have been written. The actual patterns themselves cannot be copyrighted by anyone at this point.

Quilts offer an interesting example. If a contemporary quilt designer takes a traditional quilt pattern and does something unusual with it in terms of material or colors, this new creation would qualify for a copyright, with the protection being given to the quilt as a work of art, not to the traditional pattern itself, which is still in the public domain. Thus you could take that same traditional quilt pattern and do something else with it for publication, but you could not publish the contemporary designer's copyrighted version of that same pattern.

depends largely on who has published the pattern and owns the copyright, and what the copyright holder's policy happens to be for how buyers may use those patterns.

To avoid copyright problems when using patterns of any kind, the first thing you need to do is look for some kind of notice on the pattern packet or publication containing the pattern. In checking some patterns, I found that those sold by *Woman's Day* state specifically that reproductions of the designs may not be sold, bartered, or traded. *Good Housekeeping,* on the other hand, gives permission to use their patterns for "income-producing activities." When in doubt, ask!

Whereas the general rule for selling reproductions made from commercial patterns is "no wholesaling and no sales to shops," items made from the average garment pattern (such as an apron, vest, shirt, or simple dress) purchased in the local fabric store *may* be an exception. My research suggests that selling such items in your local consignment shop or craft mall isn't likely to be much of a problem because the sewing pattern companies aren't on the lookout for copyright violators the way individual craft designers and major corporations are. (And most people who sew end up changing those patterns and using different decorations to such a degree that pattern companies might not recognize those patterns even if they were looking for them.)

On the other hand, commercial garment patterns that have been designed by name designers should never be used without permission. In most cases, you would have to obtain a licensing agreement for the commercial use of such patterns.

> *Avoid this pitfall:* In addition to problems in using copyrighted patterns, anyone who uses fabric to make a product for the marketplace has yet another concern: designer *fabrics.* Always look at the selvage of a patterned fabric. If you see a copyright notice with a designer's name and the phrase "for individual consumption only" (or similar wordage), *do not use this fabric to make any item for*

*sale without first obtaining written permission from the fabric manu-
facturer.* In many instances, designer fabrics can be used commer-
cially only when a license has been obtained for this purpose.

Be especially careful about selling reproductions of toys and
dolls made from commercial patterns or design books. Many are
likely to be for popular copyrighted characters being sold in the
commercial marketplace. In such cases, the pattern company will
have a special licensing arrangement with the toy or doll manufacturer to sell the pattern, and reproductions for sale by individual
crafters will be strictly prohibited.

Take a Raggedy Ann doll, for example. The fact that you've purchased a pattern to make such a doll does not give you the right to
sell a finished likeness of that doll any more than your purchase of a
piece of artwork gives you the right to re-create it for sale in some
other form, such as notepaper or calendars. Only the original creator has such rights. You have simply purchased the *physical property* for private use.

Avoid this pitfall: Don't *ever* make and sell *any* replica in any
material of a famous copyrighted character anywhere, such as
the Walt Disney or Warner Brothers characters, Snoopy, or the
Sesame Street gang. It's true that a lot of crafters are doing this,
but they are inviting serious legal trouble if they ever get caught.
Disney is particularly aggressive in defending its copyrights.

How-To Projects in Magazines and Books

Each magazine and book publisher has its own policy about the use
of its art, craft, or needlework projects. How those projects may be
used depends on who owns the copyright to the published projects.
In some instances, craft and needlework designers sell their original
designs outright to publishers of books, leaflets, or magazines. Other
designers authorize only a one-time use of their projects, which gives

Online Help

Today, one of the best ways to network and learn about business is to get on the Internet. The many online resources included in A "Things to Do" Checklist in the next section will give you a jump-start and lead to many exciting discoveries.

For continuing help and advice from Barbara Brabec, be sure to visit her Web site at www.barbarabrabec.com. Here you will find a wealth of information to help you profit from your crafts, including newsletters, feature articles, special tips, and recommended books.

them the right to republish or sell their designs to another market or license them to a manufacturer. If guidelines about selling finished products do not appear somewhere in the magazine or on the copyright page of a book, you should always write and get permission to make such items for sale. In your letter, explain how many items you would like to make, and where you plan to sell them, as that could make a big difference in the reply you receive.

In case you missed the special note on the copyright page of this book, you *can* make and sell all of the projects featured in this and any other book in Prima's FOR FUN & PROFIT series.

I can also tell you that readers of some magazines have the right to use the magazine's patterns and projects for money-making purposes, but only to the extent that sales are limited to places where the crafter is the only one who profits from their use. That means selling directly to individuals, with no sales in shops of any kind where a third party would also realize some profit from a sale. Actually, this is a good rule-of-thumb guideline to use if you plan to sell only a few items of any project or pattern published in any magazine, book, or leaflet.

In summary, products that aren't original in design will sell, but their market is limited, and they will never be able to command the kind of prices that original-design items enjoy. Generally speaking, the more original the product line, the greater one's chances for building a profitable crafts business.

As your business grows, questions about copyrights will arise, and you will have to do a little research to get the answers you need. Your library should have several books on this topic and there is a wealth of information on the Internet. (Just use your search button and type "copyright information.") If you have a technical copyright question, remember that you can always call the Copyright Office and speak to someone who can answer it and send you additional information. Note, however, that regulations prohibit the Copyright Office from giving legal advice or opinions concerning the rights of persons in connection with cases of alleged copyright infringement.

10. To Keep Growing, Keep Learning

Everything we do, every action we take, affects our life in one way or another. Reading a book is a simple act, indeed, but trust me when I say that your reading this particular book *could ultimately change your life.* I know this to be true because thousands of men and women have written to me over the years to tell me how their lives changed after they read one or another of my books and decided to start a crafts business. My life has changed, too, as a result of reading books by other authors.

Many years ago, the purchase of a book titled *You Can Whittle and Carve* unleashed a flood of creativity in me that has yet to cease. That simple book helped me to discover unknown craft talents, which in turn led me to start my first crafts business at home. That experience prepared me for the message I would find a decade later in the book *On Writing Well* by William Zinsser. This author changed my life by giving me the courage to try my hand at writing professionally. Dozens of books later, I had learned a lot about the art and craft of writing well and making a living in the process.

Now you know why I believe reading should be given top priority in your life. Generally speaking, the more serious you become about anything you're interested in, the more reading you will need to do. This will take time, but the benefits will be enormous. If a crafts business is your current passion, this book contains much of the information you need to know to get started. To keep growing, read some of the wonderful books recommended in the Resources section. (If you don't find the books you need in your local library, ask your librarian to obtain them for you through the inter-library loan program.) Join one or more of the organizations recommended. Subscribe to a few periodicals or magazines, and "grow your business" through networking with others who share your interests.

Motivational Tips

As you start your new business or expand a money making hobby already begun, consider the following suggestions:

- *Start an "Achievement Log."* Day by day, our small achievements may seem insignificant, but viewed in total after several weeks or months, they give us important perspective. Reread your achievement log periodically in the future, especially on days when you feel down in the dumps. Make entries at least once a week, noting such things as new customers or accounts acquired, publicity you've gotten, a new product you've designed, the brochure or catalog you've just completed, positive feedback received from others, new friendships, and financial gains.

- *Live your dream.* The mind is a curious thing—it can be trained to think success is possible or to think that success is only for other people. Most of our fears never come true, so allowing our minds to dwell on what may or may not happen cripples us, preventing us from moving ahead, from having confidence, and from living out our dreams. Instead of "facing fear," focus on the result you want. This may automatically eliminate the fear.

■ *Think positively.* As Murphy has proven time and again, what can go wrong will, and usually at the worst possible moment. It matters little whether the thing that has gone wrong was caused by circumstances beyond our control or by a mistake in judgment. What does matter is how we deal with the problem at hand. A positive attitude and the ability to remain flexible at all times are two of the most important ingredients for success in any endeavor.

■ *Don't be afraid to fail.* We often learn more from failure than from success. When you make a mistake, chalk it up to experience and consider it a good lesson well learned. The more you learn, the more self-confident you will become.

■ *Temper your "dreams of riches" with thoughts of reality.* Remember that "success" can also mean being in control of your own life, making new friends, or discovering a new world of possibilities.

Until now you may have lacked the courage to get your craft ideas off the ground, but now that you've seen how other people have accomplished their goals, I hope you feel more confident and adventurous and are ready to capitalize on your creativity. By following the sound advice in this book, you can stop dreaming about all the things you want to do and start making plans to do them!

I'm not trying to make home-business owners out of everyone who reads this book, but my goal is definitely to give you a shove in that direction if you're teetering on the edge, wanting something more than just a profitable hobby. It's wonderful to have a satisfying hobby, and even better to have one that pays for itself; but the nicest thing of all is a real home business that lets you fully utilize your creative talents and abilities while also adding to the family income.

"The things I want to know are in books," Abraham Lincoln once said. "My best friend is the person who'll get me a book I ain't read." You now hold in your hands a book that has taught you many things you wanted to know. To make it a *life-changing book,* all you have to do is act on the information you've been given.

I wish you a joyful journey and a potful of profits!

A "Things to Do" Checklist with Related Resources

INSTRUCTIONS: Read through this entire section, noting the different things you need to do to get your crafts business "up and running." Use the checklist as a plan, checking off each task as it is completed and obtaining any recommended resources. Where indicated, note the date an action was taken so you have a reminder about any follow-up action that should be taken.

Business Start-Up Checklist

☐ Call city hall or county clerk

    ☐ to register fictitious business name
    ☐ to see if you need a business license or permit
    ☐ to check on local zoning laws
      (info also available in your library)

    *Follow up:*_____

☐ Call state capitol

    ☐ secretary of state: to register your business name;
      ask about a license
    ☐ Department of Revenue: to apply for sales tax number

    *Follow up:*_____

☐ Call your local telephone company about

    ☐ cost of a separate phone line for business
    ☐ cost of an additional personal line for Internet access

☐ any special options for home-based businesses

*Follow up:*_____

☐ Call your insurance agent(s) to discuss

  ☐ business rider on house insurance
    (or need for separate in-home insurance policy)
  ☐ benefits of an umbrella policy for extra liability insurance
  ☐ using your car for business
    (how this may affect your insurance)

*Follow up:*_____

☐ Call several banks or S&L's in your area to

  ☐ compare cost of a business checking account
  ☐ get price of a safety deposit box for valuable business records

*Follow up:*_____

☐ Visit office and computer supply stores to check on

  ☐ manual bookkeeping systems, such as the
    Dome Simplified Monthly
  ☐ accounting software
  ☐ standard invoices and other helpful business forms

*Follow up:*_____

☐ Call National Association of Enrolled Agents at (800) 424-4339

  ☐ to get a referral to a tax professional in your area
  ☐ to get answers to any tax questions you may have (no charge)

*Follow up:*_____

☐ Contact government agencies for information relative to your business.

(See Government Agencies checklist.)

☐ Request free brochures from organizations

(See Craft and Home-Business Organizations.)

☐ Obtain sample issues or subscribe to selected publications

(See Recommended Crafts-Business Periodicals.)

☐ Obtain other information of possible help to your business

(See Other Services and Suppliers.)

☐ Get acquainted with the business information available to you in your library.

(See list of Recommended Business Books and Helpful Library Directories.)

Government Agencies

☐ Consumer Product Safety Commission (CPSC), Washington, DC 20207. (800) 638-2772. Information Services: (301) 504-0000. Web site: www.cpsc.gov. (Includes a "Talk to Us" e-mail address where you can get answers to specific questions.) If you make toys or other products for children, garments (especially children's wear), or use any kind of paint, varnish, lacquer, or shellac on your products, obtain the following free booklets:

☐ *The Consumer Product Safety Act of 1972*
☐ *The Flammable Fabrics Act*

Date Contacted:_____Information Received:_____

*Follow up:*_____

☐ Copyright Office, Register of Copyrights, Library of Congress, Washington, DC 20559. To hear recorded messages on the Copyright Office's automated message system (general information, registration procedures, copyright search info, and so on), call (202) 707-3000. You can also get the same information online at www.loc.gov/copyright.

To get free copyright forms, a complete list of all publications available, or to speak personally to someone who will answer your special questions, call (202) 797-9100. In particular, ask for:

☐ Circular R1, *The Nuts and Bolts of Copyright*
☐ Circular R2 (a list of publications available)

Date Contacted:_____Information Received:_____

*Follow up:*_____

☐ Department of Labor. If you should ever hire an employee
or independent contractor, contact your local Labor Department, Wage & Hour Division, for guidance on what you must
do to be completely legal. (Check your phone book under
"U.S. Government.")

Date Contacted:_____Information Received:_____

*Follow up:*_____

☐ Federal Trade Commission (FTC), 6th Street and Pennsylvania
Avenue, NW, Washington, DC 20580. Web site: www.ftc.gov. Request
any of the following booklets relative to your craft or business:

☐ *Textile Fiber Products Identification Act*
☐ *Wool Products Labeling Act of 1939*
☐ *Care Labeling of Textile Wearing Apparel*
☐ *The Hand Knitting Yarn Industry* (booklet)
☐ *Truth-in-Advertising Rules*
☐ *Thirty-Day Mail-Order Rule*

Date Contacted:_____Information Received:_____

Follow up: _____

☐ Internal Revenue Service (IRS). Check the Internet at
www.irs.gov to read the following information online or
call your local IRS office or (800) 829-1040 to get the following booklets and other free tax information:

☐ *Tax Guide for Small Business*—#334
☐ *Business Use of Your Home*—#587
☐ *Tax Information for Direct Sellers*

Date Contacted:_____Information Received:_____

*Follow up:*_____

☐ Patent and Trademark Office (PTO), Washington, DC 20231. Web site: www.uspto.gov.

For patent and trademark information 24 hours a day, call (800) 786-9199 [in northern Virginia, call (703) 308-9000] to hear various messages about patents and trademarks or to order the following booklets:

☐ *Basic Facts about Patents*
☐ *Basic Facts about Trademarks*

To search the PTO's online database of all registered trademarks, go to www.uspto.gov/tmdb/index.html.

Date Contacted:_____Information Received:_____

*Follow up:*_____

☐ Social Security Hotline. (800) 772-1213. By calling this number, you can hear automated messages, order information booklets, or speak directly to someone who can answer specific questions.

Date Contacted:_____Information Received:_____

*Follow up:*_____

☐ U.S. Small Business Administration (SBA). (800) U-ASK-SBA. Call this number to hear a variety of prerecorded messages on starting and financing a business. Weekdays, you can speak personally to an SBA adviser to get answers to specific questions and request such free business publications as:

☐ *Starting Your Business* —#CO-0028
☐ *Resource Directory for Small Business Management*—#CO-0042 (a list of low-cost publications available from the SBA)

The SBA's mission is to help people get into business and stay there. One-on-one counseling, training, and workshops are available through 950 small-business development centers across the country. Help is also available from local district offices of the SBA in the form of free business counseling and training from SCORE volunteers. The SBA office in Washington has a special Women's Business Enterprise section that provides free information on loans, tax deductions, and other financial matters. District offices offer special training programs in management, marketing, and accounting.

A wealth of business information is also available online at www.sba.gov and www.business.gov (the U.S. Business Adviser site). To learn whether there is an SBA office near you, look under U.S. Government in your telephone directory, or call the SBA's toll-free number.

Date Contacted:_____Information Received:_____

*Follow up:*_____

☐ SCORE (Service Corps of Retired Executives). (800) 634-0245. There are more than 12,400 SCORE members who volunteer their time and expertise to small-business owners. Many crafts businesses have received valuable in-depth counseling and training simply by calling the organization and asking how to connect with a SCORE volunteer in their area.

In addition, the organization offers e-mail counseling via the Internet at www.score.org. You simply enter the specific expertise required and retrieve a list of e-mail counselors who represent the best match by industry and topic. Questions can then be sent by e-mail to the counselor of your choice for response.

Date Contacted:_____Information Received:_____

*Follow up:*_____

Craft and Home-Business Organizations

In addition to the regular benefits of membership in an organization related to your art or craft (fellowship, networking, educational conferences or workshops, marketing opportunities, and so on), membership may also bring special business services, such as insurance programs, merchant card services, and discounts on supplies and materials. Each of the following organizations will send you membership information on request.

☐ The American Association of Home-Based Businesses, P.O. Box 10023, Rockville, MD 20849. (800) 447-9710. Web site: www.aahbb.org. This organization has chapters throughout the country. Members have access to merchant card services, discounted business products and services, prepaid legal services, and more.

Date Contacted:_____Information Received:_____

*Follow up:*_____

☐ American Crafts Council, 72 Spring Street, New York, NY 10012. (800)-724-0859. Web site: www.craftcouncil.org. Membership in this organization will give you access to a property and casualty insurance policy that will cost between $250 and $500 a year, depending on your city, state, and the value of items being insured in your art or crafts studio. The policy includes insurance for a craftsperson's work in the studio, in transit, or at a show; $1 million coverage for bodily injury and property damage in studio or away; and $1 million worth of product liability insurance. This policy is from American Phoenix Corporation; staff members will answer your specific questions when you call (800) 274-6364, ext. 337.

Date Contacted:_____Information Received:_____

*Follow up:*_____

☐ Arts & Crafts Business Solutions, 2804 Bishop Gate Drive, Raleigh, NC 27613. (800) 873-1192. This company, known in the industry as the Arts Group, offers a bankcard service specifically for and tailored to the needs of the arts and crafts marketplace. Several differently priced packages are available, and complete information is available on request.

Date Contacted:_____Information Received:_____

*Follow up:*_____

☐ Home Business Institute, Inc., P.O. Box 301, White Plains, NY 10605-0301. (888) DIAL-HBI; Fax: (914) 946-6694. Web site: www.hbiweb.com. Membership benefits include insurance programs (medical insurance and in-home business policy that includes some liability insurance); savings on telephone services, office supplies, and merchant account enrollment; and free advertising services.

Date Contacted:_____Information Received:_____

*Follow up:*_____

☐ National Craft Association (NCA), 1945 E. Ridge Road, Suite 5178, Rochester, NY 14622-2647. (800) 715-9594. Web site: www.craftassoc.com. Members of NCA have access to a comprehensive package of services, including merchant account services; discounts on business services and products; a prepaid legal program; a check-guarantee merchant program; checks by fax, phone, or e-mail; and insurance programs. Of special interest to this book's readers is the "Crafters Business Insurance" policy (through RLI Insurance Co.) that includes coverage for business property; art/craft merchandise or inventory at home, in transit, or at a show; theft away from premises; up to $1 million in both personal and product liability insurance; loss of business income; and more. Members have the option to select the exact benefits they need. Premiums range from $150 to $300, depending on location, value of average inventory, and the risks associated with one's art or craft.

Date Contacted:_____Information Received:_____

*Follow up:*_____

Recommended Crafts-Business Periodicals

Membership in an organization generally includes a subscription to a newsletter or magazine that will be helpful to your business. Here are additional craft periodicals you should sample or subscribe to:

☐ *The Crafts Report—The Business Journal for the Crafts Industry,* Box 1992, Wilmington, DE 19899. (800) 777-7098. On the Internet at www.craftsreport.com. A monthly magazine covering all areas of crafts-business management and marketing, including special-interest columns and show listings.

☐ *Craft Supply Magazine—The Industry Journal for the Professional Crafter,* Krause Publications, Inc., 700 E. State Street, Iowa, WI 54990-0001. (800) 258-0929. Web site: www.krause.com. A monthly magazine that includes crafts-business and marketing articles and wholesale supply sources.

☐ *Home Business Report,* 2949 Ash Street, Abbotsford, BC, V2S 4G5 Canada. (604) 857-1788; Fax: (604) 854-3087. Canada's premier home-business magazine, relative to both general and craft-related businesses.

☐ *SAC Newsmonthly,* 414 Avenue B, P.O. Box 159, Bogalusa, LA 70429-0159. (800) TAKE-SAC; Fax: (504) 732-3744. A monthly national show guide that also includes business articles for professional crafters.

☐ *Sunshine Artist Magazine,* 2600 Temple Drive, Winter Park, FL 32789. (800) 597-2573; Fax: (407) 539-1499. Web site: www.sunshineartist.com. America's premier show and festival guide. Each monthly issue contains business and marketing articles of interest to both artists and craftspeople.

Other Services and Suppliers

Contact any of the following companies that offer information or services of interest to you.

☐ American Express. For merchant account information, call the Merchant Establishment Services Department at (800) 445-AMEX.

Date Contacted:_____Information Received:_____

*Follow up:*_____

☐ Dover Publications, 31 E. 2nd Street, Mineola, NY 11501. Your source for thousands of copyright-free designs and motifs you can use in your craftwork or needlecraft projects. Request a free catalog of books in the *Pictorial Archive* series.

Date Contacted:_____Information Received:_____

*Follow up:*_____

☐ Novus Services, Inc. For merchant account information, call (800) 347-6673.

Date Contacted:_____Information Received:_____

*Follow up:*_____

☐ Volunteer Lawyers for the Arts (VLA), 1 E. 53rd Street, New York, NY 10022. Legal hotline: (212) 319-2910. If you ever need an attorney, and cannot afford one, contact this nonprofit organization, which has chapters all over the country. In addition to providing legal aid for performing and visual artists and craftspeople (individually or in groups), the VLA also provides a range of educational services, including issuing publications concerning taxes, accounting, and insurance.

Date Contacted:_____Information Received:_____

*Follow up:*_____

☐ Widby Enterprises USA, 4321 Crestfield Road, Knoxville, TN 37921-3104. (888) 522-2458. Web site: www.widbylabel.com. Standard and custom-designed labels that meet federal labeling requirements.

Date Contacted:_____Information Received:_____

*Follow up:*_____

Recommended Business Books

When you have specific business questions not answered in this beginner's guide, check your library for the following books. Any not on library shelves can be obtained through the library's inter-library loan program.

☐ *Business and Legal Forms for Crafts* by Tad Crawford (Allworth Press)

☐ *Business Forms and Contracts (in Plain English) for Crafts People* by Leonard D. DuBoff (Interweave Press)

☐ *Crafting as a Business* by Wendy Rosen (Chilton)

☐ *The Crafts Business Answer Book & Resource Guide: Answers to Hundreds of Troublesome Questions about Starting, Marketing & Managing a Homebased Business Efficiently, Legally & Profitably* by Barbara Brabec (M. Evans & Co.)

☐ *Creative Cash: How to Profit from Your Special Artistry, Creativity, Hand Skills, and Related Know-How* by Barbara Brabec (Prima Publishing)

☐ *422 Tax Deductions for Businesses & Self-Employed Individuals* by Bernard Kamoroff (Bell Springs Publishing)

☐ *Homemade Money: How to Select, Start, Manage, Market, and Multiply the Profits of a Business at Home* by Barbara Brabec (Betterway Books)

☐ *How to Register Your Own Trademark with Forms,* 2nd ed., by Mark Warda (Sourcebooks)

☐ *INC Yourself: How to Profit by Setting Up Your Own Corporation,* by Judith H. McQuown (HarperBusiness)

☐ *Make It Profitable! How to Make Your Art, Craft, Design, Writing or Publishing Business More Efficient, More Satisfying, and More Profitable* by Barbara Brabec (M. Evans & Co.)

☐ *Patent, Copyright & Trademark: A Desk Reference to Intellectual Property Law* by Stephen Elias (Nolo Press)

☐ *The Perils of Partners* by Irwin Gray (Smith-Johnson Publisher)

☐ *Small Time Operator: How to Start Your Own Business, Keep Your Books, Pay Your Taxes & Stay Out of Trouble* by Bernard Kamoroff (Bell Springs Publishing)

☐ *Trademark: How to Name a Business & Product* by Kate McGrath and Stephen Elias (Nolo Press)

Helpful Library Directories

☐ *Books in Print* and *Guide to Forthcoming Books* (how to find out which books are still in print, and which books will soon be published)

☐ *Encyclopedia of Associations* (useful in locating an organization dedicated to your art or craft)

☐ *National Trade and Professional Associations of the U.S.* (more than 7,000 associations listed alphabetically and geographically)

☐ *The Standard Periodical Directory* (annual guide to U.S. and Canadian periodicals)

☐ *Thomas Register of American Manufacturers* (helpful when you're looking for raw material suppliers or the owners of brand names and trademarks)

☐ *Trademark Register of the U.S.* (contains every trademark currently registered with the U.S. Patent and Trademark Office)

Glossary

▼▼▼

General Jewelry Making

These are terms commonly used by all who are involved with jewelry making. It's a good idea to become familiar with the jargon so you can communicate with others who make jewelry.

Alloy: Metal made up of a mixture of two or more different metals. Common examples of alloys include bronze (a mixture of copper and tin), brass (copper and zinc), and pewter (tin with antimony, copper, and sometimes lead).

Annealed: Softened by heat.

Bail: Metal triangle used to attach a bead or a pendant to a necklace.

Baroque: Irregular, rounded stone, glass, or bead.

Base metal: Non-precious metal used as a core for plated and gold-filled items. Brass and nickel are common base metals in jewelry.

Bead loom: Wood or plastic frame used to stitch warp threads for bead weaving.

Bead tip: Jewelry finding used for attaching thread to a clasp. A knot sits inside a small concave shape attached to a bent metal loop.

Beeswax: Waxy substance used to strengthen and smooth beading thread.

Bell cap: Jewelry finding used to convert a bead or stone with no hole into a pendant, using glue.

Bi-cone: Bead shape that tapers to a cone at each end.

Bib: Necklace that fits close to the base of the neck and extends over the chest in the shape of child's bib.

Bugle: Small, glass, tubular bead.

Burr: Roughness left by a tool when cutting wire or metal.

Cabochon: Round or oval stone, cut and polished with one flat side (the back) and one smooth, domed side (the front or face). A faceted cabochon is cut with faceted surfaces around the edges of the stone.

Chatoyancy: Having a changeable luster, like a cat's eye.

Choker: Short necklace, usually 15 inches long, fitting snugly at the base of the neck. Popular in the 1950s and revived in the 1970s with the addition of ornaments cascading to cover the chest.

Coil: Flat spiral of wire or metal.

Crimp bead: Small, soft metal bead that is squeezed shut to secure a loop of threading material onto a clasp.

Dog collar: Wide choker, worn tightly around the neck; popular in the 1930s and 1960s.

Eyepin: Wire finding with a loop at one end. Used for linking beads or beaded links.

Facet: Flat, polished surface cut into a stone or bead.

Finding: Catch-all term used to describe metal jewelry components. Clasps, connecting rings, the pins that hold the beads, ear wires, and posts are all findings.

Gauge: Measure of dimension.

Gold: Yellow-colored, soft, shiny metal commonly used in jewelry. The purity of gold is measured in "karats." 24 karat (or 24K) denotes **pure** or **fine** gold; 12K is 50% gold; 14K is about 58% gold. Gold that is less than 24K is actually an alloy.

Gold-filled: Thin layer of gold bonded to a base metal core. In gold-filled products, the gold layer must be at least 1/20th (5%) of the overall product, by weight.

Gold-plated: Very thin layer of gold bonded to a base metal core.

Lampwork: Technique for making glass beads by hand. A glass rod or cane is held to a flame or "lamp" and wound around a mandrel. The bead is shaped or smoothed by rotating the mandrel through the flame.

Lapidary: Cutting, shaping, polishing, and creating jewelry from precious and semi-precious stones.

Lavaliere: Necklace with a drop of a single stone suspended from a chain, also called a neglige.

Lazy stitch: Bead embroidery stitch that attaches several small beads on each short stitch.

Loaf: block of clay with a pattern throughout; usually a square shape.

Log: Roll of clay that is thicker than a cane.

Matinee: Necklace 24 to 26 inches long; in Europe, 30 to 35 inches.

Mokume: Japanese word used in metalsmithing to describe the look of growth rings in trees.

Opera: Necklace 28 to 30 inches long; in Europe, 48 to 90 inches, can extend to 120 inches.

Opacity: Quality of not allowing light to pass through (the quality of being opaque).

Opaque: Not allowing light to pass through; solid.

Papier roule: Beads made of rolled up paper triangles.

Parure: Set of several matching types of jewelry (i.e. necklace, earrings, and bracelet).

Paste: Jewelry made of glass, imitating faceted gemstones.

Perfumed beads: Beads that release a scent when warmed by the body.

Peyote stitch: Honeycomb beadwork stitch, worked in a spiral fashion to produce a beadwork tunnel.

Princess: Necklace 20 to 21 inches long.

Sautoir: Long necklace popular in the 1920s; usually made of chains, beads, or pearls and ending in a tassel or fringe.

Silver: White-colored, soft, shiny metal, commonly used in jewelry. Like gold, silver is available in different levels of purity: the purest form, **Fine** silver, is 99.9% silver. **Sterling** silver is 92.5% silver, with other metals (usually copper) making up the remaining 7.5%. **Coin** silver is 90% silver with 10% copper. *Nickel* silver is an alloy of copper (65%), nickel, and zinc—no silver at all.

Silver-plated: A very thin layer of silver bonded to a base metal core.

Split ring: Small base metal finding that resembles a key ring.

Torsade: Combination of several strands of pearls, chains, or beads twisted together into a single necklace.

Translucent: Allowing some light to pass through; objects seen through translucent material are diffused or indistinct.

Transparent: Easily seen through; allowing light to pass through without obscuring the ability to see objects on the other side.

Tools of the Trades

No matter what you craft, you'll need a tool or two to make your work easier. Stick this list in your handy, dandy toolbox and let your friends know you "saw" it here! Just remember, the one with the most tools—wins!

Abrasives: Family of smoothing tools including sandpaper, grit paper, steel wool, sand sticks, sand blocks, taping, and cording. Abrasives can be dry or wet.

Adhesive: Substance or chemical mixture used to temporarily or permanently bond two surfaces or items.

Awl: Sharp, pointed, usually metal tool for hand punching holes or openings.

Bevel: Instrument to balance or make centered.

Blending stump: Paper or soft textile stick used to blend pencil colors, chalk, pastels, or charcoal.

Bone: Hard, wood tool used to score other materials.

Bow saw: Hand-held saw with thick blade anchored onto angled metal bridge, used for rough cutting.

Brad point bit: Bit used on rounded surfaces for a smoother cut or boring.

Brayer: Similar to a rolling pin, used to smooth or flatten materials.

Brush: Natural or man-made bristles, gathered and clamped together and used to transport one medium to another medium. Brush types include: sponge, round, flat, stencil, and more.

Burnisher: Metal or wood instrument used to smooth, shape, embellish, polish, or transfer one material to another; also referred to as a embossing tool.

Calipers: Metal instruments used in measuring dimensions. Inside and outside measurements use different calipers.

Chisel: Metal tool used to create decorative edges or designs in wood.

Circular saw: Hand-held power tool, with round or circle blade, used for making rough to detailed cuts.

Clamp: Work-holding device. Some types of clamps are C-clamp, bar, pipe, hand-screw, band, web, and specialty.

Coping saw: Hand-held saw with thin cutting blade that is anchored across a metal bridge, used for fine cutting.

Drill: Portable tool that can be hand held or placed in a press and used to bore holes. Many other applications are possible with the variety of bits available today.

File: Tool made of hardened steel with rows of finely-spaced cutting teeth for smoothing, trimming, and sharpening.

Hammer: Tool with a hard or soft head, mounted on a handle, used to pound smooth or force one item into another. There are over 30 varieties of hammers for specific tasks, including the rubber-headed mallet.

Kiln: Oven used to heat or fire ceramics.

Lathe: Tool that turns a piece of wood, allowing it to be carved or decorated.

Loom: Frame used to weave materials or hold materials in place.

Miter box: Guide created to give an accurate cutting angle.

Needle: Instrument with an eye on one end, which can be threaded with thin materials, and a sharp or blunted point on the other end for piercing fabric or other materials.

Palette knife: A knife, shaped like a pie cutter, that is used to transfer a medium, smooth a medium, or texture a medium to a surface.

Plane: Used to smooth or flatten wood. Can be hand-held or power.

Radial arm saw: Power saw with round blades used where the material is stationary and the saw moves to make cuts.

Ribs: Smooth, hand-size, wood pieces with edges in different degrees of texture; used to shape clays or other modeling mediums.

Rifflers: Files with very small heads and large hand grips, used for detail work.

Router: Portable power tool with changeable bits for a variety of tasks, from cutting to edging.

Ruler: Hard or soft device for measuring in inches and meters. Soft form is also referred to as a tape.

Sabre saw: Hand-held power tool with a straight blade.

Soldering iron: Heating tool used to melt metals or transfer metal to a surface.

Square: Flat measuring tool with a 90-degree angle, used to measure wood or metal so precise corner and edge cuts can be made.

Staple gun: Hand or power tool that shoots staples or nails into material.

Stylus: Metal, round-tipped, hand-held tool, used to create perfect, consistent depressions in leather or other soft materials.

Table saw: Stationary saw with a round blade used to cut wood, which is moved across the blade.

Tack cloth: Very sticky cloth or fabric used to remove fine particles or dust from wood, metal, ceramic, and so on.

Tjanting: Holds wax to use in applying lines of wax to materials, as in batik.

Wheel: Table with flat top that rotates or spins.

Design Terms

Design is basic to jewelry making. You will need to know the following terms as you learn more about the different technique and style options. These terms are used in all craft mediums.

Asymmetrical balance: Informal, natural, somewhat abstract design.

Composition: The arrangement of the various parts that make up the whole piece.

Focal point: The main area of a design or arrangement that dominates the design and draws the eye; usually a single element. In a symmetrical design, the focal point is at the center. In an asymmetrical design, the focal point is placed toward the high side of the arrangement.

Free form: Having no focal point.

Harmony: A state in which the parts of a design or arrangement do not conflict with each other, but flow together and compliment each other.

Proportion: The relationship between the elements (size, color, quantity, and setting) of an arrangement.

Symmetrical Balance: Formal design; in which an arrangement can be divided into two equal parts.

Texture: Refers to the physical surface qualities of materials used in a design or arrangement. A texture can be smooth, glossy, rough, or soft. Also refers to the size of the pieces that make up a design or arrangement.

Metal-Smithing

Artists who work with metals have their own set of terms. The most common metals used are gold, silver, and copper. In its purest form, no materials or supplies other than metal are used.

Annealing: The heat treating (softening) of metal after it has been work-hardened with steel tools. Annealing is necessary between the raising and forging stages. Annealing is also used to remove tension in a piece of metal before brazing, helping to reduce warping.

Brazing: A form of soldering that utilizes high-temperature alloys to join high-temperature metals. When brazing sterling, care must be used to prevent firescale, which is formed at higher temperatures than soldering.

Chasing: The technique of detailing the front surface of a metal article with various hammer-struck punches.

Checking: The hammering down onto the edge of a form. This technique strengthens and visually thickens the edge.

Crimping: A rapid metal-raising process that forms radiating valleys from the center to the outer edge of a metal object. Generally used on thinner gauge metal.

Cross-peen hammer: Hammer with a long, narrow face running perpendicular to the handle, used for raising, forming, and planishing.

Die Forming: The process of stamping or hammering a sheet of metal into a form which has the outline of the object. Also used when making duplicate objects.

Drawbench: A narrow, waist-high bench equipped with a chain that drags a pair of drawtongs (large coarse-toothed pliers), used to grip the end of a piece of wire. This wire is then pulled through a series of consecutively smaller dies (round, square, triangular, and so on) reducing its thickness. Patterned dies may also be used to produce moldings, borders, and so on.

Engraving: The process of cutting shallow lines into metal with a sharp graver, reproducing artwork which has been drawn on a metal article. Unlike machine engraving, hand engraving removes metal when cutting. Bright cutting is another form of engraving which, when viewed, is very reflective because of its flat, angled cut.

Firescale: A purple stain that develops in sterling silver when oxygen penetrates the outer surface of an object during brazing, thus oxidizing the copper content. Fine silver is left on the surface when sulfuric acid chemically removes the oxidized copper, though copper may be oxidized below the surface. Colonial pieces will show this purple stain after many years of polishing.

Head: A short, polished, cast metal mushroom-type stake that fits into a horse and is used for planishing and burnishing metal objects.

Horse: Held in a vise, this straight or L-shaped holding device accommodates heads. The length of a horse varies, depending on the size or depth of the piece being fashioned.

Mokume cane: Laminated metals that have been fused or brazed together like a sandwich and passed through a flat or wire-forming rolling mill to make the material easier to fabricate or raise. The sandwich, or "billet," can also be forged without the use of the rolling mill. Patterns are then punched, filed, and hammered to produce a desired pattern.

Planishing: The act of hammering or refining the surface of a metal object with highly polished hammer faces. This process refines the surface after raising and may be used as a decorative element. Great care must be used, for even a speck of dust will make an impression in the metal being hammered.

Polishing: The process of refining a metal surface by use of a polishing wheel attached to a long-spindled motorized arbor which runs at high speed. Various finishes may be obtained with a wide variety of abrasive compounds applied to the polishing wheels such as rouge—this compound imparts the brightest finish. Other polishing compounds will produce matte finishes, emphasizing the form, which will be rendered less reflective.

Raising: The technique of forming a flat sheet of metal over a cast iron T-stake or head, forming and compressing the metal to take a hollow form. This labor-intensive process is the purest form of silversmithing.

Repoussé: A process used to roughly emboss a metal object from the back or inside with larger punches than those used in chasing.

Rolling mill: A hand- or motor-driven cast iron mill with polished or patterned hardened steel rollers that reduce the thickness or impart a texture on a metal sheet or wire. Functions like a hand-cranked clothes ringer.

Scratch brush: A long-spindled, motorized arbor using fine wire wheels, rotating at slow speed, that burnish the surface of a metal object after soldering. Soapy water is used as a lubricant between the wheel and object. May also be used as a texturing wheel to soften the luster of metal.

Silversmith: One who fashions silver objects and wrought items such as forged flatware. The first silversmiths who settled in this country set up our banking system and produced its first coinage.

Sinking: The hammering of a flat piece of metal into a concave hemispherical shape in the top of a tree stump or any dished form. A small bowl shape is formed in the center of the sheet, producing a lip, enabling the piece to "ride" the end of a raising stake, aiding in the raising process.

Snarling: The embossing from underneath or inside an object with a long-armed steel tool, with one end placed in a vise. Snarling is accomplished by placing a form over the snarling iron's tip (which may be any shape) and tapping the back end of the arm which is secured in the vise. The vertical vibration that results gives a "kick," raising a bump on the outside of the object. This technique is usually used in conjunction with chasing.

Soldering: A low-temperature form of brazing. This technique is used for joining low-temperature base metal, such as pewter, and does not possess the strength of brazing solders when joining higher temperature metals such as silver.

Spinning: The forcing of a flat disc of metal over a profiled steel or wooden form (chuck) with long-handled, polished steel tools. The horizontal spinning lathe generally runs at high-speed and is also used to turn the chucks. This technique takes much less time than raising.

Spring hammer: A 5-foot, cast iron beam, supporting a long-handled, highly polished pivoting hammer with a 3-inch diameter face. The hammer is mounted on a spring mechanism, allowing the hammer head to bounce off a highly polished adjustable anvil used to flatten the bottoms of trays and anything else that requires a perfectly flat surface. The spring hammer head bounces off the anvil perfectly flat, avoiding a costly crescent-shaped miss-hit of a hand-held hammer head's edge.

Stake: Any polished cast iron or steel tool placed in a vise and used for forming and planishing metal. This tool is generally large enough to be used without a horse.

Sterling silver: An alloy of fine silver (92.5%) and copper (7.5%); most commonly used when fashioning holloware and flatware because of its strength. Fine silver (99.99% pure) is generally too soft when producing large functional objects. U.S. law states that all objects marked "sterling," "925," or "925/1000" must contain no less than 92.5% fine silver.

Surface gauge: A vertical steel rod mounted with an adjustable arm fastened to a heavy base. The adjustable scribe-type pivoting arm can be raised or lowered to check the height or to scribe a level line around an object in order to mount a wire or anything else that must be level. Often used on top of a surface plate.

Surface plate: A perfectly level, steel, cast iron, or granite table of any dimension; used to check the level and flatness of an object. Often used in conjunction with a surface gauge.

T-stake: Any polished, cast iron or steel tool in the form of an elongated "T"; used in a vise for raising, forming, or planishing metal.

Decorative Painting and Faux Finishes

A creative palette of terms to know when painting. This list covers the spectrum and adds depth and meaning to all the instructions you may read for decorative painting patterns. It may seem like a strange language, but brush away your worries.

Acrylic: Water-based paint that dries quickly.

Antiquing: Product used in finishing a painted item that gives an aged or darkened look to the paint. Available in sprays and cremes. Usually applied to the wood and then rubbed off.

Basecoat: Color applied to an entire piece; for example, a background color that then has other colors or detailing work added, usually one or two coats of paint.

Binder: Component of paint. Binders in latex products are acrylics and binders in alkyd products are oils.

Blending: Toning down imprints or hue of glaze or paint by sponge brush or cloth to get a softer effect or to combine different colors on a surface.

Bronze powders: Fine metallic powders from gold to copper.

Chisel: Tool used to shave edges from wood.

Color: Another word for hue or paint.

Crackle glaze: The appearance of old paint that has cracked and peeled to reveal a different color of paint underneath.

Crackle varnish: A finish or varnished layer that appears cracked and aged.

Criss-crossing: Applying paint or glaze smoothly and evenly over a surface by working top-to-bottom and then side-to-side.

Distressing: Deliberately inflicting dents and knocks on a new surface; also accomplished with over sanding.

Dragging: Applying glaze, then removing some of the glaze by sweeping with a metal graining comb, dry brush, or feathers.

Dry brushing: Technique of using a dry brush with a minimal amount of paint to add shading or highlighting details to a design. The brush is dipped in paint and a paper towel is then used to remove most of the paint from the brush.

Eggshell finish: Slight sheen that reflects low amounts of light.

Fan: A brush with bristles shaped like a fan, used to create texture. A fan brush is used dry or with only the tips of the brush loaded with paint.

Ferrule: Metal part of a brush where the bristles meet the brush handle.

Filbert: Brush in the shape of a flower petal or leaf, used to create soft edges and blend colors.

Flat brush: A brush with a flat or crimped ferrule, used in stroke work, basecoating, and shading/highlighting.

Flat finish: No sheen or gloss; will not reflect light and is very porous.

Flip float: Technique of floating one side of a brush, then flipping it, and floating the opposite side as when painting chair legs.

Float: Technique in which one side of a flat brush is loaded with paint and the brush is stroked on a palette until a blended color is achieved. Floating is used to shade or highlight.

Flogging: Technique in which glaze is manipulated by striking a surface with a long, bristled brush.

Gesso: Thick, chalky liquid medium that is smooth and porous, absorbs color, and is used to add texture or design to a piece.

Gilding: The application of gold, silver, or other metal leaf to a surface.

Glaze: Transparent coat of paint that is thinly brushed or sponged over a basecoat or raw surface.

Gloss finish: Shiny, lustrous finish that reflects light.

Gold leaf: Gold and other metals on a thin sheet of transfer paper for gilding or foiling.

High gloss finish: The most reflective of all finishes with a shine that appears almost like a glass layer over the surface.

Highlight: To lighten a painted area as if sunlight were falling across it, giving a more realistic effect to the appearance of a painted piece. The color used to highlight is lighter than the base color.

Intarsia: Highly developed form of wood inlay.

Liming: Treating a wood surface with a limewash for protection.

Liner: Round, thin-haired brush used to create straight or curved lines with consistency.

Liquid gold: Bronze powder suspended in medium that must be shaken before use.

Load: To dip a brush into paint so that the bristles pick up and hold the paint.

Luster powders: Powders containing mica to add luster.

Matte: Dull finish without gloss or luster.

Medium: Usually a liquid substance that is added to paint to give it a desired quality. For example, a textile medium is added to paint to allow the paint to adhere to fabric and to hold up to washing.

Milk paint: Paint made from curds with tint added to achieve the desired color.

Palette: 1. Colors used to create a design. **2.** A surface for holding and mixing colors such as plastic lids, ceramic tiles, and freezer paper. Palette paper is a coated paper designed to help blend colors, make washes, and is usually disposable.

Round brush: A brush with a round ferrule and pointed tip, used for stroke and detail work such as comma strokes, writing, vines, or eyelashes.

Satin finish: A finish that has a sheen, but is not as shiny as a gloss finish.

Sealer: Finish that is sprayed or brushed on to seal raw wood before paint is applied.

Shade: Darkening an area in order to give the appearance of a shadow or shading.

Spattering: Technique of flicking paint off from a brush onto another surface to distress or age the surface.

Sponging: Applying paint with a sponge to give a textured effect.

Sponging out: Soaking up paint with a sponge or paper towel to remove areas of pigment in order to create a special effect.

Stains: Transparent liquids which allow a base surface to show through the color.

Stippling: The technique of dry-brushing paint onto a surface, using short dabs in order to create highlights and shading.

Stylus: Tool used to make dots of paint, emboss, or transfer a design. A stylus may have a small metal ball at the tip. A brush tip can also be used as a stylus.

Technique: Method used to achieve a specific look, texture, or feel to a piece. Techniques include: stripping, sponging, marbleizing, and antiquing.

Tint: 1. Transparent color. **2.** A hint of color.

Tole: A technique of painting on tin or metal.

Tooth: To give a surface a dull finish, usually by sanding, in order to help paint adhere to a glossy surface.

Transfer paper: Paper that is coated on one side with gray, black, white, blue, or red material that aids painters in transferring a design to a surface. Transfer paper is placed color side down, a design is placed on top of the transfer paper, and a stylus or pencil is used to trace the design.

Variegated wash: Different colors applied in such a way that they run into each other.

Verdigris: Bluish-green patina formed on copper, brass, and bronze by corrosion from exposure to air or saltwater.

Wash: Thinned paint used for transparent basecoating or aging.

Working dry: Technique done by adding new glaze or paint to dry glaze or paint. Also, working with a dry brush; not one wet with water.

Working wet: Technique done by adding glaze or paint to wet glaze or paint; also referred to as wet on wet.

Business Terms

It's important to "speak" with the correct business jargon and terms when communicating with your clients and suppliers. Nothing to it—just use this list!

Accounts payable: Money owed for goods or services received.

Accounts receivable: Money owed to your business for goods or services delivered.

Back order: Items not available to be shipped immediately to the buyer, which are usually shipped at a later date.

Break-even: Point at which a business is not making or losing money; the total revenue equals the total expenses.

Budget: Financial plan to control spending.

COD account: Cash or check on delivery. Payment is due upon receipt from a common carrier.

Common carrier: Transportation service or company that will deliver supplies, such as UPS.

Consumer: End user.

Cost of goods sold: Direct cost to business owner of items that will in turn be sold to consumers.

CPD: Certified Professional Demonstrator.

Dealer minimum: Also called minimum order. The lowest quantity of an item that must be purchased, or the lowest dollar amount that must be spent to place an order with a supplier.

Distributor: Middleman that markets and sells to retailers.

Gross price: Price of product before discounts, deductions, or allowances.

Invoice: Itemized statement from supplier/vendor stating charges for merchandise.

Manufacturer: Business that makes product(s) from raw materials.

Net price: Actual price paid for products/supplies after deductions, discounts, and allowances are subtracted.

Open account: Credit extended to a business for a specific billing period.

Purchase order: A record of agreement made between supplier and buyer.

Retailer: Business that sells directly to the consumer.

Sales representative: Person who sells a product(s) for a commission, usually in a specific geographic area. Company representatives work for a specific manufacturer/distributor. Independent representatives handle more than one product line.

SKU: Stock Keeping Unit. A unit assigned to a product/item, usually designated with a bar code for inventory control.

Terms of sale: Conditions of a sale, including who can purchase goods and the method of payment.

Trade association: An organization of businesses in the same line of work that promotes common interests.

Trade publication: Printed material intended for trade-only consumption.

Trade show: A gathering of individuals and businesses in a common industry to display, educate, and sell products/services to other members within the common industry.

Wholesaler: Business that sells to others who then resell the products.

Abbreviations and Acronyms

SOS! What the heck do all these initials mean? FYI. Here's your guide to all the acronyms you'll encounter in the craft industry.

ACCI: Association of Crafts & Creative Industries

AHSCA: American Home Sewing & Craft Association

CCD: Certified Craft Designer (awarded by SCD)

CCHA: Canadian Craft & Hobby Association

CK: Check

COD: Cash or check on delivery

CPD: Certified professional demonstrator (awarded by HIA)

COGS: Cost of goods sold

CSM: Craft Supply Magazine (business journal for the professional crafter)

FOB: Free on board

HCR: Home craft retailer (one who purchases raw craft supplies at wholesale to resell from the home)

HIA: Hobby Industries of America or Hobby Industries Association (trade association)

ICCPSA: International Cake, Candy, & Party Association

MATCH: Mid-Atlantic Craft & Hobby Industry Association (regional trade association)

MIAA: Miniatures Industry Association of America

MO: Money order

NECHIA: Northeast Craft & Hobby Association (regional trade association)

NWCHA: Northwest Craft & Hobby Association (regional trade association)

PACC: Professional Association of Custom Clothiers

PC: Professional Crafter (one who buys raw craft supplies to incorporate supplies into finished craft items)

PCP: Professional Craft Producer (HIA's official trade association name of a PC)

POP: Point of purchase display (a showcase of product placed where the consumer can see the product and buy it)

PPFA: Professional Picture Framers Association

PPD: Postage paid

SCD: Society of Craft Designers

SKU: Stock Keeping Unit (number assigned to a specific item, designated by a bar code, used to control inventory)

SECHA: Southeast Craft & Hobby Association (regional trade association)

SEF: Southeastern Fabric, Notions, & Craft Association

SASE: Self-addressed, stamped envelope

SEYG: Southeastern Yarncrafters Guild

SDP: Society of Decorative Painters

SIP: Special Interest Publication (one time publication on a specific event, theme, or subject)

TKGA: The Knitting Guild of America

TNNA: The National Needlework Association

Computer Terms To Know

A bit here and a byte there. One needs to learn a few new words in order to understand what's going on online. Here's a database of terms and jargon. For most of us, it's more information than we need to know, care to know, or wish to store in our memories, extended or expanded. Just input, file, and be sure to backup the information! A computer is one of the most important tools a crafter can use!

Access code: Also known as Password or PIN. An identification number or set of characters that are sometimes required to gain entry into a computer program or system. Individuals and companies use an access code to protect data and resources. The computer accepts the code, but can't determine who entered the code.

Backup or backup files: Copies of data and program files. Usually the information on a hard drive or disk is stored on a separate disk. It is very helpful to back up important files and data in case of computer system or human error.

Batch file: A set of commands which are stored in a disk file for execution by the operating system. A batch file is created to save time and reduce error for tasks that are executed frequently. For example, AUTOEXEC.BAT is automatically executed by DOS each time the system is started.

BBS: Bulletin Board System. Port of many Web sites. Allows you to post messages for others to read and respond.

Bit: Binary digit, and the smallest unit of information.

Boot: A procedure that starts the computer. Turning the power on allows the computer to boot.

CD-ROM: a device that uses a compact disc (CD) to store large amounts of data. Eight hundred megabytes of information equals more than 200,000 printed pages.

Chat or chat room: Area online where you can communicate with others. Chat rooms may be public for all users to enter, or private for users who know the name of the room.

Clobber: 1. To write new data over the top of good data in a file. **2.** To wipe out a file.

Compatible: As in IBM compatible. Allows programs written for one computer to run on another computer even though the computers are not from the same manufacturer.

Computer literate: Person who knows and understands the world of computers.

COM port: A communications channel over which data is transferred between remote computer devices. Usually a serial port used with a modem to establish a channel over telephone lines.

Computer: Electronic device that can perform high-speed arithmetic and logical operations. A computer is made up of a processor, memory, input/output, disk storage, and software.

Crash: Malfunction of a computer system or program, making it inoperable.

Cursor: The blinking or flashing indicator on screen which identifies a location in the text. Usually a thin, vertical line or box. The cursor is controlled by the arrows on the keyboard, a mouse, trackball, or joystick.

Cybernetics: 1. Field of science that explores the similarities and differences between human beings and machines. **2.** Robots that imitate human behavior.

Database: A set of interrelated data records stored on a direct access storage device that allows multiple applications to access the data. For example, a large collection of information on a particular subject organized to allow search and retrieval of any one field.

Disk: Also disc. A direct access storage device of varied storage capacity, from a single-sided, floppy diskette to a high-capacity fixed disk.

E-mail: Electronic mail. Information is sent via one computer to another computer by a network of computer systems. E-mail is rather quick when compared to snail mail (the post office). You need the correct address of the recipient to get your mail delivered.

Emoticon: Using different symbols on the keyboard like :-) to make a smiley face or :-(to make a sad or angry face.

FAQ: Frequently asked questions, listed with answers in an area online.

FAX: Facsimile machine that allows images to be sent over telephone wires. Facsimile transmission can be done from a personal computer with an internal or an external FAX board. The image is scanned at the transmitter, reconstructed at the receiving station, and duplicated on paper.

Field: A unit of information in a database like zip codes or last names.

Floppy disk: Disk made of mylar and coated with a material that can be magnetized to store bits of information. Can be single or double-sided and double or quad-density. High capacity disks store even more information.

Formatting: Preparing a disk so the operating system can find the data. A disk is unusable until formatted.

Hard disk: A disk made of a rigid base and coated with magnetic material. The rigid, rotating platter of a hard drive is capable of storing megabytes or more data than a floppy disk.

Hardware: The physical parts of a computer: printer, keyboard, monitor, scanner, hard or floppy disk, power supply, memory chips, modem, and math coprocessor.

Internet: Also the net or the information super highway. Systems of computer systems that are linked together around the world to share information.

Microsoft: Largest software company in the world.

Modem: Modulator-Demodulator. A device that converts digital data from a computer into analog data that can be transmitted over telephone lines. It can dial and answer a phone call to send or receive data. Also FAX/modem which allows for fax and modem communication.

Motherboard: Main circuit board of a microcomputer. This board holds the CPU and memory.

Newbie: Individual new to the Internet.

Newsgroups: A collection of world-wide discussion groups made up of people with common interests or expertise.

Software: Programs, languages, or routines that control the operations of a computer. Software is often stored on disks or loaded into a computer's hard drive.

Surfing: As in surf the net. Browsing the Internet, looking at files, listings, chat rooms, Web sites, bulletin boards and so on with little or no interaction.

SYSOP: System operator. The person who operates an electronic bulletin board.

Techspeak: The very formal technical language of computers.

User-friendly: A computer program that is easy to understand by the average person who may not be familiar with the program.

Operating system: The first or lowest level of software that runs on the computer. This software defines the devices the system has such as: disks, graphics cards, serial ports, and parallel ports and allows program access to the devices. It also defines how disk files are stored and named.

WWW: World wide web. A source through the Internet that allows for browsing. Organized to make access and finding information on Internet more user-friendly.

Resources

Recommended Books

The Artist's Way by Julia Camerson (Putnam, 1992).

The Art of Jewelry Making: Classic & Original Designs by Alan Revere (Sterling Publishing Company Inc., 1999).

The Art of Polymer Clay by Donna Kato (Watson-Guptill Publications, 1997).

The Art of Silk Ribbon Embroidery by Judith Baker Montano (C & T Publishing, 1993).

Basic Beadwork for Beginners by Mitsuko Muto (Ondorisa Publishers/Kodansha America, 1996).

Beadwork Basics by Ann Benson (Sterling Publishing Company, 1995).

Beautiful Beads: How to Create Original Gifts and Jewelry for Every Occasion by Alexandra Kidd (Quarto, 1994).

The Best Little Beading Book, Techniques and More: A Practical Guide for Bead Lovers by Wendy Simpson Conner (Interstellar Trading & Publishing Company, 1995).

The Book of Beads by Janet Coles and Robert Bydwig (Simon & Schuster, 1990).

Crafting For Dollars by Sylvia Landman (Prima Publishing, 1996).

Crafts Market Place: Where and How to Sell Your Crafts edited by Argie Manolis (Betterway Books, 1997).

Creative Bead Jewelry: Weaving, Looming, Stringing, Wiring, Making Beads by Carol Taylor (Sterling Publishing Company Inc., 1995).

Creative Clay Jewelry: Designs to Make from Polymer Clay by Leslie Dierks (Lark Books, 1994).

The Designer's Common Sense Business Book by Barbara Ganim (North Light Books, 1995).

Drawing on the Artist Within Revised Edition by Betty Edwards (Simon & Schuster, 1989).

Drawing on the Right Side of the Brain Revised Edition by Betty Edwards (Simon & Schuster, 1989).

The Encyclopedia of Jewelry Making Techniques: A Comprehensive Visual Guide to Traditional and Contemporary Techniques by Jinks McGrath (Simon & Schuster, 1995).

Fifteen Beads: A Guide to Creating One-of-a-Kind Beads by Jane Dunnewold (Martingale & Company, 1998).

Foundations in Polymer Clay by Donna Kato (Watson-Guptill Publications, 1997).

Handcrafts by James E. Seitz, Ph.D. (TAB Books, 1993).

How to Make Soft Jewelry by Jackie Dodson (Chilton Book Company, 1991).

How To Open and Operate A Home-Based Craft Business by Ken Oberrecht (The Globe Pequot Press, 1994).

How to Sell What You Make: The Business of Marketing Crafts by Paul Gerhards (Stackpole Books, 1996).

The Jeweler's Art: A Multimedia Approach by Alice Sprintzen (Davis Publications Inc., 1995).

Jewelry: Two Books in One by Madeline Coles (Quarto Publishing, 1999).

Make Wire Beads by Lisa Van Herik (BeaDifferent Press, 1999).

Making Wire Jewelry by Helen Clegg and Mary Larom (Lark Books, 1997).

Making Your Own Jewelry by Wendy Haig Milne (New Holland Publishers/Storey Communications, 1993).

The New Beadwork by Kathlyn Moss and Alice Scherer (Abrams, 1992).

The New Clay: Techniques and Approaches to Jewelry Making by Nan Roche (Flower Valley Press, 1991).

The New Ribbon Embroidery by Victoria Adams Brown (Watson-Guptill Publications, 1997).

Organizing for the Creative Person by Dorothy Lehmkuhl and Dolores Cotter Lamping (Crown Trade Paperbacks, 1993).

The Polymer Clay Techniques Book by Barbara A. McGuire (Krause Publications, 1999).

Promoting & Marketing Your Crafts by Edwin M. Field and Selma G. Field (Macmillan Publishing Company, 1993).

Selling What You Make: Profit from Your Handicrafts by James E. Seitz, Ph.D. (TAB Books, 1993).

Working From Home by Paul and Sarah Edwards (Putnam, 1994).

Recommended Magazines

Aardvark Territorial Enterprise Newspaper
P.O. Box 2449
Livermore, CA 94550

Bead 'n Button
Kalmbach Publications
Phone: (888) 558-1544

Canadian Jeweler
1448 Lawrence Avenue E Suite 302
Toronto, Onterio Canada M4A 2V6
Phone: (416) 755-5199
Fax: (416) 755-9123
Web site: www.canjewel.polygon.net

Crafts Magazine
Published by Primedia Publications
News Plaza Box 1790
Peoria, IL 61656
Phone: (309) 682-6626
Fax: (309) 682-7394

Craftworks
Paintworks
Woodworks
Published by All American Crafts, Inc.
243 Newton-Sparta Road
Newton, NJ 07860-2748
Phone (201) 383-8080

Fairs and Festivals
Published by Division of Continuing
Education
University of Massachusetts
Amherst, MA 01003
Phone: (413) 545-2360
Fax: (413) 545-3351
Web site: www.umass.edu

Fiberarts
50 College Street
Asheville, NC 28801

Jewelry Crafts
Published by Miller Publications
4880 Market Street
Ventura, CA 93003-7783
Phone: (805) 644-3824
Fax: (805) 644-3875

Jewelry Making, Gems, and Minerals
c/o Jewelers Bench
Box 226
Cortaro, AZ 85652-0226

Lapidary Journal
Published by Primedia Publications
2 News Plaza Box 1790
Peoria, IL 61656
Phone: (309) 682-6626
Fax: (203) 682-7394
E-mail: LJmagazine@aol.com
Web site: www.lapidaryjournal.com

National Jeweler Magazine (Trade Only)
Phone: (800) 250-2430
Web site: www.national-jeweler.com

Ornament Magazine
230 Keystone Way
Vista, CA 92083
Phone: (619) 599-0222

Piecework
201 East Fourth Street
Loveland, CO 80537
Phone: (970) 669-7672
Fax: (970) 667-8317
Web site: www.interweave.com

Popular Ceramics
Box 5000
North 7450 Aanstad Road
Iola, WI 54945
Phone: (715) 445-5000
E-mail: jonespub@gglbbs.com
Web site: www.popularceramics.com

Sew News
P.O. Box 1790
Peoria, IL 61656

Sunshine Artist
2600 Temple Drive
Winter Park, FL 32789
Phone: (800) 804-4607

Surface Design Journal
4111 Lincoln Boulevard Suite 426
Marina del Rey, CA 90292

Threads
Box 355
Newton, CT 06470

Web Sites

The Web has opened a whole new world of jewelry artists and craft people. With a click of your mouse, you can find hundreds of sites for information and resources.

Beads/Jewelry

www.beadage.com

www.bourgetbros.com

www.eebeads.com

family.go.com

www.genesisglass.com

hometown.aol.com

www.kornelys.com

Business

artsandcrafts.miningco.com

www.ebay.com

www.sunshineartist.com

Fiber-Textile/Jewelry

www.boazfurn.com

www.creativeneedle.com

www.fabricartdesign.com

www.hempsupply.com

www.joann.com

www.makestuff.com

members.tripod.com

www.purewhimsy.com

www.sulky.com

www.tias.com

General Jewelry

www.albritons.com

www.antique-estatejewelry.com

www.craftassoc.com

www.craftsitedirectory.com

www.fwkc.com

www.ganoksin.com

jewelrymaking.about.com

jewelrymaking.miningco.com

www.jewelrynet.com

www.jewelryspokenhere.com

www.jsritter.com

www.lapidaryjournal.com

professionaljeweler.com

www.tripps.com

www.wampumworks.com

www.jewelrycrafts.com

www.wehug.com

www.galleryofjewelry.com

Mail Lists, BBS, and Newsgroups

www.egroups.com

Polymer Clay/Jewelry

www.beadsoftime.com

www.ccmaui.com

www.geocities.com

www.gwengibson.com

pages.ivillage.com

www.jaedworks.com

www.jmjgifts.com

www.brass-Stencils.com

www.mcs.com

www.moonarts.com

Wire and Metal/Jewelry

www.beadage.com

www.goldbenders.com

jewelrymaking.about.com

jewelrymaking.miningco.com

www.jewelrytrends.com

www.livewirejewelry.com

www.microsculptures.com

www.otramac.com

silvermine.hypermart.net

www.wag.on.ca

www.wigjig.com

www.wire-sculpture.com

www.mamibeads.com

www.wire-sculpted-jewelry.com

www.wire-world.com

Wood and Decorative Painting/Jewelry

www.artitems.com

www.busybee.ns.ca

www.busybrushes.com

www.decordelights.com

folkart.tqn.com

www.handcraftersvillage.com

www.handmade.addr.com

members.aol.com

members.home.net

www.paintbox.co.uk

www.ppi-free.com

www.priscillahauser.com

roo.com

www.shasta.cc.ca.us

www.somersetcounty.com

www.sunco.com

www.tolenet.com

woodworking.miningco.com

Recommended Search Engines

Web sites may change addresses or even disappear. Here is a list of general and specialized search engines that can help you find a re-located Web site or find a new Web site for the information you may be looking for.

General Search Engines

AltaVista: www.altavista.com

Direct Hit: www.directhit.com

Excite: www.excite.com

Google: www.google.com

GoTo: www.goto.com

HotBot: www.hotbot.com

Infoseek: www.infoseek.com

Inktomi: www.inktomi.com

LookSmart: www.looksmart.com

Lycos: www.lycos.com

Mamma: www.mamma.com

MegaSpider: www.megaspider.com

Northern Light: www.northernlight.com or www.nlsearch.com

Open Directory (NewHoo): www.dmoz.org

Search.Com: search.cnet.com

Snap: www.snap.com

WebCrawler: www.webcrawler.com

Yahoo: www.yahoo.com

Specialized Search Engines

Art and Craft Show Net: www.artandcraftshows.net/ (Search database of over 2000 shows)

Deja News: www.dejanews.com/ (Deja News is devoted to searching newsgroup discussions, with archives stretching back to March 1995.)

FindMail: www.findmail.com/ (Similar to DejaNews, only for mailing lists. FindMail allows you to search for mailing lists of interest, or to read actual messages and post via an online interface.)

Information Please: www.infoplease.com/ (Information Please almanacs are favorites among researchers who need trustworthy facts. This site allows searching across Information Please's various almanacs, its encyclopedia, and its dictionary.)

Liszt: www.liszt.com/ (Long a favorite for those looking for mailing lists.)

Publicly Accessible Mailing Lists (PAML): www.neosoft.com/internet/paml/ (Another well-known place to find mailing lists.)

U.S. Trademark Search Page
trademarks.uspto.gov/access
/search-mark.html
(Enter a few words, and you can quickly
discover if a U.S. trademark has been
registered containing them. It's free, easy,
and comes courtesy of the U.S. Patent and
Trademark Office. The link above is to the
"Combined Marks" search page, which is
very easy to use.)

When.com: www.when.com/
(An events directory and personal
calendar Web site. Users can browse
events listings, ranging from Internet
chat sessions to upcoming trade shows.
Events can then be linked to a web-based
personal calendar.)

World Wide Art Resources:
wwar.com/index.html
Artists, museums, galleries, art history,
arts education, antiques, performing arts
ranging from dance to opera, classified
ads, resume postings, and more.

Suppliers/Product Resources

General Supplies

Artifacts
P.O. Box 3399
Palestine, TX 75802
Phone: (903) 723-4178

Craft King
P.O. Box 90637
Lakeland, FL 33804
Phone: (888) 272-3891
Web site: www.craftking.com

National Artcraft
7996 Darrow Rd.
Twinsburg, OH 44087
Phone: (888) 937-2723
E-mail: nationalartcraft@worldnet.att.net

Sax
P.O. Box 510710
New Berlin, Wisconsin 53151-0710
US Fax: (800) 328-4729
Canada Fax: (905) 356-3700

Sunshine Discount Crafts
12335 62nd Street North
Largo, FL 33773
Phone: (800) 729-2878

Zim's
Box 57620
Salt Lake City, UT 84157
Phone: (801) 268-2505
E-mail: ranae@interserv.com

Jewelry Supplies

Beads

Bead Bazaar
1345 Spruce Street
Boulder, CO 80302
Phone: (303) 444-80302

Beadalon
205 Carter Drive
West Chester, PA 19382
Phone: (610) 692-7551

Beaders Paradise
4201 Guinn Road
Knoxville, TN 37931
Phone: (800) 859-5254

Beads Unique
308 Roberts Lane
Bakersfield, CA 93308
Phone: (805) 399-6523

Beadsmith
1501 S Park Ave,
Linden, NJ 07036
Phone: (908) 474-1000

Garden of Beadin'
P.O. Box 1535
Redway, CA 95560
Phone: (707) 923-9120

Love To Bead
P.O. Box 8492
Asheville, NC 28814
Phone: (704) 252-0274

Fabrics/Soft Jewelry

Bond America
178 Maple Street
Glens Falls, NY 12801
Phone: (518) 798-3767

Elsie's Exquisiques
208 State Street
Chester, NJ 07930
Phone: (908) 879-4700

Lacis
3163 Adeline Street
Berkeley, CA 94703
Phone: (510) 843-7178

Leather Factory
643 East 10th Street
Houston, TX 77008
Phone: (713) 880-8235

RibbonSmyth
P.O. Box 416
Fountainnville, PA 18923
Phone: (215) 249-1258

Zucker Feather
512 N. E Street
California, MO 65018
Web site: www.zuckerfeathers.com

Findings/Wire

Artistic Wire
752 North Larch Ave
Elmhurst, IL 60126
Phone: (630) 530-7500

Beadworks
139 Washington Street
South Norwalk, CT 06854

Rings & Things
P.O. Box 450
Spokane, WA 99210
Phone: (509) 624-8565

River Gems and Findings
6901 Washington NE
Albuquerque, NM 87109
Phone: (800) 443-6766

TSI
101 Nickerson Street
Seattle, WA 89109
Phone: (800) 426-9984

Westrim Crafts
9667 Canoga Avenue
Chatsworth, CA 91311

Packaging

Action Bag Co.
Phone: (900) 824-BAGS
Carries packaging

Associated Bag Company
Phone: (800) 926-6100
Source for packaging

PT BAG
Phone: (800) 448-5891
Source for packaging

Paper/Jewelry

Cache Junction
1717 South 450 West
Logan, UT 84321
Phone: (800) 333-3279

Daniel Smith, Inc.
4150 First Avenue South
P.O. Box 84268
Seattle, WA 98124-5568
Phone: (800) 426-6740

The Japanese Paper Place
887 Queen Street West
Toronto, Ontario Canada M6J 1G5
Phone: (416) 703-0089
Fax: (416) 703-0163

Oblation Earthworks
6503 SW Luana Beach Drive
Vashon Island, WA 98070

Paper Adventures
P.O. Box 04393
Milwaukee, WI 53204
Phone: (800) 727-0699

PaperDirect, Inc.
205 Chubb Ave
Lyndhurst, NJ 07071
Phone: (800) 272-7377

Paper Journey
450 Raritan Center Parkway
Edison, NJ 08837
Phone: (800) 827-2737

Paper Reflections/DMD Industries
1207 ESI Drive
Springdale, AR 72789
Phone: (501) 750-8929

PaperSource, Ltd
1506 West 12th Street.
Los Angeles, CA 90015
Phone: (213) 387-5820

Twinrocker Handmade Paper
P.O. Box 413
Brookston, IN 47923
Phone: (317) 563-3119

Polymer Clay And Stamps

All Night Media
454 Du Bois
San Rafael, CA 94901
Phone: (415) 459-3013

American Art Clay
4717 West 16th Street
Indianapolis, IN 46222
Phone: (800) 374-1600

ClearSnap, Inc.
509 30th Avenue
Anacortes, WA 98221
Phone: (800) 448-4862

Co-Motion Rubber Stamps
2711 East Elvira Road
Tucson, AZ 85706
Phone: (520) 746-0515

Embossing Arts Company Inc.
31961 Rolland Drive
Tangent, OR 97389
Phone: (541) 928-9898

Hampton Art Stamps
19 Industrial Boulevard
Medford, NY 11763
Phone: (800) 229-1019

Kemper Enterprises
13595 12th Street
Chino, CA 91710
Phone: (800) 388-5367

Personal Stamp Exchange
360 Sutton Place
Santa Rosa, CA 95407
Phone: (707) 763-8058

Polyform Products
1901 Estes
Elk Grove Village, IL 60007
Phone: (847) 427-0020

Prairie Craft Company
865 North Hermitage Street
Chicago, IL 60622
Phone: (800) 779-0615

Rubber Stampede
967 Stanford Avenue
Oakland, CA 94608
Phone: (510) 420-6800

Rycraft Stamps
4205 SW 53rd Street
Corvallis, OR 97333
Phone: (541) 753-6707

Stampa Rosa
2322 Midway Drive
Santa Rosa, CA 95405
Phone: (707) 527-8267

Stampendous
1357 South Lewis Street
Anaheim, CA 92805
Phone: (714) 563-9501

Specialty Supplies

Adhesive Technologies
3 Merrill Industrial Drive
Hampton, NH 03842-1995
Phone: (603) 926-1616
Fax: (603) 926-1780
Sells low-temperature glue guns and
specialty glues with Magic Melt

American Traditional Stencils (Stencils
and Brass Templates)
442 First New Hampshire
Northwood, NH 03261
Phone: (800) 448-6656
E-mail: amtrad@amtrad-Stencil.com

Art Institute Glitter
720 N. Balboa Street
Cottonwood, AZ 86326

B & B Products, Inc.
18700 North 107th Avenue #13
Sun City, AZ 85373-9759
Phone: (888) 382-4255
Fax: (877) 329-3824
International Fax: (602) 815-9095
Sells etching supplies

Christy's Crafts
P.O. Box 492
Hilsdale, IL 60521
Phone: (630) 323-6505
Carries pinpricking, quilling paper, tools

Creative Beginnings
P.O. Box 1330
Morro Bay, CA 93443
Phone: (800) 367-1739
Sells charms

Creative Paperclay Co.
79 Daily Drive Ste 101
Camarillo, CA 93010
Phone: (805) 484-6648
Source for paper clay

Crystal Creations
23727 19th Avenue NE
Arlington, WA 98223
Phone: (360) 435-83327

Dremel
4915-T 21st Street
P.O. Drawer 1468
Racine, WI 53406
Phone: (800) 747-6344 Ext. 2

Environmental Lighting Concepts
3923 Coconut Palm Drive
Tampa, FL 33619
Phone: (800) 842-8848
Carries true spectrum lighting/OTT Lite

Fiskars
7811 W Stewart Avenue
Wausau, WI 54402-8027
Phone: (725) 842-2091
Fax: (715) 848-3657
Sells ergonomically correct tools

Highsmith Inc.
W5527 Highway 106
Ft. Atkinson, WI 53538-0800
Phone: (800) 554-9332
Source for cardboard storage systems
for supplies

McGill, Inc.
P.O. Box 177
Marengo, IL 60152
Phone: (800) 982-9884
Sells punches

Ranger Ink
15 Park Road
Tinton Falls, NJ 07724
Phone: (732) 389-3535
Fax: (732) 389-1102
Carries inks, inkpads, embossing powders,
embossing tools

Xuron Corp.
60 Industrial Park Rd
Saco, ME 04072
Source for scissors

Wood Shapes, Turnings, Paint

Cabin Craft
1500 Westpark Way
Euless, TX 76040
Phone: (800) 877-1515
Fax: (817) 571-4925

Delta Technical Coatings
2550 Pellissier Place
Whittier, CA 90601
Consumer Information Line:
(562) 695-7969
Web site: www.deltacrafts.com

Dick Blick Art Materials
P.O. Box 1267
695 Route 150
Galesburg, IL 61402
Phone: (309) 343-6181
Orders: (800) 447-8192

Dove Brushes
1849 Oakmont Avenue
Tarpon Springs, FL 34689
Phone: (800) 334-3683
Fax: (727) 934-1142

Forster, Inc.
P.O. Box 657
Wilton, ME 04294-0657
Phone: (207) 645-2574
Fax: (207) 645-2775

Loew-Cornell
563 Chestnut Avenue
Teaneck, NJ 07666-2490
E-mail: loewcornell@aol.com

Silver Brush, Ltd.
P.O. Box 414
Windsor, NJ 08561-0414
Phone: (609) 443-4900
E-mail: brushlady@aol.com

Stan Brown Arts & Crafts
13435 NE Whitaker Way
Portland, Or. 97230
Phone: (800) 547-5531

Woodworks
4521 Anderson Blvd
Ft. Worth, TX 76117

Trade and Consumer Associations, Societies, and Guilds

I've spent hours searching out different groups and organizations under the umbrella of art and craft. You will not have a need for every one of these groups, but it's a great reference list for you and your friends. The trade-only groups will have an asterisk. Trade only means you will have to qualify for membership within the craft industry. Trade associations are for promoting the business of a trade.

American Association of Woodturners
3200 Lexington Avenue
Shoreview, MN 55126
Phone: (651) 484-9094
Fax: (651) 484-1724

American Gem Society
Phone: (702) 255-6500
E-mail: AGSwein@aol.com.

American Sewing Guild
Box 8476
Medford, OR 97504
Phone: (503) 772-4059

American Society of Artists
Box 1326
Palatine, IL 60078

Artists and Craftsmen Associated
9420 Shoreview
Dallas, TX 75238
Phone: (214) 348-0829

Canadian Craft & Hobby
Box 44
4044 12th Street NE
Calgary, Alberta Canada T2E-6K9
Phone: (403) 291-0559
Fax: (403) 291-0675

Gemological Institute of America
The Robert Mouawad Campus
5345 Armada Drive
Carlsbad, California 92008
Phone: (800) 421-7250
Phone: (760) 603-4000
Fax: (760) 603-4153
E-mail: eduinfo@gia.edu

HIA/Hobby Industries Association
319 East 54th Street
Elmwood Park, NJ 07407
Phone: (201) 794-1133
Fax: (201) 797-0657

Home Sewing Association
1350 Broadway Suite 1601
New York, New York 10018
Phone: (212) 714-1633
Fax: (212) 714-1655

The Jewelry Information Center (JIC)
1185 Avenue of the Americas 30th Floor
New York, NY 10036-2601
Phone: (800) 459-0130
Fax: (212) 398-2324
e-mail: jic@jewelryinfo.org

Manufacturing Jewelers & Suppliers of America
45 Royal Little Drive
Providence, RI 02904
Phone: (800) 444-MJSA
Fax: (401) 274-0265
E-mail: mjsa@mjsainc.com

National Academy of Design
1083 Fifth Avenue
New York, NY 10028

National Artists Equity Association
P.O. Box 28068
Central Station
Washington, DC 20038-8068

The National Arts Club
15 Gramercy Park South
New York, NY 10003

NGD/National Guild of Decoupageurs
1017 Pucker Street
Streetowe, VT 05672

Polygon.net
P.O. Box 4806
Dillon, CO 80435
Phone: (970) 468-1245
E-mail: customerservice@polygon.net
Web site: www.Polygon.net

National Polymer Clay Guild
1350 Beverly Road, Suite 115-345
McLean, VA 22101
Phone: (202) 895-5212
Web page: www.npcg.org/home.htm

Local Guilds

California
San Diego Polymer Clay Guild
Phone: (619) 534-2715

Illinois
Chicago Area Polymer Clay Guild
Phone: (708) 771-8932

Michigan
Metro Detroit Polymer Art Guild
Phone: (810) 645-9308

Texas
Austin Guild
Phone: (512) 836-7775

Houston Polymer Clay Guild
Phone: (218) 536-8541

Washington
NW Polymer Clay Guild
Phone: (206) 287-9170

The National Quilting Association
P.O. Box 398
Ellicott City, MD 21041-0393

National Wood Carvers Association
P.O. Box 43218
Cincinnati, OH 45243

SCD/Society of Craft Designers
Contact: Offinger Management
P.O. Box 2188
Zanesville, OH 43702
Phone: (614) 452-4541

SDP/Society of Decorative Painters
P.O. Box 808
Newton, KS 67114
Phone: (316) 283-9665
Fax: (316) 283-5048

Craft Malls

Craft malls and galleries are a great way to market handmade goods. Most shops have a program for out-of-town or out-of-state vendors. Craft malls listed here were in business at the time this book went to print. Please understand that every effort was made to only include shops that have been in business for at least one full year. Businesses sometimes close or relocate, so keep updated by using the Internet to check craft mall directories and Web sites. Many of the shops listed below also have, as an additional service, the ability to become part of their established company Web sites. Average fees for this service range from $60.00 to $100.00 per six-month commitment for up to six pages on a site.

American Craft Malls

6851 East Reno Rd
Midwest City, OK 73110

103 Ash Creek Dr. West
Azle, TX 76020

2395 SW Wilshire Blvd.
Burleson, TX 76028

3307 Wurzbach
San Antonio, TX 78238

7900 IH-35 North
San Antonio, TX 78218

American Crafters
1919-B Emmitsburg Road
Gettysburg, PA 17325

American Indians Arts & Crafts
2765 North Scottsdale Road
Scottsdale, AZ 85257

Apple Tree Mall
1830 West Highway 76
Branson, MO 65616

Arts & Crafts Emporium
234 Bull Street
Savannah, GA 31401

Bayberry Junction Crafter's Gallery
248 Morro Bay Boulevard
Morro Bay, CA 93442

The Bunny Patch
2100 Highway 35
Sea Girt, NJ 08750

Coomers Craft Mall

    19785 Stevens Creek Boulevard
    Cupertino, CA 95014

    8001 South Broadway
    Littleton, CO 80122

    525 Lincoln Highway
    Fairview Heights, IL 62208

    9800 Quivera Rd.
    Lenexa, KS 66215

    35323 Plymouth Road
    Livonia, MI 48150

    40700 Van Dyke
    Sterling Heights, MI 48313

    P.O. Box 9068
    Walled Lake, MI 48390

    1668 Clarkson Road
    Chesterfield, MO 63017

    2805 West Park Row
    Arlington, TX 76013

Countryside Craft Mall
4333 Miller Road
Flint, MI 48507

The Crafter's Cottage
2550 Prospect Avenue
Helena, MT 59601

Crafter's Market
2791 32nd Avenue South
Unit B
Grand Forks, ND 58201

Crafter's Village
1029 Blossom Hill Road
San Jose, CA 95123

Crafter's Marketplace and Gifts
1403 West Glen Avenue
Peoria, IL 61614
Phone: (309) 692-7238

Cooper Street Craft Mall
1701 South Cooper
Arlington, TX 76010

Crafter's DeLight
1110 Green Run Square
Virginia Beach, VA 23452

Crafts for All Occasions
1329 Fifth Avenue
Garner, NC 27529

Craftworks

    1600 Ocean Outlets
    Rehoboth Outlet III
    Rehoboth Beach, DE 19971

    Liberty Tree Mall
    Danvers, MA 01923

    The Mall @ Rockingham Park
    Salem, NH 03079

    120 Laconia Road
    Tilton, NH 03276

    1270 Fording Island Road
    Hilton Head Factory Stores
    Bluffton, SC 29910

    Landmark Mall
    Alexandria, VA 22304

Creations Craft Mall
6804 Green Bay Road
Kenosha, WI 53142
Phone: (414) 942-9420

Homespun Crafters Mall

    5110 West Franklin Road
    Boise, ID 83705

    856 NW Bond Street
    Bend, OR 97701

    410 Valley River Center
    Eugene, OR 97401

    2117 SE Burnside
    Gresham, OR 97030

    3298 Lancaster NE
    Salem, OR 97305

    5729 Little Rock Road SW
    Turnwater, WA 98512

    8700 NE Vancouver Mall Drive
    Vancouver, WA 98662

    3710 Tieton Drive
    Yakima, WA 98902

Homespun Treasures
3650 Boston Road Suite Q
Lexington, KY 40514

Nostalgia Crafts and Antiques
971 West Centerville Road
Garland, TX 75041

On The Corner Craft Mall
7996 Darrow Road
Twinsburg, OH 44087

The Quilted Bear

    821 East Lake Street
    Wayzata, MN 55391

    3661 South Maryland Parkway
    Las Vegas, NV 89109

    14002 East 21st Street
    Tulsa, OK 74134

    1110 Newgate Mall
    Ogden, UT 84405

    1172 Brickyard Road
    Salt Lake City, UT 84106

    145 W 7200 South
    Salt Lake City, UT 84047

Southern Creations Craft Mall
2853 Bartlett Blvd.
Memphis, TN 38134

Village Craft Mall
4409 North Highway 7
Hot Springs, AR 71910
Phone: (501) 984-5248

Windmill Crafters
P.O. Box 435
West Dennis, MA 02264

Acknowledgments

Many thanks to the special people and companies who have provided quality products, sage advice, great tips, wonderful hints, brilliant ideas, insightful wisdom, endless patience, pep talks, listening ears, quick responses, and much appreciated support in writing this book:

Ken Nerius; Elizabeth Conklin; Denise Sternad, Michelle McCormack, and Prima Publishing; Jane Guthrie, Marilyn Russell, and her girls; Creative Beginnings; American Art Clay Company; Polyform Products; Artistic Wire; Rubber Stampede; Victoria Adams Brown; Dr. Underill; The Palm Bay Senior Center; Design Originals; Uncle Ron Given; Aunt Wanda Cusack; Jeff Given; Jeff Nerius; Hazel Pearson-Williams; Patricia Nimocks; The Society of Craft Designers; Handeze Gloves; and all the wonderful people who over the years were kind enough to buy our work.

Index

About the Authors

LYNDA S. MUSANTE has worked in the craft and creative industries as a freelance designer and consultant for over 18 years. Her experience includes working in a family-owned independent craft store, and in her own self-publishing and consulting business.

Lynda is former president of the Society of Craft Designers, and serves the Association of Craft and Creative Industries (ACCI) as chair of the Education and Nominating Committees. She is a member of the ACCI Designs for Living Committee, and is also a designer member of HIA (Hobbies Industries Association). She lives in Richmond, Virginia, with her husband, Lou, and their two children, Laurel and Robbie.

MARIA GIVEN NERIUS graduated with a degree in Advertising and worked in that field briefly before discovering her love of crafting. She sells her original folk wood dolls at craft shows in Florida and has published over 1,000 of her designs. Maria has helped establish education and information resources for the crafter in consumer magazines, on television, and on the Internet. In Maria's own words, "Crafting is the expression of care, love, and joy straight from the heart." Feel free to contact Maria Nerius by mail: P.O. Box 100205, Palm Bay, FL 32907 or by e-mail: Mnerius@aol.com.

About the Series Editor

BARBARA BRABEC is one of the world's leading experts on how to turn an art or craft hobby into a profitable home-based business. She regularly communicates with thousands of creative people through her Web site at www.barbarabrabec.com.